D1521845

Spain and the Protestant Reformation

For Charles V and Philip II, both of whom expected to continue the momentum of the *Reconquista* into a campaign against Islam, the theology and political successes of Martin Luther and John Calvin menaced not just the possibility of a universal empire, but the survival of the Habsburg monarchy. Moreover, the Protestant Reformation stimulated changes within Spain and other Habsburg domains, reinvigorating the Spanish Inquisition against new enemies, reinforcing Catholic orthodoxy, and restricting the reach of the Renaissance and Scientific Revolution.

This book argues that the Protestant Reformation was an existential threat to the Catholic Habsburg monarchy of the sixteenth century, and the greatest danger to its political and religious authority in Europe and the world. Spain's war on the Reformation was a war for the future of Europe, in which the Spanish Inquisition was the most effective weapon. This war, led by Charles V and Philip II, was in the end a triumphant failure: Spain remained Catholic, but its enemies embraced Protestantism in an enduring way, even as Spain's vision for a global monarchy faced military, political, and economic defeats in Europe and the broader world.

Spain and the Protestant Reformation will appeal to researchers and students alike interested in the history and society of Early Modern Spain.

Wayne H. Bowen is the Director of Interdisciplinary Studies in the College of Undergraduate Studies and a Professor in the Department of History, University of Central Florida, US.

Routledge Research in Early Modern History

The Trial of Giordano Bruno
Germano Maifreda

A Genlis Education and Enlightenment Values
Mrs Chinnery (1766–1840) and her Children
Denise Yim

Anti-Jacobitism and the English People, 1714–1746
Jonathan Oates

The Eye of the Crown
The Development and Evolution of the Elizabethan Secret Service
Kristin M.S. Bezio

Parliamentarism in Northern and East-Central Europe in the Long Eighteenth Century
Volume I: Representative Institutions and Political Motivation
Edited by István M. Szijártó, Wim Blockmans, and László Kontler

The Culture and Politics of Regime Change in Italy, c.1494–c.1559
Edited by Alexander Lee and Brian Jeffrey Maxson

Spain and the Protestant Reformation
The Spanish Inquisition and the War for Europe
Wayne H. Bowen

Royal Journeys in Early Modern Europe
Progresses, Palaces and Panache
Edited by Anthony Musson and J. P. D. Cooper

For more information about this series, please visit: https://www.routledge.com/Routledge-Research-in-Early-Modern-History/book-series/RREMH

Spain and the Protestant Reformation

The Spanish Inquisition and the War for Europe

Wayne H. Bowen

Routledge
Taylor & Francis Group

LONDON AND NEW YORK

First published 2023
by Routledge
4 Park Square, Milton Park, Abingdon, Oxon OX14 4RN

and by Routledge
605 Third Avenue, New York, NY 10158

Routledge is an imprint of the Taylor & Francis Group, an informa business

British Library Cataloguing-in-Publication Data
A catalogue record for this book is available from the British Library

ISBN: 978-1-032-05473-5 (hbk)
ISBN: 978-1-032-05474-2 (pbk)
ISBN: 978-1-003-19767-6 (ebk)

DOI: 10.4324/9781003197676

Typeset in Times New Roman
by SPi Technologies India Pvt Ltd (Straive)

Contents

Preface

The idea for this book came from a discussion in 2011 with Dr Peter Lillback, President of Westminster Theological Seminary. He encouraged me to research the history of the Protestant Reformation in Spain and sponsored my participation in the 2nd Annual International Conference on the Spanish Protestant Reformation, held in Madrid in late 2012. I remain grateful for his inspiration and support. At the same conference, I was inspired by the work of Frances Luttikhuizen, as well as by her generosity of sources and ideas. While I did not expect this book to take a decade to complete, I am hopeful that the time has enabled the final work to be more measured.

I want to thank former colleagues at Southeast Missouri State University, especially Steven Hoffman, Vicky McAlister (now at Towson University), and Lissette Acosta Corniel (now at CUNY) for their encouragement as I embarked on a new topic four centuries removed from my primary period of research. Craig Nakashian, at Texas A&M University-Texarkana, graciously invited me to deliver my first lecture on this topic. The writing and structure of this book benefitted from discussions in 2015 with scholars, especially John Edwards and Jessica Fowler, at the "III Simposio Internacional de Estudios Inquisitoriales" (Third International Symposium of Inquisitorial Studies), Universidad de Alcalá.

Research funding for this book came from the Program for Cultural Cooperation between Spain's Ministry of Education, Culture, and Sports and United States Universities, the Grants and Research Funding Committee of Southeast Missouri State University, and the College of Undergraduate Studies and the Department of History at the University of Central Florida. I am grateful to all three sources. Special thanks to Melody Bowdon and Theodorea Regina Berry, in their successive roles as dean of the College of Undergraduate Studies, for securing research funds for this project, as well as for their allowing me time for travel to Spain. I am also much in debt to Joan Maria Thomàs Andreu, Professor of Contemporary History at Universitat Rovira i Virgili, for his years of support and encouragement.

Most of all, thanks to my wife Kendra, and my boys, Sam and Nathan, who have endured my plodding through this project, forgiven me for research trips to Spain, and witnessed my late nights of writing. We are all delighted that our time with the Spanish Inquisition is at an end.

Introduction

Franciscan friar Diego de Arce delivered a sermon in Spain at the height of Habsburg wars against Elizabeth of England, Dutch Calvinist rebels in the Netherlands, and Protestants in Spain and Spanish colonies. This message was an exposition of how Spanish Catholics, including King Philip II, viewed the threat at hand. The arrival of Martin Luther was evidence for the coming of the Apocalypse, Friar Diego argued, as the Protestant Reformation increasingly destroyed the unity of Christianity. Through his actions and his sins, Luther was "the author of all contemporary ills:" heresy, vice, gluttony, greed, and sexual immorality. Anyone within Christendom that questioned or refused to obey the instructions and wisdom of the Catholic Church, emanating from the Pope, and carried out by bishops and priests, were "friends of Lutherans" and equally damnable as heretics. Friar Diego's description of Luther as a beast collaborating with "avaricious and ambitious princes" echoes other descriptions and imagery of Protestants in Catholic literature and public exhortations. For devout Catholics, especially in Spain, the arrival of Protestantism did not reflect religious differences within the family of Christendom; this was an imminent danger, inspired by Satan and emanating from the pit of Hell: a plague on true Catholicism.[1]

To Friar Diego and, more importantly, Emperor Charles V and King Philip II, the Protestant Reformation was an existential threat to the Habsburg Empire of the sixteenth century. Faithful Catholics saw themselves in a war for Europe, and the broader world, with the Spanish Inquisition serving as the most effective and trusted weapon against Protestant heresies. Although Europe's Protestants were diverse in their origins and theological beliefs, these new religious movements challenged Spain's religious and geo-strategic trajectory, forcing a shift of the empire from a Mediterranean crusade to a global war within Christendom. Whether initiated by theologians or monarchs, from Luther to Calvin to Henry VIII, their impact spread across Europe, bringing institutional and theological innovations that directly threatened the structure and legitimacy of the Habsburg state and the connection between crown and Catholic Church. The Protestant Reformation accelerated the division of the Habsburg realms into Spanish and Austrian components, each with their own Protestant challenges. Although the challenge to Catholic Europe began with the "evil heretic"

DOI: 10.4324/9781003197676-1

Martin Luther, what would become the umbrella of Protestantism spread and multiplied in multiple manifestations from the 1520s to the 1550s.[2]

For Charles V and Philip II, both of whom expected to continue the momentum of the *Reconquista* (Reconquest) of Spain, into a campaign against Islam, the irruption of Martin Luther and John Calvin menaced not just the possibility of a universal empire, but also the survival of Habsburg monarchy. Protestants within Spain were a threat to the monarchy, and Spanish Protestants elsewhere in Habsburg lands undermined the potential for universal empire and the legitimacy of the reigns of Charles V and Philip II.[3] In reaction to this danger, the Protestant Reformation stimulated changes within Spain and other Habsburg domains, reinvigorating the Spanish Inquisition against new enemies, reinforcing Catholic orthodoxy, and restricting the reach of the Renaissance and Christian humanism. The defiant stands of Luther, Calvin, and their followers altered the history of Christianity and Europe. These Protestants who in the face of threats of being called heretics, excommunicated, and punished up to the death penalty, defied papal bulls and openly argued with Charles V.[4] While some historians have concluded that Habsburg Spain was "barren territory for the northern reform movement," for a brief period during the mid-sixteenth century the Protestant challenge was as direct and consequential as it was in the Holy Roman Empire, the Netherlands, France, and England, where new faiths clashed with Catholicism in civil wars, insurrections, and dynastic clashes over the fate of thrones and nations.[5]

Indeed, arguably without the questions raised by Luther, Calvin, and other Protestant theologians, there might never have emerged a clarified version of Catholic orthodox beliefs. This body of doctrine was eventually determined and updated at the sessions of the Council of Trent, which concluded its work in 1563 after almost two decades of sporadic efforts. Prior to the Tridentine effort, and especially before the Protestant theological insurgency, there seemed little need to define Catholicism, as nearly everyone in western and central Europe was in the only existing Church. The handful of openly heretical movements, such as the Cathars and Bogomils, did not threaten Christianity on a wide scale. Within Spain, the Inquisition could easily manage individual heretics, without requiring the Church to standardize what this meant beyond general devotion, obedience to ecclesiastical authorities, and avoiding blatant violations of understood doctrines such as the sanctity of the Holy Eucharist.

Indeed, had the Council of Trent been called years earlier, perhaps in the 1520s, it might have addressed the challenge of Luther's calls for reform and avoided a century of warfare between Catholics and Protestants. Martin Luther initially hoped his *Ninety-Five Theses* would bring about change within the Roman Catholic Church, rather than leading to a theological insurgency against it. While Luther's excommunication likely would have remained in place, accommodating some of his demands for reform, such as an end to indulgences, a reassertion of the role of faith in salvation, allowing the use of the vernacular, and defining Church teachings more clearly, could have limited the attractiveness of new religious denominations. A Catholic Reformation that began in 1525 might have overcome these challenges in much of Europe internally, addressing many of the concerns initially raised by Luther. The Holy Roman Empire was especially fertile terrain for change within Catholicism in the 1530s and 1540s.[6]

As one historian noted, at the time that Luther posted his *Ninety-five Theses*, there was significant ambiguity in Christendom and particularly in Spain about what it meant to be a Roman Catholic:

> ... there were no Catholic seminaries to educate Catholic priests, no con-clusive explanation of the Catholic doctrine of salvation, no description of the standard Catholic Bible, and no official demarcation of Church tradition. ... Spanish Catholics could embrace a variety of doctrinal pri-orities and depend upon a variety of customary references. None of these emphases and texts had to mesh with each other in every detail; all of them could be uttered by a clergy whose theological training ranged from the thorough to the vacuous.[7]

This study leaves to other scholars the role of evaluating change over time within the theology and structure of the Catholic Church throughout Christendom. Debates over the use of terms such as Catholic Reformation versus Counter-Reformation, and ostensibly progressive and pastoral reform-ers vs. reactionary scholastics, are ably pursued elsewhere.[8] Similarly, other historians have successfully wrestled with the codification of the main Protestant tendencies into specific denominations, with distinctive theologies, religious structures, and relationships to the state.[9] The lines between Catholic and Protestant, and just as much within the various groups within the Reformation, were unclear in the early decades after 1517; not until the 1550s or 1560s were these definitions explicit within the respective camps.[10]

Despite the centrality of the Protestant Reformation in re-shaping Spanish foreign policy and domestic affairs, the impact of the Protestant Reformation on Spain has previously received only limited historiographical treatment.[11] The main narratives of the Reformation focus on the rise of Lutheranism in northern Europe, the impact of Calvin's Geneva on France and the Netherlands, and Henry VIII's Church of England. Inasmuch as Spain enters the picture, it is as the leading defender of the Catholic Church, engaged in episodic conflict at sea and on land against England and Calvinist rebels in the Netherlands, sending theologians to Church councils at Trent and elsewhere to reinforce orthodoxy, intervening in French territories to oppose Huguenots, and supporting the operations of the Spanish Inquisition against other faiths and all forms of heresy. As one historian noted, Philip II's Spain was "a greater part of the power behind the Catholic Reformation," contributing not only its military strength in campaigns against Dutch and English Protestants, but its diplomatic efforts against French and Navarrese Huguenots, its theologians in the conciliar movement, its priests, nuns, monks, and friars in religious and secular orders, and its territories for the operation of the Spanish Inquisition and affiliated tribunals.[12]

Some historians have argued that the Protestant Reformation was, rather than a primary cause for conflict, more of an accelerant to existing rivalries. France, England, and even the Low Countries, despite the latter's status as a Habsburg territory, were rivals of Spain in commerce, maritime communications, and strategic position, even before the irruptions of Luther, Calvin, and Henry VIII. Smuggling to Spanish colonies, piracy, and the drive for markets in the Americas by English, French, and Dutch merchants and raiders preceded the Reformation by some years, albeit on a small scale. Many merchants and buccaneers, as well, were hardly paragons of religious practice, whether before or after religious warfare struck Europe in the sixteenth century, although certainly they took advantage of the "element of religious fanaticism" in their efforts to form crews, gain government authorization for their endeavors, and justify their violations of Spanish laws and territories. Spain, which characterized illegal trade as piracy, lumping merchants with the violent raiders who plundered and attacked colonial towns and ports, applied the same broad categorizations in the Reformation. They were no longer just English, Dutch, or French pirates, but also heretics, doubly condemned in Habsburg eyes for both secular and religious activities against Spanish settlements and colonies from the Caribbean to the west coast of the Americas.[13]

The sources for this book include published and unpublished letters of Charles V, Philip II and other Habsburg leaders, which discuss the challenge of Protestant Reform within their lands and as an external enemy. Also important for this work are the writings of Spanish Reformers such as Juan de Valdés, Antonio del Corro, and Casiodoro de Reina, who led internal and diaspora communities of Spanish Protestants. Records of trials of Protestants by the Spanish Inquisition are also useful sources that illustrate the deep concern of the Catholic Church for these new movements. This study also integrates in a limited way the writings and correspondence of other Reformers and Christian humanists, such as John Calvin, Martin Luther, Erasmus, and Michael Servetus. Finally, *Spain and the Protestant Reformation* makes extensive use of existing historiography in Habsburg and broader European political, military, and religious history. Indispensable, too, is the *Bibliotheca Wiffeniana*, a three-volume compilation of Spanish Protestant texts, by Eduard Boehme, Benjamin Barron Wiffen, and Benjamin B. Wiffen.

The Protestant Reformation – the rise of new religious movements led by men such as Martin Luther, John Calvin, and Henry VIII, along with women such as Queen Elizabeth of England and Queen Jeanne of Navarre – has long been associated as an external enemy of Spain. In popular images dating back to the sixteenth century, nefarious and black-robed Spanish priests plot against enlightened Reformers, with Spain a land of "ignorance, tyrannized over by superstition, and a prey to every crime."[14] The 1998 film *Elizabeth*, for example, was an award-winning version of this trope. In practice, the

Spanish were consistently at war with lands that had adopted Reformation theology. The Spanish Armada tried – and failed dramatically – to defeat the British at sea partly to restore Catholicism in England. The Spanish army, and its sporadically paid German, Swiss and Italian mercenaries, fought, and eventually lost, an 80-year war in the Low Countries to prevent Dutch Calvinists from becoming independent.

The Spanish Inquisition, other religious tribunals and Inquisitions throughout the Habsburg Empire, and the Spanish-based Jesuit order, used every intellectual and coercive tool available, from the most erudite to the brutal, to prod Protestants, suspected Protestants, and the theologically uncertain to return to the Roman Catholic Church. These associations between Spain and the Protestant Reformation, told with frequency and effectiveness by historians for hundreds of years, have been primarily episodic. Few historians have attempted to consider the global impact of the Reformation not just on Spain's foreign policy and wars, but on the territory of Spain itself. While for many readers, Spain represents the nation of the Inquisition, its role as the vanguard of the Counter-Reformation not only shaped events throughout Europe, but comprehensively within Spain itself.[15] Spain's external image as the "champion of Catholicism" and home to the Spanish Inquisition earned it the ongoing enmity not only of Protestants across Europe and the world, but later of Enlightenment writers, based on the anti-clericalism and skepticism that were the enemies of Catholic faith.[16]

Many historians have written about conflicts between the Spanish Empire and Protestants throughout Europe and beyond: struggles between Emperor Charles V and Martin Luther, Spanish campaigns against Dutch Calvinism in the Low Countries, and Habsburg naval warfare against England in the Atlantic and the Caribbean. However, the impact of the Reformation within the physical boundaries of the Spanish states, especially Castile, the largest and most significant of Philip's Iberian realms, has received less attention and is often not integrated into internal and external contexts. The existential threat of Protestantism played a significant role not only in shaping the foreign policy of the Habsburg monarchy, but the internal operations and development of the state and Catholic Church. Even though the Protestant Reformation is, as one historian noted, "one of history's most well-chronicled events," the role of Spain within and against these movements has been less comprehensively developed.[17]

At times, Spain's struggle against Protestantism is subsumed in the broader Habsburg account, with the initial conflict between Charles V and Luther leading to an emphasis on the confessional fight within the Holy Roman Empire. Historians such as Gábor Ágoston take this approach, with little mention of Spain in the campaigns against the Ottomans or in the global confrontation with the forces of the Protestant Reformation. Even when Spain was not a direct belligerent in the wars of central and south-eastern Europe, however, its strategic position, strength in the Mediterranean and beyond, and role as a counterweight to the Ottoman Empire reduced the available forces that the sultans could devote to their campaigns.[18] In other words, every Ottoman soldier and sailor fighting Spain and its allies in Malta, Tunis, or at Lepanto was one fewer arrayed against Christian lands in the Balkans, the approaches to Vienna, or elsewhere in south-eastern Europe.

Within the Catholic Church, and encouraged by the Inquisition, suspicion of Reformation influences encouraged strident orthodoxy, putting even high-ranking priests and bishops at risk. Despite the small numbers of Protestants within Spain, they played a disproportionate role in transforming Spain's Inquisition and the monarchy after 1517. Philip II saw Protestantism as a pervasive enemy, undermining not only the Catholic Church, but the kingdom, the broader empire – even the royal family. Philip II was correct, but in unanticipated ways. Despite what most historians have considered a minimal impact, the Protestant Reformation shaped the Spanish Inquisition, and other institutions of political, social, and religious authority, in far greater ways than has been previously accepted. Indeed, for good reason Emperor Charles V considered Protestantism, in the words of one Spanish historian, "*la fisura abierta en el cuerpo de la Cristianidad*" (the open fissure in the body of Christianity).[19]

To Emperor Charles V and King Philip II, the Protestant Reformation was a collection of foreign and heretical theologies, opposed across Europe by a semi-united, and constantly shifting, front of Spanish Catholics and their allies. Depending on the moment, these monarchs could find themselves alone in the struggle, leading a coalition of Catholic powers against Islam, or allied with some subjects, while others rebelled openly against the Catholic Church and Spanish Habsburg rule. For Charles V, Philip II, and their supporters, religious warfare in Europe was not a separate realm of struggle from the actions of the Spanish Inquisition. Devout Catholics, whether fighting "battles in northern Europe" or as clerics engaged in "the Spanish Inquisition's trials," saw their efforts as "part of a conflict against Protestants of global dimensions."[20] The war of Spanish Catholicism against the Protestant Reformation was arguably the first world war, with Spanish military and theological campaigns against the new heresies in Europe, the Americas, and the Pacific.

The war was not always consistent or fought against all Protestants with equal resolve. The Duke of Alba, Philip II's merciless commanding general in a repressive war against Dutch Calvinists, advocated for peace with England. Spain and the papacy, despite their common interest in purging Europe of the theological heresy of Protestantism, were often at odds in military and political campaigns. France was the most inconsistent in the connection of its Catholic kings and majority to foreign policy, at times allying with the Muslim Ottoman Empire, intervening on behalf of Protestants in opposition to Catholic Spain, and introducing limited religious toleration for its own Huguenot Protestants, only to reverse these decrees with remarkable harshness.[21]

The fight against the ideas of the Protestant Reformation had a deleterious impact on intellectual life within Spain, forcing into retreat what had been a vibrant humanist tradition in the late fifteenth and early sixteenth centuries.

As noted by historians such as Lu Ann Homza, prior to Luther and Calvin, Spain was fully immersed in the ideas and practices of the Renaissance. While this vibrancy was on a smaller scale and theologically focused, Christian humanism within Catholic thought was at the center of Spanish intellectual life until the global threat of the Protestant Reformation made many innovative ideas, even ones from Catholic writers such as Erasmus, seem bridges to heresy.[22]

The history of the Spanish Inquisition has been perhaps better documented than any institution of the Roman Catholic Church, except for the papacy. While the initial accounts were often sensationalized works by Protestants, exhibiting hagiography for what they considered martyrs of the Spanish Inquisition, later historians redressed this approach. Henry Kamen, E. William Monter, Joseph Pérez, Mary Giles, Clive Griffin, Benzion Netanyahu, Richard Kagan and Abigail Dyer, among others, have contributed monographs and edited collections on the Spanish Inquisition. Most of these have focused on the institution's campaigns against formerly Jewish *conversos* or been more general narratives of the Holy Office from its fifteenth-century origins to its nineteenth-century dissolution, examining the contrary impulses of the Inquisition, torn between the "belief in the fallen nature of humankind and in human perfectibility."[23]

While essential in describing the structure, operations, and intent of the Spanish Inquisition, most include only limited discussions of the Protestant Reformation, as a relatively small group of victims over the 350-year Spanish history of the Holy Office. Given the greater numbers of those convicted, *conversos*, Moriscos, and those committing moral offenses, such as bigamy and homosexuality, receive more attention. Even less so do these scholarly contributions present the struggle between Catholicism and Protestantism as an existential threat to Spain, and the prime reason for Spain's grand strategy and role in leading this global fight against heresy. The campaign against Protestantism initiated the second major phase of the Spanish Inquisition, shifting from persecuting *conversos*. After the decline of Protestantism as an open threat, the seventeenth century saw reinvigorated efforts against *conversos* from Portugal and the Portuguese Empire, followed by a brief fight against the Enlightenment, often at odds with the Spanish Bourbon monarchy of the eighteenth century, who ruled Spain from the end of the War of Spanish Succession until their overthrow by Napoleon Bonaparte.[24]

While Spain consistently figures in the story of Catholic Europe's reaction to the Reformation, rarely do these accounts examine the ways in which the rise of Protestantism changed Spain, beyond causing it to fight against the English navy, Dutch rebels, and Swedish infantry across the continent. In a sense, historians have agreed with Spanish autocrats, from Philip II to Francisco Franco, that the Protestant Reformation was something external, foreign, and totally non-Spanish. Most histories of sixteenth-century Spain describe it as an enemy of the Reformation, but not as threatened by it. Other works on Christianity do not mention the existence of Protestants within Spain at all, not even as victims of the Spanish Inquisition. From Philip II's dispatch of the Spanish Armada, to the fight against Calvinists in the Low Countries, to Spanish joy at the St. Bartholomew's Day Massacre, the Reformation is elsewhere, distant, and entirely alien. From the Catholic redoubt of the Iberian Peninsula, Spain's priests, soldiers, and *conquistadores* set forth upon the world, determined to claim (or reclaim) it for Catholicism and Philip II, with the security of a loyal Spain behind them and supporting their far-flung campaigning and crusading.[25]

The Spanish Inquisition may have been more justified than most historians have been willing to concede, in seeing Protestants throughout Spain as the primary threat to Catholic orthodoxy and the legitimacy of the Habsburg kingdom. The Pyrenees were no magical wall, holding back heresy. Absent the diligence of the Spanish Inquisition, there was no obvious reason why Protestantism could not have become as widespread as in France. In this regard, Habsburg Spain was different: "At the dawn of the Reformation era … Spain was the only nation in Europe that had an extensive and experienced bureaucratic institution whose explicit mission was the eradication of religious heterodoxy."[26] With Protestantism increasingly organized in universities, urban centers, and under the protection of Lutheran princes in the Holy Roman Empire and Scandinavia, in French Huguenot fortified towns, from Holland to the city walls of Calvin's Geneva, and in England under Henry VIII and Elizabeth, a systemic and institutionalized response by Catholicism was the best response to protect the Church.

Individually, most of those accused in Spain of being Protestants over the course of the sixteenth century were an unimpressive lot. Apart from a cluster of educated and well-connected believers, caught in Inquisitorial sweeps during the 1550s and 1560s, most of those tried for Protestantism were semi-literate, ignorant of theology, and no more familiar with Luther's doctrine than they were with the Catholic Church's. Many of those brought before the Spanish Inquisition were itinerant laborers – printers, sailors, soldiers, tailors – often without families or a stable upbringing grounded in any organized faith. A disproportionate number were foreigners, even if in many cases they were subjects of the far-flung Habsburg Empire or allied states – such as Germans from the Holy Roman Empire or Flemish from the Low Countries. As foreigners from hostile states, French and English were even more vulnerable. The denunciations that brought alleged Protestants to the attention of the Inquisition frequently came from those they had wronged, often themselves from among the geographically and theologically rootless. While on their own these individuals were hardly a threat to Catholicism or the Spanish state, they were emblematic of an empire tied together with fragile bonds of religion and dynastic authority, fetters under considerable pressure in the sixteenth century.

Had the Inquisition ignored men and women such as these, allowing their individually harmless behavior – describing Luther as a "good man," questioning why Spanish priests remained unmarried when German ones married, and avoiding the obligation to attend Mass – the potential for widespread social dissolution could have emerged. As with other contemporary institutions, the Inquisition employed physical cruelty, harsh interrogation, and psychological tricks to entice confessions. Its main goal, to eliminate heresy in a state dependent on religious unity, was buttressed by theological imperatives, a mandate from Rome, and the political needs of a crusading monarchy.

In *Underground Protestantism in Sixteenth Century Spain*, the most complete work on the Reformation in Spain, independent historian Frances Luttikhuizen recounts the story of the small groups of Spaniards that initially studied the works of Luther and Calvin, formed cells to worship and pray together, and for these actions came under the intense and eventually deadly scrutiny of the Spanish Inquisition. While her account at times inclines towards historical advocacy, the work provides a detailed narrative of the men and women most associated in Spain with the Reformation.[27] Hers is the only full-length contemporary survey on Spanish Protestant Reformers in English or Spanish, although the latter language has seen an increase in recent publication on the subject.

The independent scholar and Spanish Protestant pastor Manuel de León de la Vega completed an even more comprehensive study in the two volumes of *Los protestantes y la spiritualidad evangelica en la Espana del siglo XIV*. His 1,600-page book includes regional surveys examining the varied approaches by the Spanish Inquisition across the peninsula, as well as the conflation of the ideas of Erasmus, the *Alhumbrados*, and others with those of Luther, Calvin, and other Protestants.[28] A more documented two-volume work on the same subject, although focused on only one city, is Tomás López Muñoz, *La Reforma en la Sevilla del XVI* (Seville: Editorial MAD, 2011).

The persistent fear that Habsburg Spain could become like France, and face civil wars like those between French Catholics and Huguenots during the sixteenth century, was quite real. This danger motivated the actions of Spanish Inquisitors and their supporters, including Philip II and Charles V, to be consistent and merciless in the pursuit of Protestant Reformers. The stakes were too high for them to exercise tolerance or magnanimity in their actions; the weight of Christendom and its possibilities for revival rested on their shoulders. Habsburg Spain faced "wars associated with Protestantism abroad and the perceived danger of a Reformist fifth column at home" with these multiple threats challenging not only the existence of this far-flung Catholic empire, but the foundational justifications for its existence.[29] With Protestant theologies finding converts in Spanish territories, among Spain's traditional enemies, and in the populations of antagonists such as England, these ideas were spreading rapidly and in a concerning way. Protestantism even came to the New World, which initially had been exclusive terrain for Spanish clerics and their Portuguese co-religionists. The Reformation was a global threat to the first global empire.

As Philip II confronted the Protestant Reformation in Europe and beyond, he faced not only a theological conflict, but one based on personalities and informed by gender. Among his most determined and frustrating opponents were Protestant women, including two queens: Jeanne of Navarre

and Elizabeth of England. While Habsburg domains were not entirely encir-
cled by Protestant kingdoms, the Reformation and its followers were on all
fronts where the king turned his attention. Indeed, the existence of
Protestants was in many cases why Philip remained so fixated on the Low
Countries, France, and England. Only the transfer of the Holy Roman
Empire to another monarch, his uncle Ferdinand, prevented this from being
another front line for Spain.

Although few historians have noted this connection, there was an important gender element to the Reformation, with women in Spain and elsewhere
contributing as a key audience, and at times as contributors, to these new
ideas. It was not just monarchs such as Elizabeth and Jeanne that embraced
the new faiths in the sixteenth century: French noblewomen, wives of Dutch
artisans, and German market women found new meaning and opportunities.
Calvinism, Lutheranism, and Anglicanism brought women new opportunities to be actively religious without taking on religious orders as nuns,
enhanced the status of women within the family and the Church, and at times
even saw women as writers or preachers.[30] There was a wide variety of practice among Protestant women. Elite Englishwomen were more likely to write
both for public dissemination and for their own private reflective journals,
French Huguenots more likely to engage in direct action amid France's religious civil wars, and Dutch Calvinists, while literate, to embrace charitable
works in support of their community.

At the same time, however, devout Catholic women remained active,
lamenting the closure of convents by Henry VIII, reduced opportunities for
pilgrimages, the sidelining of reverences for the Virgin Mary, Mother of
Jesus, and female saints in worship and devotion, and the diminished space
for mystery and liturgy in the new denominations.[31] Female mystics, most
notably the Spanish nun Teresa of Ávila, wrote of their contemplative relationship with God and in praise of the interior life, withdrawing from society.
Teresa, later sainted by the Catholic Church, organized her Carmelite order
into a more austere rule, through her writings inspiring both women and men
to seek deeper spiritual lives through prayer, self-sacrifice, and meditation.
Because of her claims of individual communion with God, even Teresa was
suspected at times by the Spanish Inquisition. The tribunals saw the danger
of allowing women, or men, to assert direct inspiration by the Holy Spirit,
without the intermediation of the Church.[32]

Both Catholic and Protestant women saw opportunities to find their own
religious understanding not just as dependencies of men, but "as individual
Christians to secure their own salvation," with rising literacy among both
communities, at least among women of the nobility and middle classes, opening up additional areas for participation and reflection.[33] While the Spanish
monarchy did allow for a limited role for Catholic women as exemplars of
religious devotion – the faith of Queen Isabel being notable in this regard –
even in these roles it was their faithfulness, rather than their theological leadership or innovations in practice that drew reverence and respect. For
Philip II, however, his main interest in prominent women during this era was

not in elevating Catholic role models, but instead in pursuing the advocates for the Reformation with all military, political, and religious means at his disposal; they were theological enemies of his vision. This vision was reciprocated by Protestant women, with Philip II's Spain portrayed as the embodiment of evil, including as allegorically representing the ancient mythological sorceress Medea, whose betrayal by Jason (of Greek Argonaut fame) let to a murderous quest for revenge, death, and destruction.[34]

Elizabethan propagandists, who followed Dutch Calvinists in associating Spain with the cruelty of the Spanish Inquisition, successfully shaped these two images for centuries to come. English writers wrote eloquently of the Spanish Inquisition and its victims, employing fears about this institution as "the major weapon in the anti-Spanish armoury," a message that echoed essentially unchallenged in the English-speaking world from the time of Queen Elizabeth until the late twentieth century.[35] Despite the evidence that the Holy Office was less likely to impose physical punishments or the death penalty than secular tribunals at the time, it became identified with torture and executions of its victims. Notwithstanding the Inquisition's objectives of truth seeking and reconciliation of those it investigated, and the willingness of many tribunals to consider mitigating factors during its cases, it is still linked to idea of merciless questioning, a refusal to acknowledge innocence, and a rush to judgment. From exaggerated ideas about the extent of Inquisitorial persecutions of English sailors and merchants in the sixteenth century, to the broader cultural and political meaning of more contemporary discussions, the Spanish Inquisition has evoked powerful historical memory, even if in doing so its history has been just as widely misunderstood.

Even in the case of English Protestants, during the years of war between Spain and England, there were relatively few arrested by the Inquisition: only 57 imprisoned between 1587 and 1604 by the Holy Office in Seville, Spain's largest port. Similarly, on the Canary Islands, only 47 English subjects were in prison between 1574 and 1624. Typically, only the most provocative types of behavior, such as openly mocking the Catholic Church or attempting to proselytize Spaniards, would lead to an arrest. There are almost no cases involving English residents of Spain, who presumably were aware of the need to tread carefully over religious sensitivities if they were Protestant. English Catholics in Spain faced even fewer challenges; indeed, some had moved to Spain to seek refuge from religious persecution in England.[36]

The Spanish Inquisition nonetheless retains an image in Western popular culture of cruelty and ferocious persecution, becoming synonymous with any institution or practice of persistent questioning, especially under duress. This perception has been expressed in a range of media from the comic such as *History of the World, Part I*, and episodes of *Monty Python's Flying Circus*, to the horrific, as with the various film versions of Edgar Allen Poe's *The Pit and the Pendulum*.[37] The term "Spanish Inquisition" remains in common parlance, useful for making negative comparisons against other tribunals and investigations. Merely asking questions can be met with a reference to the Spanish tribunals, implying that the interrogatory was excessive or even torture. The theme continues to resonate in history and popular culture, from films to graduate seminars.[38]

For example, defense attorneys and opponents of trials at the US detention facility at Guantanamo Bay drew analogies linking the use of water boarding by the US government during the War on Terror to this method's original use by the Holy Office in the fifteenth and sixteenth centuries. While the techniques of the medieval and early modern Spanish Inquisitors differed from those employed in modern interrogations, there were shared elements in the early modern and twenty-first-century processes. Both included the overarching goals of coaxing the individual into a confession and to volunteer names of co-conspirators; both also were aimed at perceived global conspiracies emblematic of an existential threat.[39]

In another contemporary example, at the National Prayer Breakfast in 2015, US President Barack Obama used the medieval Crusades to the Holy Land and the Spanish Inquisition as examples of Christian terror, comparing both to the terrorist violence of the insurgent Islamic State in the Middle East. These analogies drew both support and criticism from across the political spectrum, but especially strong critiques from historians, who noted the presentism and ahistoricism of the President's remarks.[40]

As historians have noted, the terms that refer to the religious transformation of the sixteenth century are themselves imprecise. "Protestant" initially referred to a coalition of princes at the Diet of the Holy Roman Empire in 1529, the terms Lutheran, Calvinist, and Anglican were originally insulting, and nearly every religious leader of the sixteenth century would have described themselves at Catholic. Even the words "Reformation" and "Reformers" could just as well apply to those within the Roman Catholic Church attempting to promote institutional and theological changes, to reinforce and standardize the definition of orthodox Christian theology, and to do away with practices such as indulgences, priestly concubinage, and the selling of religious offices. Erasmus, for example, was if nothing else a voice for reform within the Catholic Church, even as he rejected the title of Reformer, and explicitly denounced Luther and Calvin. Even so, this book uses these words conventionally, in keeping with historiography over the past few decades, while admitting they remain contested.[41]

With the emergence of the Protestant Reformation, the primary antagonist of these new religious movements was the Habsburg Empire of Charles V. Beginning in 1517, these efforts transformed what had been on the verge of claiming universal empire into a state focused on ending the Protestant danger. It would be under King Philip II of Spain, however, that this tendency under Charles V was confirmed as a primary strategic driver of Spanish Habsburg behavior. The conflict between Habsburg Catholicism and Reformation Protestantism would begin in the 1520s, accelerate to its height from the 1540s to the 1570s, then fade thereafter as European confessional lines consolidated. By the end of the sixteenth century, the Spanish fear of Protestantism was subsumed into conflicts with external enemies, rather than being seen as connected in a global struggle that also threatened Spain internally. This study, therefore, begins with a portrait of Spain just prior to the beginning of the Protestant Reformation, and ends with the death of Philip II in 1598. While there were echoes of this existential threat after the passing of this monarch, it never approached the dimensions of the global war against Protestantism begun through a confrontation between Charles and Martin Luther, and which continued through the rest of the sixteenth century.

Notes

1 Gwendolyn Barnes-Karol, "Religious Oratory in a Culture of Control," in Anne J. Cruz and Mary Elizabeth Perry, eds., *Culture and Control in Counter-Reformation Spain* (Minneapolis: University of Minnesota Press, 1992), 64–66. The sermon was given sometime between 1578 and 1606.
2 Letter, Suprema, Spanish Inquisition to Inquisition Tribunals, "Carta acordada enviada por el Consejo a los distintos tribunales inquisiciones ante la sospecha de aparición de libros luteranos en la Península," 28 March 1534, Archivo Histórico Nacional (AHN), Inquisición, lib. 573, f.14, in Tomás López Muñoz, *La Reforma en la Sevilla del XVI*, Vol. II (Seville: Editorial MAD, 2011), 43.
3 Doris Moreno Martinez, "Entre política y religión. La inquisición española y la reforma en tiempos del emperador," in Cristina Borreguero Beltrán and Asunción Retortillo Atienza, *La memoria de un hombre. El Burgalés Francisco de Enzinas en el V centenario de la reforma protestante* (Burgos, Spain: Universidad de Burgos, 2019), 184–185.
4 Michael Massing, *Fatal Discord: Erasmus, Luther, and the Fight for the Western Mind* (New York: HarperCollins, 2018), x, 398–400.
5 Andrew Pettegree, ed., *The Reformation World* (London and New York: Routledge, 2000), 3.
6 Michael Mullett, *The Catholic Reformation* (London and New York: Routledge, 1999), 30–31.
7 Lu Ann Homza, *Religious Authority in the Spanish Renaissance* (Baltimore: Johns Hopkins University Press, 2000), 11–12.
8 On the debate over terms see, for example, Homza, *Religious Authority in the Spanish Renaissance*, 117–120.
9 Peter Marshall, *Religious Identities in Henry VIII's England* (Aldershot, UK: Ashgate, 2006), 3.
10 Peter Marshall and Alec Ryrie, eds., *The Beginnings of English Protestantism* (Cambridge: Cambridge University Press, 2002), 5–7.
11 The most complete contemporary bibliography is Frances Luttikhuizen, *La Reforma en España, Italia, y Portugal, Siglos XVI y XVIII: Bibliografía Actualizada* (Seville: Editorial MAD, 2007).
12 Mullett, *The Catholic Reformation*, 181.
13 Peter Gerhard, *Pirates on the West Coast of New Spain, 1575-1742* (Glendale, California: Arthur H. Clark, 1960), 12–13.
14 No Author, *Protestantism in Spain, its Progress and its Extinction by the Inquisition, with an Account of the Principal Martyrs*. Translated from the French (Dublin: J. Porteous, 1835), 7.
15 Manuel Fernández Álvarez, *España del Emperador Carlos V (1500-1558, 1517-1556)*, Vol. XX (Madrid: Espasa Calpe, 1999), 106.
16 William S. Maltby, *The Black Legend in England: The Development of Anti-Spanish Sentiment, 1558-1660* (Durham, North Carolina: Duke University Press, 1971), 4.
17 Massing, *Fatal Discord*, xv.

18 Gábor Ágoston, *The Last Muslim Conquest: The Ottoman Empire and its Wars in Europe* (Princeton: Princeton University Press, 2021).

19 Fernández Álvarez, *España del Emperador Carlos V*, Vol. XX, 719.

20 Kimberly Lynn, *Between Court and Confessional: The Politics of Spanish Inquisitors* (Cambridge: Cambridge University Press, 2013), 42.

21 Manuel Rivero Rodríguez, "El imperio en su apogee," in David García Hernán, ed., *La historia sin complejos: La nueva visión del Imperio Español* (estudios en honor de John H. Elliott) (Madrid: Actas, 2010), 136–175.

22 Homza, *Religious Authority in the Spanish Renaissance*, 2–4.

23 Lynn, *Between Court and Confessional*, 3.

24 Lynn, *Between Court and Confessional*, 21–22.

25 See, for example, Carter Lindberg, *The European Reformations*, 2nd edition (Chichester, UK: Wiley-Blackwell, 2010), 279, 284–285, 291, 315, and James Tracy, *Europe's Reformations, 1450-1650* (Lanham, Maryland: Rowman and Littlefield, 1999), 8, 141–143. Vivian Green, *A New History of Christianity* (New York: Continuum, 1996), 124–159.

26 David Coleman, "Spain," in Pettegree, ed., *The Reformation World*, 298.

27 Frances Luttikhuizen, *Underground Protestantism in Sixteenth Century Spain* (Bristol, Connecticut: Vandenhoeck & Ruprecht, 2017). On page 350, she notes her goal "to vindicate the memory" of Protestants persecuted by the Spanish Inquisition.

28 Marcel Bataillon, *Erasmo y España: Estudios sobre la historia espiritual del siglo xvi* (Mexico City: Fondo de Cultura Económica, 1965), 701–703. Manuel de León de la Vega, *Los protestantes y la spiritualidad evangelica en la Espana del siglo XIV*, Vol. 1 and 2 (Oviedo, Spain: Self-published, 2012).

29 Clive Griffin, *Journeymen-Printers, Heresy, and the Inquisition in Sixteenth-Century Spain* (Oxford: Oxford University Press, 2005), 6, 10–12.

30 "A Discoverie of Six Women Preachers, in Middlesex, Kent, Cambridgeshire, and Salisbury," in Joyce Irwin, ed., *Womanhood in Radical Protestantism, 1525-1675* (New York: Edwin Mellen Press, 1979), 210–214.

31 Susan Broomhall, *Women and Religion in Sixteenth Century France* (New York: Palgrave Macmillan, 2006), 3, 7, 47, 71–73, 145.

32 Mullett, *The Catholic Reformation*, 183–184.

33 Broomhall, *Women and Religion in Sixteenth Century France*, 70–71,143.

34 Broomhall, *Women and Religion in Sixteenth Century France*, 122.

35 Pauline Croft, "Englishmen and the Spanish Inquisition 1558-1625," *The English Historical Review*, April 1972, Vol. 87, #343, 249.

36 Croft, "Englishmen and the Spanish Inquisition 1558-1625," 257–258, 261.

37 *History of the World, Part I*, 92 minutes, Directed by Mel Brooks, Original release 14 June 1981, Twentieth Century Fox; *Monty Python's Flying Circus*, "The Spanish Inquisition," Season 2, Episode 2, 31 minutes. Original release 22 September 1970, BBC.

38 "Imagining the Inquisition," Special Faculty of Theology, Radboud University, accessed 28 March 2022, https://www.ru.nl/theology/society/imagining-the-inquisition/.

39 https://www.npr.org/2007/11/03/15886834/waterboarding-a-tortured-history; https://www.latimes.com/world/la-fg-na-waterboarding-backgrounder-20170127-story.html; Adam Gopnik, "Inquiring Minds: The Spanish Inquisition revisited," *The New Yorker*, 16 January 2012. https://www.newyorker.com/magazine/2012/01/16/inquiring-minds.

40 Barack Obama, "Remarks by the President at National Prayer Breakfast," 5 February 2015, Washington Hilton, Washington, D.C., accessed 4 April 2022, The White House, Office of the Press Secretary, https://obamawhitehouse.

archives.gov/the-press-office/2015/02/05/remarks-president-national-prayer-breakfast. Evan Simon, "Historians Weigh in on Obama's Comparison of ISIS Militants to Medieval Christian Crusaders," *ABC News*, 6 February 2015, accessed 4 April 2022, https://abcnews.go.com/Politics/historians-weigh-obamas-comparison-isis-militants-medieval-christian/story?id=28787194.

41 Diarmaid MacCulloch, *The Reformation: A History* (New York: Viking 2003), xvii–xviii.

1   Spain and the World in 1516

At the ascension of Charles I as King of Spain in 1516, the monarch's empire was already vast, including the combined states of Castile and Aragon, southern Italy, the Netherlands, much of the Caribbean, redoubts in North Africa, and with growing enclaves in both North and South America. The king would soon add the title of Holy Roman Emperor (as Charles V), as well as significant territories in Germany, Burgundy, Italy, and Austria. During the first two decades of his rule, to this were added new conquests in North and South America and Asia, including over the Aztecs in Mexico and the Incas in Peru. By almost any measure, these lands comprised one of the ten largest empires in world history. With tremendous wealth in people, land, and resources, including silver and gold from the Americas, the potential at his hands exceeded that of any rivals. Only the ambitions of the emperor exceeded his means. Even the monarch's motto, "*Plus Ultra*" (Farther), using the pillars of Hercules, was emblematic of his ambitious vision. With honor and reputation the measures Charles employed to judge his successes or failures, he continued to be embroiled in far more conflicts than he could win. Consistently beleaguered by France, obsessed with campaigns against the Ottomans and their allies, and beset by the Protestant threat across his domains in Europe, he engaged everywhere with the powerful armies and other instruments of state power at his command, but rarely won decisively.[1]

Leading European scholars, including Erasmus, played a role in the education and administration of Charles, praising his merits while advising the young Catholic prince on how to manage his far-flung state. The Dutch theologian, the most popular author in Western Christendom at the time, dedicated the work *The Education of a Christian Prince* to the young ruler.[2] As one historian noted, Charles V's contemporary monikers "Lord of the World," "King of Kings," and "Monarch of the Universe" were not entirely hyperbole.[3] While the largest and most powerful state among his realms was Castile, Charles was the king of many rich and populous regions, able to contribute men, resources, and prestige toward his grand imperial goals. His hope was to bring all Catholic Europe, if not under his direct rule, at least in coalition against the Ottoman Empire and its Muslim allies, on a Crusade against Islam. The success of his grandparents, Ferdinand of Aragon, Isabella of Castile, Maximilian I of the Holy Roman Empire and Mary of

DOI: 10.4324/9781003197676-2

Burgundy, contributed to the possibilities for Charles V, even as some observers noted the young ruler's lack of charisma, unfamiliarity with Spain, and his inexperience; indeed, there were calls in the peninsula for Ferdinand, the younger brother of Charles, who had been raised in Spain and taught by Cisneros, to take the throne instead. Even Charles recognized the competence of Ferdinand, successfully nominating him to be his heir as Holy Roman Emperor, a position elected by the leading nobles of the central European confederation.[4]

The world Charles inherited was a legacy of several factors, including successful Habsburg marriages, battlefield conquests and, in the case of his Spanish possessions, centuries-long Christian reconquest of Spain from Islam. This process, completed by Queen Isabella I of Castile and King Ferdinand II of Aragon, culminated in the defeat of Muslim Granada in 1492, a year that witnessed the unification of Spain, the voyage of Columbus, and the expulsion of the Jews from Spain. Charles was also the heir to the Spanish Inquisition, founded by order of Pope Sixtus IV in 1478. This religious body, created at the request of Ferdinand and Isabella, investigated cases of false Christian conversions by Jews, a mandate expanded later to include converts from Islam. Unlike other religious tribunals or previous inquisitions established in France, the Spanish Inquisition was "an ecclesiastical court placed under the authority of the State."[5]

Rather than serving under bishops, or even under the Pope, the Grand Inquisitor served Spain's monarchs directly. While the clerics who served in this office were formally named by the Pope, they did so upon receiving a royal nomination. Once the Grand Inquisitor was named, he in turn nominated to the king the members of the Suprema, the highest body and court of the Inquisition, who made the appointments of these officials. The Grand Inquisitor named other key national officials of the Spanish Inquisition; chief Inquisitors for regional tribunals appointed officials at the local level as well. Also unique to the Habsburg monarchy, no local laws (*fueros*) could limit its legal and practical operations. In this, the Spanish Inquisition faced fewer constraints than Charles V and Philip II, both pledged to respect regional traditions and laws that limited their authority.[6] The majority of priests who served within the Holy Office were secular: clerics appointed by bishops and trained within the dioceses or bishoprics of Spain, rather than belonging to religious orders, such as the Dominicans, Franciscans, or Jesuits. This reinforced control by the Spanish monarchy, avoiding split loyalties among the friars and others within national and international religious orders.[7]

At any one time, approximately 50 priests served as regional Inquisitors in Spain, leading as many as 21 tribunals: 14 in peninsular Spain, three in Spanish colonies in the Americas, and one each in Sicily, Sardinia, the Balearics, and Canaries. Normally, each tribunal had three Inquisitors. Any one of the three could initiate an investigation or even initiate an interrogation, but major decisions, including torture, detention, and final sentence required at least two Inquisitors.[8] Inquisitors made their careers through their writing, summarizing evidence in cases, and arguing theology and religious practice. Their reputations depended on their successful navigation through issues of heresy and faith, responsive not only to their religious peers and superiors, but to local mood, national and international events, and on the position and behavior of those who came before their tribunals. Judgments had to stand on the strength of their written arguments, sometimes appealed as far as the Vatican. Inquisitors who were either too harsh or too lenient could be removed by the Grand Inquisitor or at the recommendation of the *Suprema*, a humiliation that clerics were keen to avoid.[9]

This change in terms of organization was significant, but the theological shift from the previous policy of legal tolerance of Jews and Muslims under Christian kingdoms, which coexisted with commensurate toleration of Christians under Islamic rule, was not as stark as some historians would argue. Christians under Islam before 1492, and Muslims under Christianity during the same period, did not enjoy religious freedom or legal equality; their status was clearly subordinate, more heavily taxed, and subject to episodic persecution. Faced with these challenges, individuals did convert from one faith to another, seeking the advantages this would bring, or determined by their own convictions and reason. Even so, the Spanish Inquisition was something entirely new among secular and religious tribunals.[10]

This Catholic institution built on earlier royal decrees that ordered the followers of Judaism and Islam to embrace Christianity or go into exile – after a hefty set of exit fines and penalties, which often amounted to effective confiscation of a family's entire means. Given the strong financial incentive to stay in Spain, many Jewish families did convert to Catholicism; some became genuine in their devotion to their new faith, but others continued to hold their Jewish traditions secretly, a practice known and feared by the Catholic Church.[11] Given that prior to 1492, the Iberian Peninsula had hosted Europe's largest Jewish population of Jews, the fear that there was a mass of secret Jews, masquerading as Christians, was on the minds of Spain's monarchs and Inquisitors.[12]

Along with concern about Jews pretending to be Christians, Spain's monarchs and the Catholic Church were worried about genuine converts among their Jewish subjects, who despite their good intentions were ignorant of Christian doctrines and practices, and who because of this lack of information might default to the traditions of Judaism. A serious effort to educate new Christians into the faith also accompanied the introduction of the Inquisition, although many priests and bishops acknowledged the inadequacy of these efforts. How could they hold accountable for heresy those who had never received a full Christian education in the sacraments, prayers, and rituals of the Catholic Church?

These questions concerned not only Ferdinand and Isabella, but officials of the Inquisition; tribunals regularly imposed lighter sentences in cases of ignorance, rather than willful disobedience.[13] Even so, some Inquisitors acted without mercy; within the first decade of the Spanish Inquisition, as many as one thousand former Jews were executed for heresy, guilty of incomplete or false conversion. Pope Sixtus IV and his successor Innocent VIII, appalled by these widescale killings, considered revoking the Spanish Inquisition, reversing these plans after assurances that the convicted could appeal judgments to the Grand Inquisitor.[14]

For Charles, the threat of a secretive internal enemy, *conversos* (converts) who retained their Judaism while masquerading as Christians, was only one of his many global challenges. Viewing himself as the heir of the *Reconquista* (Reconquest of the Roman Empire), Charles V looked east toward the lands held by the Ottoman Empire as potentially, even rightfully, his. Although Charles was born almost 50 years after the fall of Constantinople and its transformation into the Ottoman capital of Istanbul, the surrender of that citadel to Islam still was seen as a reversible loss in Western Christendom. Some historians have referred to this struggle between Habsburgs and Ottomans as one between two rival claimants to the legacy of Rome; indeed, at times Ottoman sultans referred explicitly to this legacy as theirs by conquest.[15] Driven by an "unwavering sense of duty" and the conviction that in his hands rested responsibility for uniting Christendom, the young king hoped not only to build a universal monarchy, but to strengthen the Church, no matter the costs to his treasury, kingdoms, or himself.[16]

Charles, therefore, was a man of tremendous goals, ruling over an empire of vast resources, but possessed of only modest talents. He was neither remarkably intelligent nor wise, handsome, or strong, or known for exuding charisma or charm. He was, however, dedicated, devout, and serious, making less time for frivolities such as mistresses, elaborate ceremonies, or costly luxuries than his fellow monarchs. While he did enjoy music and hunting, these modest pastimes cost little and rarely diverted him entirely from his responsibilities as king and emperor. In his devotion to his obligations, he compensated for many of his weaknesses, but in the end even his virtues proved insufficient to achieve his overly ambitious objectives. Uniting Christendom and repelling Islam from its redoubts in North Africa and the Holy Land were goals even the most powerful man in the world could not achieve.[17]

For Charles, restoring Jerusalem and Constantinople to Christian hands, uniting all Christendom under his rule, and defeating Islam were one and the same mission. He embraced this vision of a united Christianity at war as his destiny early in his reign, listening to the siren song of royal courtiers, flatterers, and millenarian prophets of his day.[18] This idea was hardly unique to Charles. Countless medieval kings during the crusading era hoped to use these movements for their own political gains, with the war against Islam as a unifying theme. Even after the end of the crusading era, monarchs and popes attempted multiple times to call upon this religious fervor to encourage Europe's warriors to put aside their internal differences to fight against the greater external enemy; Pope Leo X attempted in 1518 to promote a European-wide Crusade against the Ottoman Empire, proposing to unite French, Spaniards, Italians, English, and Germans not only in this military campaign, promising religious favors to those who participated, but also through collecting a special tax through the Catholic Church with revenues expressly devoted to the cause.[19]

The next Pope, Adrian VI, in his brief time in office (1522–1523), promoted the same crusading idea, albeit with the same lack of success in raising revenues and willing soldiers. Europe's monarchs were, for the most part, focused on fighting each other, as well as warring over Luther and his ideas. Indeed, one of the most multinational campaigns that took place in Europe was the sack of Rome by imperial forces in May 1527; far from conquerors of Islam, the forces of Charles V, in conflict over Italy, conquered and looted the capital of Christendom. Pope Clement VII and cardinals fled Rome, and Charles V's army, made up of many German mercenaries, killed 6,000–8,000 people in the violence that followed the assault on the Vatican on 6 May. This was a disaster for the reputation of the emperor, who cut short celebrations in Spain for the birth of his son, the future Philip II, in mid-June. Charles left Spain on 27 July 1529; almost four years would pass before he would see his son and heir again.[20]

Luther could only be amazed at his good fortune, with Catholics slaughtering Catholics, as the Protestant cause drew more of the faithful to its banners.[21] Indeed, Luther would on several occasions benefit from Charles V devoting resources to fighting France, the Ottoman Empire, or Muslim states of North Africa, rather than against Protestant forces.[22] Soon after assuming Spain's crowns, he faced revolts in Aragon and Castile, by peasants and urban residents against Charles and the nobility. Although crushed by the end of 1521, the rebellions, known as the Germanias and the Comuneros, respectively, were distractions to Charles V from the Lutheran threat.[23]

The cause of retaking Jerusalem through what became known as the Spanish Road was especially dear to the heart of his Spanish grandmother; some of Isabella's interest in sponsoring Columbus might have been because of his claims that through reaching the Indies he could help fund a new Crusade against the Ottomans. Contemporary maps of North Africa often showed a straight coastline, interrupted only by cities and rivers, perhaps contributing to the sense that a serious of marches or episodic conquests could extend the *Reconquista* into this region.[24] This was hardly an other-worldly dream; the Ottomans had conquered Constantinople and the last outposts of the Byzantine Empire when Isabella was a child; around the time of her marriage to Ferdinand, Ottoman forces invaded Austria and conquered what was left of Orthodox Christian Greece, conducting additional assaults in the Mediterranean over the next few decades with their vast navy and Muslim allies.[25] Corsair forces such as the North African-based Barbarossas, who launched attacks from Tunis, Algiers, and Djerba against southern Europe and Christian vessels, and enslaved tens of thousands of Christians, provided a frequent auxiliary to the main Ottoman fleets.[26]

Campaigning against Islam was the emperor's intention, but events closer to home, and threats more proximate, forestalled this dream. While Charles viewed himself as the secular leader of all Christendom, his bitter rival, the French King Francis I, loomed large and concerning. While Pope Leo hoped to unite Christendom in a revived Crusade against the Ottoman Empire, rivalries between the Christian monarchs of western and central Europe mitigated against this call. After all, if Europe's princes, kings, and emperors had stood by when Constantinople, the last redoubt of the Roman Empire, fell to the Turks, why would they initiate a war against them, now immeasurably stronger?[27] Indeed, on several occasions, including in 1518, the Imperial Diet rejected requests from the Catholic Church and from Charles V to endorse special funds to pay for a renewed Crusade. War fatigue, suspicion of the Pope, and more proximate fears of French invasions into central Europe, at times in alliance with certain states within the empire, trumped this objective.[28]

As King Ferdinand of Aragon, Charles V's grandfather, had warned, confrontation with France could easily sidetrack the Habsburg monarchy from its destiny to fight against Islam. Even though as King of Spain and Holy Roman Emperor Charles V had greater wealth and resources than did the French monarchs, France had the advantage of interior lines, fewer non-contiguous territories to defend, and agricultural self-sufficiency, as well as the willingness to seek allies, even in the Islamic world, to confound the intentions of Charles V. Despite this, both Charles V and Philip II were tempted by the possibility of a final victory over France, as a triumph over the other major European power would be a powerful vindication of their authority, potentially providing leverage to unite Christendom against Islam.[29] Although Charles shared his grandfather's hope of continuing the *Reconquista*, the new monarch's geographic sense was different. Unlike the Aragonese Ferdinand, Charles was born in Flanders, spoke Flemish and French, and was less focused on the Mediterranean world centered on Aragon.[30]

Even so, the wars between the Habsburgs and the French Valois could later not help but provide, as one historian noted, "encouragement" to the Protestants, who rejoiced at Catholics warring upon Catholics while heresy flourished elsewhere. The dream of both Ferdinand of Aragon and Charles V, to recreate the ancient Visigothic Empire on both sides of the straits of Gibraltar, proceeding thereafter to conquer North Africa and eventually the Holy Land, did not come to fruition.[31] Not only did France at times grant some religious freedoms to Protestant Huguenots; more shockingly it formed an alliance with the Ottoman Empire, sharing resources, strategic plans, and campaigns with the most powerful Islamic state in the world against Christian powers, principally Spain.

While the reach of the Habsburg Empire was massive, it also required vast resources for its defense. Spain's European territories faced multiple military challenges in the sixteenth century, from land wars with France to naval conflicts against the Ottoman Empire, to Corsair raids against its Caribbean possessions, to rebellions in the Netherlands and Aragon, to attempts by French, Dutch, and English expeditions to seize Spanish overseas possessions, which had themselves been taken from indigenous rulers. Added to these concerns was a concern initially entirely spiritual, but which would become all too temporal: the rise of the Protestant Reformation. Although Isabella and Ferdinand had launched Spain into the Americas, it was during the reign of Charles V that Spanish enclaves, huddled along the coastlines and ephemeral in the face of disease, infighting, and conflicts with the indigenous population, became an established empire. Pizarro launched against the Incas and Cortes against the Aztecs: these *conquistadors* brought riches, glory, trade, and vast territories, but also long-standing infamy to Habsburg rule over the Americas.[32]

While Spain could raise armies, deploy ships, and exert diplomatic and commercial means against its military foes, this new danger did not yield itself to the same kinds of material calculations. While Protestant princes and kings would soon pose a strategic challenge for the Holy Roman Empire in central Europe, and other monarchs, such as Elizabeth of England and Jeanne of Navarre, would threaten Habsburg frontiers, initially the insurgency of Reform seemed confined to the realm of theology. Charles V's preference for negotiation, conciliation, and collaboration with local elites in many cases served him well in negotiating settlements and treaties to forestall and end wars through terms of compromise, but it was not an ideal approach to a theology and, eventually, political world view that saw the Catholic Habsburgs as hopelessly corrupt and sworn to a Rome that was, in the view of Martin Luther, in league with the Antichrist.[33]

The Protestant perspective on the Catholic Church and the Holy Roman Empire was not entirely consistent with the record, especially considering these institutions in the years before Luther's public efforts. Indeed, early in his reign Charles had considered restricting, or even eliminating, the Spanish Inquisition, given not only the dearth of genuine heretics in Spain, but also its chilling effect on intellectual revival within Catholicism. From 1516 to 1519, he received petitions from his subjects, most notably from Valladolid and Aragon, supporting the Inquisition's abolition. These protests complained of corruption among Inquisitors and other Church officials and recommended that the Holy Office be forced to proceed more moderately with those accused. Some complaints noted that even if one was found innocent, or guilty of mild offenses, the long process, deprivation of the ability to work, and accompanying privations could leave even those with wealth destitute. Skilled master craftsmen, merchants, and others could find themselves and their families in abject poverty after the years-long investigations and trials that often followed what seemed initially to be mere inquiry based on a misunderstood incident, denunciation by an acquaintance under torture, or comment made in jest or under the influence of alcohol.[34]

Other concerns focused on the methods of the Inquisitors. Rather than resorting immediately to torture and other painful measures with those who might be found innocent, the tribunals were supposed to first use all other means to determine guilt. There is some evidence that, with the strong support of nobles and even some clerical figures, Charles actively considered abolishing, or at least constraining, the Spanish Inquisition several times during the period 1516–1520; even Pope Leo X expressed concerns about the Holy Office, at a time when others proposed the institution at least be more constrained by civil authorities.[35] Was it time to revoke the papal bulls allowing and empowering this unique body? Could heresy and other theological threats to the Church be fought through other means, such as tribunals under the direct authority of bishops, as was the case elsewhere in Christendom?

Elsewhere in Charles' domains there was open rebellion against the Inquisition. In 1516, a mob attacked the tribunal in Palermo, Sicily, destroying the seat of the Viceroy and the Spanish Inquisition. The chief inquisitor fled for Spain, the archive and offices were destroyed, and all activities ceased in Sicily for three years. This level of opposition prompted a three-year delay before the Spanish Inquisition restarted its activities in Sicily. It began to operate again in 1519 but was less active than tribunals in Spain. There was no similar uprising against it in Spain, where the Holy Office rarely lacked for informers, familiars, or volunteers from among the clergy and general population. It seems to be Sicily where it was singularly loathed, perhaps because many of the chief Inquisitors were from Spain. Seeing another rise in opposition in the early 1530s, and perhaps fearing a repeat of 1516, Charles V suspended the activities of the Spanish Inquisition for five years. After allowing it to restart in 1540, he nonetheless held in abeyance its ability to issue death sentences for another five years. However, fearing the spread of Protestantism in Italy, the emperor did not renew this limitation, approving *autos da fe* against Lutherans and Jews in 1541. Full authorization, including the ultimate punishments, resumed in 1546.[36]

Persuaded by the hierarchy that the institution could reform itself, realizing that some of the proposed changes would limit his own authority, and consumed by other issues after he took on the role of Holy Roman Emperor in 1520, Charles did not implement any significant changes to the policies or processes of the Spanish Inquisition. Charles was also persuaded that the rumblings from Germany around Martin Luther showed that the time was not appropriate for the weakening of an institution that had preserved Spain's Catholicism. Had Charles acceded to the petitions from his subjects, if not to eliminate it, then to limit its authority and autonomy, the Holy Office would have been weaker when the Protestant Reformation began in earnest shortly thereafter, with unknown consequences during the sixteenth century.[37] Charles did instruct the Holy Office to moderate its campaigns against *Moriscos* (Muslims that had converted to Christianity) for several decades. In practice, this enabled many former Muslims to return to Islam, practicing openly in Valencia and other regions. In exchange, these communities paid annual tribute and remained allied to the Crown. Even though the campaign against the Ottoman Empire and its allies was initially the driving force in Charles V's campaigns, he was willing to tolerate this population, with the fiction that they were loyal Christians, a point he preferred not to press during this period.[38]

Despite its later image as a land of strict Roman Catholic orthodoxy, in the late fifteenth and early sixteenth centuries Spain experienced a vibrant intellectual period, with the writings of Erasmus and other Christian humanists published, read, taught, and embraced by the Crown, seminary and university faculty, and educated readers among the nobility and others with the means to purchase books. The most famous sponsor of this burst of Renaissance and Christian humanism within Spain was Francisco Ximénez de Cisneros, primate of Spain, Inquisitor General, regent of Spain, confessor of Queen Isabel, and leader of the Spanish Franciscans. More than any other figure, he dominated the religious life of Spain for the two decades prior to the Reformation.[39]

A Dominican friar, pastoral in his approach and initially focused on improving the ethical behavior of both secular and regular clergy, Cisneros expanded his vision to include support for a revival of education across Spain.[40] Erasmus was at the height of his popularity in Spain from 1520 to 1530, and was considered standard reading among educated Spaniards. His most popular work there was *Enchiridion militis christiani* (Handbook of the Christian Knight), translated into Spanish and printed by Miguel de Equia in Alcala in 1524. The vision of Erasmus to promote "spiritual renovation, an endeavor of intellectual culture dominated by an idea of piety" converged and inspired the plans of Cardinal Ciseneros.[41] Spain seemed open to ideas of reform within the Catholic Church, informed by reason and inspired by both compassion and attention to scripture.[42]

In his role as Archbishop of Toledo, the highest-ranking ecclesiastical position in Spain, Cisneros sought to promote religious and secular education. In 1499 he founded in Alcalá de Henares, about 30 kilometers northeast of Madrid, a school that in 1508 would become a university. The core of this institution was the College of San Ildefonso, a center that supported scholars engaged in advanced reading, translation, debate, and other theologically related subjects within the budding humanist tradition in Spain.[43] Promoting classical education, devotion to mysticism, "focused piety and his determination to proclaim his vision of the Christian faith to the peoples of the Spanish kingdoms," at the same time he was an ardent supporter of the work of the Spanish Inquisition.[44] The study of Erasmus and other Christian humanists, as well as the expansion of this perspective to other fields of study beyond theology, was at the core of the Cisnerian project, "a period of renewed vitality and intellectual freedom."[45] The approach of Erasmus, "to strengthen the walls of faith" through reason, careful thought, and even humor, provided the intellectual support and validation for the project at Alcalá. Cisneros invited Erasmus to come to Spain to teach and promote Christian humanism, but the scholar declined.[46]

Encouraging printing presses and supervising the creation of a multilingual Bible, with the Latin translation alongside the original Hebrew and Greek, the last volume of which was published in 1517, Ximénez Cisneros promoted a literate, but nonetheless enthusiastically orthodox form of Catholicism intended not only to reach to all subjects of Spain's kingdoms, but also for export to the New World.[47] In this Cisneros was following the Christian humanist example of Erasmus, an author who not only wrote thoughtful satires such as *In Praise of Folly*, but also compiled a Greek and Latin New Testament that, despite its flaws, would serve as a standard edition for many centuries.[48]

During Cisneros' term as Grand Inquisitor, head of the Spanish Inquisition, he attempted to reform the institution, reducing corruption, improving literacy among the clerics attached, and "dismissing some of the more obnoxious inquisitors" with reputations for cruelty or venality. Despite his leadership role, he was limited in his capacity to humanize the Holy Office given his other roles, the rotation of officials, the lack of unanimity within the hierarchy for these changes, and the decentralized nature of the tribunals.[49] Although Charles V inexplicably shunned the aged cardinal during the king's first year in office, this likely had more to do with court conflicts between Spaniards and Burgundians over policy, personnel, and proximity to Charles. The king himself had shown sympathy toward Erasmus and Christian humanism; perhaps with time the two could have formed a connection and aligned their policies, but the passing of the cardinal in 1517 prevented this.[50] While some would argue that the Erasmian ferment would undermine the Church, making it more vulnerable to the ideas of Luther and other Protestant Reformers, the efforts of Cisneros and his clerical and academic supporters was aimed at strengthening Catholicism and providing it with a stronger foundation in both the spirit and reason.[51]

One key reason why Spain's intellectual environment had become more vibrant at this time was that temporal and religious threats from the other two Abrahamic faiths had declined. As religious rivals, Islam and Judaism had subsided as imminent dangers after 700 years of intermittent warfare between Christian and Muslim states. All non-converted Jews had been expelled in 1492; Muslim communities faced the same result after 1502 in Castile and other lands under Queen Isabella. The efforts of the Spanish Inquisition to target false or incomplete conversions to Catholic Christianity had been thorough and effective. The number of trials declined as religious orthodoxy prevailed. Spain's Catholicism was militant and militaristic in a way that had already begun to fade elsewhere in Europe, where the crusading spirit of the eleventh to fourteenth centuries had declined.[52]

Two key movements within the Catholic Church, the mystics of the *Alumbrados* (Enlightened Ones) and the Christian humanists in the tradition of Erasmus, embraced this opportunity. While the *Alumbrados* were declared heretical in 1525, and persecuted by the Inquisition, the Erasmians were more complicated.[53] The scholar whom the latter imitated, and whose work and reputation initially flourished in Spain within the Catholic intellectual tradition, was the Dutch theologian Desiderius Erasmus Roterodamus, more commonly known then and later as Erasmus. His works were quite popular in Spain, both in Latin and in translation, selling thousands of copies.[54] Initially embraced by Cardinal Francisco Ximénez de Cisneros and other Catholic theologians, his encouragement of piety, devotion, and learning to simplify Christian life converged with Spanish efforts to promote spiritual education, theological engagement, and general knowledge among the clergy and nobility. In the early years of the sixteenth century, especially in the early 1520s, Erasmus "became a virtual idol in the Iberian Peninsula," with his writings, Christian philosophy, and translations of the New Testament in circulation among the educated upper class, universities, and clerics.[55]

By the late 1520s, however, as fear began to grow about the potential impact of the Reformation in Spain, conservative Spanish religious figures, including many affiliated with the Inquisition, began to see troubling parallels between the work of Luther and that of Erasmus.[56] This posed challenges for university faculty, printers, and priests who had identified with, praised, or promoted the work of Erasmus. In 1527–1528, the Inquisition convened a body of experts that reviewed his writings, eventually verifying that Erasmus was not himself a heretic. Ruffled at being questioned in this way, Erasmus produced a bitter response, *Defense Against Some Spanish Monks*, which made his case for his devotion to reforming the Church from within, but also angered those at whom it was directed with comments about the hypocrisy and corruption of religious figures who opposed even the most basic application of true Christian love and humanism to the institutions of Rome and to the transformation of the faith of believers in Christ.[57]

While Emperor Charles V around the same time wrote to Erasmus to assure him of his safety and orthodoxy, it was clear that Spain was no longer so friendly. Prior to Martin Luther's public activity, a scholar like Erasmus would not raise significant suspicions; given the "religious unease" that permeated Spain and Europe, anyone who questioned the Catholic Church or the papacy could be considered a threat and Protestant vector, regardless of the author's claims or loyalty to the Church.[58] Some theologians continued to question the writings of Erasmus, including the Spanish scholar Diego López Zúñiga (also known as Stunica), who in Rome published *Erasmi Roterodami blasphemie o impietates* (*The blasphemy of Erasmus of Rotterdam*), denouncing his errors and identifying his Luther-like positions. In Spain, even if his enemies could not attack him directly, opponents of Erasmus felt comfortable enough to pursue his less protected acolytes through the mechanisms of the Holy Office.[59]

Among the Spaniards most influenced by Erasmus was Juan de Valdés. As an imperial official in the court of Emperor Charles V, he had served the most powerful man in Christendom in the 1520s. It was perhaps during his time in this exalted position that that he gained a feeling of protection from the tribunals of the Spanish Inquisition, a security that proved ephemeral. In 1527, he left the employ of the emperor, beginning studies at the University of Alcalá de Henares. This institution attracted many scholars interested in Erasmus and the general causes of educational reform, bringing Renaissance thought to Spain, enhancing the level of literacy among priests, and reviving classical Greek and Roman studies. A vibrant printing community was also present in Alcalá de Henares, with publications of Erasmus, classics of Greek and Roman literature, the polyglot (Hebrew, Latin, and Greek) Bible translation authorized and funded by Cardinal Cisneros, and a wide range of other classical and modern works, including some translated by Valdés, whose studies of Latin and especially Greek had been quite successful.[60]

In early 1529, Juan de Valdés, with the help of local printer Miguel de Eguía, published in Alcalá de Henares his first original manuscript, *Dialogo de doctrina Christiana*, which soon came to the attention of the Spanish Inquisition. Although this work was initially cleared of accusations of heresy, and indeed received approval from the Holy Office to continue as a published work, the investigation concerned Valdés. Indeed, he should have been concerned, given that some passages of this week were close paraphrases of Luther's writings. Even though the book claimed inspiration from Erasmus, and therefore from within orthodox Catholicism, this was a façade, given its closer reliance on Luther's theology, interpretation of scripture, and implicit critique of official doctrine. The main point of this work – justification by faith – clearly does coincide with Luther. [61]

Juan first consulted with his brother, Alfonso de Valdés, still an official in the court of Emperor Charles V, who exhorted him to defend himself and encourage friendly theologians to weigh in on *Dialogo*. The Inquisition invited scholars and clerics to read and comment on this work, which they found consistent with the teachings of the Church. Even Erasmus sent a letter of support, "expressing his joy" that the inquiry had not found grounds to accuse Valdés of unorthodox theology. Given the Erasmian approach of this book, this exculpation assured Erasmus of his own safety from the Spanish Inquisition.[62] For both men, this relief proved short-lived, as suspicion of the Dutch theologian and his Spanish disciple would soon revive.

In 1531, the Spanish Inquisition launched a new investigation of the work of Juan de Valdés, which now included accusations against his brother Alfonso. As an imperial court official, Alfonso had joined Charles V and defended Erasmus against suspicion of heresy, which by the 1530s was a dangerous role to have played.[63] The departure of Charles from Spain in 1529 had weakened the pro-Erasmus camp immeasurably, as the monarch's focus was elsewhere. The premature death of Alfonso in 1532, by some accounts from the plague, ended the concern of the tribunal over his potential heresies. Unlike others accused by the Spanish Inquisition, he was not convicted or burned in effigy after his death. Juan de Valdés remained under suspicion, even more so given that he had moved to Rome in 1531, beyond the immediate reach of the Holy Office's investigations and tribunals.[64]

While unable to defend himself, and therefore to question the work of the tribunal, no doubt he considered the opportunity to save his own life more vital than preserving his orthodox reputation within Spain. In Italy, he attracted a small group of devotees and continued to teach and write theology. His writing, originally in Spanish, was translated into Italian, English, French, and several other languages. Although he did not directly argue against the existence of the Catholic Church, nor embrace Luther or Calvin, his works would later be considered by the Church as heretical. Valdés was neither Lutheran nor Calvinist, although his theology strayed from orthodox Catholicism. Not declared a heretic during his lifetime – Juan de Valdés died in 1541, never having returned to Spain – his works were later included on the index of forbidden books by both the Roman and Spanish Inquisitions.[65]

Shortly after the death of Valdés, Italy soon became dangerous territory for Protestants and those sympathetic to new ideas; not only the Roman Inquisition, but a revived Catholic Church throughout the peninsula, invigorated by Counter-Reformation initiatives such as the Council of Trent, no longer tolerated those who strayed from the faith. The last city-state where some freedom of worship and of the press for Protestants endured in limited ways was Venice, but even there such practices were no longer safe after 1550. Printers, priests, and lay citizens that had participated in Protestant efforts found themselves in danger from local tribunals, if they did not have the means to leave. Just as Spanish Protestants fled into exile, so too did Italians of the same inclinations, seeking refuge in Geneva, England, or the Protestant states of the Holy Roman Empire. One more state was no longer safe for the unorthodox.[66]

By the 1530s, the Spanish Inquisition had launched cases against almost all the leading Erasmians in Spain, equating them to Lutherans and the *Alhumbrados* in heresy and perdition. The *Alhumbrados* (Illuminated Ones) were Spanish mystics who believed themselves to be in direct connection with Christ, and therefore no longer able to sin or be bound by Church law. Seeing themselves as obedient only to God, they embraced the immediate guidance of the Holy Spirit, rather than the authority of the Catholic Church, its sacraments, or priests. Along with Erasmians, the *Alhumbrados* rejected the scholasticism, formalism, and ritual of the Church, following a simpler form of mystical piety. Led by local priests, and in some cases by inspired women mystics (*beatas*, or blessed ones) and self-identified prophets, these believers organized small groups for worship, prayer, and shared spirituality. Most practitioners were poorly educated, relying on moments of exuberant charisma, putting them in jeopardy of accusations of heresy. Beginning in the late 1520s, the Spanish Inquisition launched efforts to investigate and prosecute this movement as heretical. Within a decade the Holy Office had crushed, driven into exile, or forced underground the last known *Alhumbrados*. Inquisitors at times conflated these mystics with Protestants, dual heresies against the Church, even though *Alhumbrados* believed themselves to be within the Church, if outside its formal structure, parish life, and orthodox theology.[67]

The followers of Erasmus, however, were both more numerous and more prominent in Spain. They also were not as obviously vulnerable to prosecution, given their higher levels of education and outspoken devotion to the Church. Realizing this, some *Alhumbrados* had tried to claim, with little success, that they were Erasmians, and therefore within Catholic orthodoxy.[68] Even so, men such as Juan de Vergara, one of the editors of the Polyglot Bible of Cisneros, were investigated and then prosecuted with vigor. Vergara, who had been chaplain in the court of Charles V, had attended the Diet of Worms, had worked directly for three archbishops, and was considered the leading theological scholar at Alcalá de Henares, could not depend on his prestige, imperial pedigree, or connections to keep him out of the inquisitorial lines of inquiry.[69] Indeed, it was Vergara's earlier defense of Erasmus that caused him great challenges when facing his own investigation. Absent the prestige and imperial protection of his intellectual colleague and facing the additional personal disadvantage of being of *converso* heritage, Vergara was in a weak position to continue fighting the Spanish Inquisition. After a long investigation, in December 1535, Vergara publicly admitted his errors, including possessing Lutheran and other heretical books, speaking positively of Protestant ideas, disrespecting the institution of the Church, and mocking the Pope.[70]

There was some evidence that the Spanish Inquisition in Toledo had tired of jousting with Vergara, whose theological and legal knowledge was superior to that of his adversaries; he was not a semi-literate *Alhumbrado*, susceptible to being trapped into confessing heresy; there was also concern that in the event of a harsh judgment, he might be successful in an appeal to the *Suprema* to overturn his conviction, a defeat which would be humiliating to Toledo's Inquisitors. In return for this confession, which also ended his imprisonment and the expense of a long defense, he was given the mild sentence of a year's monastic seclusion. Erasmus himself died in 1536, leaving his former intellectual fellow travelers more vulnerable, just as the Spanish Inquisition revived its efforts to enforce orthodoxy against the rising threat of the Protestant Reformation and the worldly princes that endorsed the new heresy.[71] No one was immune from the Inquisition as it turned its gaze on Erasmians. Pedro de Lerma, scholar and former chancellor of the University of Alcalá de Henares, faced the Inquisition in 1537 and was ordered to denounce Erasmus. Forced to recant his previous support for Erasmus, but fearing further interrogation, he fled for Paris that same year, assuming a leadership among the theology faculty at the University of the Sorbonne.[72]

As one historian has noted, it was not Erasmus himself that posed a danger to Roman Catholicism. After all, the philosopher was a devout Catholic in addition to being a scholar and popular writer. Erasmus had pledged his loyalty and piety in service to Rome, even if his satires, gentle chidings, and other writings could at times prick the sensitivities of Catholic audiences and the Church hierarchy. The early embrace of Erasmus by ecclesiastical and political leaders in Spain and elsewhere, including by Charles V, showed promise of enabling sincere reform within the Catholic Church; it was the carrying forward of Erasmian ideas in the form of the Protestant rebellion that broke the ostensible unity of Christendom. Initially, it was also the reluctance of Erasmus to take sides in the conflict between Luther and the Roman Catholic Church that caused the Spanish Inquisition and other ecclesiastical leaders to question the true devotion of the humanist scholar Erasmus to orthodox Catholicism.

Holding similar beliefs to those of Luther on the primacy of scripture, the need to combat corruption and abuse within the Church, as well as the intellectual dominance of scholasticism, Erasmus was intrigued by Luther's arguments on theology and the structure of the Church. Despite correspondence between Erasmus and Luther, the Dutch writer eventually backed away from the German's more confrontational style, theology, and direct involvement in politics within the Holy Roman Empire and throughout Christendom. Luther, for his part, rebuffed the admonitions from Erasmus that he should confine his scathing criticism to individuals within the Church, rather than painting all of Catholicism as corrupt, faithless, and out of harmony with the Gospel.[73]

In 1524, Erasmus finally yielded to Catholic ecclesiastical pressure and his own sense of survival and responded to Martin Luther in formal public writing. His reply to Luther's claims came specifically in Erasmus' work *De libero arbitrio* (*Of Free Will*), an attempt to nudge Luther back into the Church. However, the humanist scholar's gentle criticisms infuriated Luther without appeasing orthodox Catholic opinion. Having undertaken an attack on the Protestant Reformer to protect his own reputation and the possibility of travails within the Catholic Church, Erasmus found his anti-Lutheran comments did not achieve either result. Erasmus himself commented, "both camps barricaded themselves, and I received the blows from both sides," with "monks and theologians" calling him "the father of Luther" and Luther referring to Erasmus as "an atheist, a skeptic" and a "blasphemer."[74] Perhaps Erasmus would have been happier not to have been drawn into the debate, given the irreconcilable positions across Europe.

The crossfire from both Catholics and Protestants against Erasmus was both effective and demoralizing. While Erasmus retained his personal liberty and was never directly interrogated or imprisoned by the Spanish Inquisition or similar tribunals, his personal position and privileges were not the same as in early decades. Gone were the early years of the Dutch scholar's fame, when Europe's monarchs competed to bring him to their courts, boasted of their correspondence with him, and hired Erasmians as tutors to their heirs and the sons of prominent nobles. The transition from European celebrity to anathema was as abrupt as it was surprising and disheartening to Erasmus.

Saddened by the hardening of attitudes, and the humorless enforcement of a new orthodoxy, Erasmus was unable to find a middle ground for a reformist consensus that could not only cleanse the Church but reunite it. In one sense, his Catholic critics were correct; absent the foundation built by Erasmus, calling for a more peaceful and spiritual Church, ending compulsion, and simplifying the Christian experience, it is harder to imagine the later successes of Luther, Calvin, and other Reformers. Ironically, the initial hesitation among some theologians to condemn Erasmus, fearing this might drive him to embrace Luther, seems to have ebbed after Erasmus criticized Luther. Having staked his position so clearly against Luther, and with little chance he would embrace the Reformation or be able to seek protection from Lutheran princes, Erasmus left himself vulnerable to criticism, even persecution, by his own side. Given his prestige, he was never arrested, but worth noting is that he never traveled to Spain, where presumably the Spanish Inquisition would have found him too attractive and popular a target to ignore.[75]

By the mid-1530s, even Erasmus was considered one step away from anathema for good Catholics in Spain, even as his writings and ideas gradually faded from their earlier significance and popularity. Not only was he no longer acceptable to the Church, but his musings and style were overcome by events and changing appetites among readers. By the 1550s, some of the author's works even found their way into the Spanish Inquisition's *Index of Forbidden Books*.[76] Having in some ways paved the road for Luther, Erasmus was bypassed by Protestants in Europe, who demanded even greater changes, more provocative denunciations of Catholic corruption and errors, and a new literary genre of martyrology of both Catholic and Protestant victims of Europe's religious wars. Erasmus was also increasingly ignored by Catholic leaders, who despite initial enthusiasm for his ideas, feared that any reforms could lead to an ecclesiastical crisis.

Even more significantly, his calls for reform within the Church were shunted aside amidst fear of Protestant theological insurgencies. While one can see the influence of Erasmian ideas in the Catholic institutional and religious reforms later incorporated through the Council of Trent, this came well after the passing of the Dutch humanist in 1536.[77] As for the Spanish Inquisition, it would soon move beyond the ostensible threat of Erasmus and focus on a more dangerous heresy – Protestantism, which had arrived not only in Europe, but even within the boundaries of Spain itself, an irruption that the Holy Office could not and would not tolerate.[78]

Notes

1 James D. Tracy, *Emperor Charles V, Impresario of War: Campaign Strategy, International Finance, and Domestic Politics* (Cambridge: Cambridge University Press, 2002), 26, 38.
2 Massing, *Fatal Discord*, 402.
3 Martyn Rady, *The Habsburgs: To Rule the World* (New York: Basic Books, 2020), 64. Massing, *Fatal Discord*, ix.
4 John Lynch, *Spain 1516-1598: From Nation State to World Empire* (Oxford: Blackwell, 1991), 51. Fernández Álvarez, *España del Emperador Carlos V*, Vol. XX, xxi. Esteban Sarasa Sanchez, "La Casa Real de Aragon y Castilla: Los Trastámara (1410-1516)," in Redondo Veintemillas and Morte Garcia, *Reyes de Aragón*, 180–181.
5 Joseph Pérez, *The Spanish Inquisition: A History* (New Haven, Connecticut: Yale University Press, 2005), 101. The first reasonably accurate summary, by a former official who advised Napoleon Bonaparte to abolish the Inquisition, is Jose A. Llorente, *La Inquisicion y los espanoles*. Originally published 1812 (Madrid: Castellote, 1973).
6 Pérez, *The Spanish Inquisition*, 102–103, 108–109. Lynn, *Between Court and Confessional*, 18. Schäfer, *Protestantismo Español e Inquisición en el Siglo XVI*, Vol. 1, 239–240.
7 Pérez, The Spanish Inquisition, 115.
8 Schäfer, *Protestantismo Español e Inquisición en el Siglo XVI*, Vol. 1, 245.
9 Lynn, *Between Court and Confessional*, 8, 10–11, 16–17.
10 Pérez, *The Spanish Inquisition*, 1–4.
11 Downey, *Isabella*, 202, 205–207.
12 Homza, *Religious Authority in the Spanish Renaissance*, 76, 99–100.
13 Pérez, *The Spanish Inquisition*, 19–21.
14 Pérez, *The Spanish Inquisition*, 27–28.
15 Alan Mikhail, *God's Shadow: Sultan Selim, His Ottoman Empire, and the Making of the Modern World* (New York: W.W. Norton, 2020), 145–146.
16 Massing, *Fatal Discord*, 407.
17 John Julius Norwich, *Four Princes: Henry VIII, Francis I, Charles V, Suleiman the Magnificent and the Obsessions that Forged Modern Europe* (New York: Atlantic Monthly Press, 2016), 20–22, 25–26.
18 Rady, *The Habsburgs*, 69.

19 Massing, *Fatal Discord*, 312–313. Garrett Mattingly, *Catherine of Aragon* (New York: Quality, 1990. Originally published in 1941), 196–197.
20 Benton Rain Patterson, *With the Heart of a King: Elizabeth I of England, Philip II of Spain, and the Fight for a Nation's Soul and Crown* (New York: St. Martin's Press, 2007), 2–4.
21 Massing, *Fatal Discord*, 560–564, 697–704. Norwich, *Four Princes*, 98–99.
22 Tracy, *Emperor Charles V, Impresario of War*, 311, 315.
23 Ricardo Garcia Cárcel, "Lutero y Carlos V," in Borreguero Beltrán and Retortillo Atienza, *La memoria de un hombre*, 49.
24 Esteban Sarasa Sanchez, "La Casa Real de Aragon y Castilla: Los Trastámara (1410-1516)," in Redondo Veintemillas and Morte Garcia, *Reyes de Aragón*, 176–177.
25 Downey, *Isabella*, 175–177, 235.
26 Ágoston, *The Last Muslim Conquest*, 141–142.
27 Mikhail, *God's Shadow*, 329, 372–373.
28 Ágoston, *The Last Muslim Conquest*, 143.
29 M.J. Rodríguez-Salgado, *The Changing Face of Empire: Charles V, Philip II and Habsburg Authority, 1551-1559* (Cambridge: Cambridge University Press, 1988), 1, 28–30.
30 Encarna Jarque Martínez, "La Casa Real de Aragón y Austria. Aragón en la monarquía universal (1516-1700)," in *Reyes de Aragón*, 183–184.
31 Rodríguez-Salgado, *The Changing Face of Empire*, 26, 253–254.
32 Downey, *Isabella*, 433.
33 Rady, *The Habsburgs*, 65.
34 Griffin, *Journeymen-Printers*, 52–53.
35 Pérez, *The Spanish Inquisition*, 60–61.
36 Henry Charles Lea, *A History of the Inquisition of Spain and the Inquisition in the Spanish Dependencies*, Vol. V, 22, 24–25. D.G. Del Valle, *Anales de la Inquisición* (Madrid: Gregorio Hernando, 1848), 245.
37 John Longhurst, *Erasmus and the Spanish Inquisition: The Case of Juan de Valdés* (Albuquerque: University of New Mexico Press, 1950), 61–70.
38 Fernández Álvarez, *España del Emperador Carlos V*, Vol. XX, xxviii–xxxix, 319–324.
39 Bataillon, *Erasmo y España*, 1.
40 Michael Mullet, *The Catholic Reformation* (London: Routledge, 1999), 22.
41 Luttikhuizen, *Underground Protestantism in Sixteenth Century Spain*, 45–46, 70.
42 Jesús Alonso Burgos, *El luteranismo en Castilla durante el siglo XVI: autos de fe de Valladolid de 21 de mayo y de 8 de octubre de 1559* (San Lorenzo de El Escorial: Editorial Swan, 1983), 14–26.
43 Homza, *Religious Authority in the Spanish Renaissance*, 1–3. Cruz and Perry, eds., *Culture and Control in Counter-Reformation Spain*, xii.
44 MacCulloch, *The Reformation: A History*, 59.
45 Pérez, *The Spanish Inquisition*, 65. Cruz and Perry, eds., *Culture and Control in Counter-Reformation Spain*, xii.
46 R. Olivar-Bertrand, *La revolución erasmista y los españoles* (Quito, Ecuador: Casa de la Cultura Ecuatoriana,1976), 10, 14.
47 MacCulloch, *The Reformation*, 66–67, 80–81.
48 Massing, *Fatal Discord*, 255–256, 262.
49 Longhurst, *Erasmus and the Spanish Inquisition*, 59–60.
50 Lynch, *Spain 1516-1598*, 51. Pérez, *The Spanish Inquisition*, 60.
51 Emilio Martínez, *Recuerdos de Antaño: los mártires españoles de la Reforma del Siglo XVI y la Inquisición* (Valladolid: Consejo Evangélico de Castilla y León, 2009), 11.
52 MacCulloch, *The Reformation*, 56–57.

53 Homza, *Religious Authority in the Spanish Renaissance*, 6–11; Longhurst, *Erasmus and the Spanish Inquisition*, 70–71.

54 Massing, *Fatal Discord*, 679.

55 Longhurst, *Erasmus and the Spanish Inquisition*, 7.

56 John Edwards, *The Inquisitors: The Story of the Grand Inquisitors of the Spanish Inquisition* (Stroud, Gloucestershire, UK: Tempus, 2007), 99.

57 Massing, *Fatal Discord*, 711–712.

58 Pérez, *The Spanish Inquisition*, 66.

59 Longhurst, *Erasmus and the Spanish Inquisition*, 15, 72–75. Homza, *Religious Authority in Renaissance Spain*, 49–50, 52–55. Massing, *Fatal Discord*, 509–510.

60 Longhurst, *Erasmus and the Spanish Inquisition*, 28–32. José C. Nieto, *Juan de Valdés y los orígenes de la Reforma en España e Italia* (Mexico City: Fondo de Cultura Económica, 1979), 152–153, 167–169, 178–179.

61 Pérez, *The Spanish Inquisition*, 68. Carlos Gilly, "Juan de Valdés, traductor y adaptador de escritos de Lutero en su Diálogo de Doctrina christiana," in *Miscelánea de Estudios Hispánicos, Homenajée de los hispanistas de Suiza, a Ramon Sugranyes de Franch* (Carrer Ausiàs Marc, Catalonia: Publicacions de L'Abadia de Montserrat, 1982), 85–86, 89–93, 95, 97–99.

62 Longhurst, *Erasmus and the Spanish Inquisition*, 35–44.

63 Eduard Boehmer, Benjamin Barron Wiffen, and Benjamin B. Wiffen, *Bibliotheca Wiffeniana. Spanish Reformers of Two Centuries from 1520; Their Lives and Writings, According to the Late Benjamin B. Wiffen's Plan and with the Use of His Materials*, Vol. I (New York: B. Franklin, 1971), 65–66.

64 Nieto, *Juan de Valdés y los orígenes de la Reforma en España e Italia*, 40, 233, 234–235, 237.

65 Longhurst, *Erasmus and the Spanish Inquisition*, 47–50, 54. Boehmer, Wiffen, and Wiffen, *Bibliotheca Wiffeniana*, Vol. I, 68–70, 76–77, 115–116. Nieto, *Juan de Valdés y los orígenes de la Reforma en España e Italia*, 44,51–53, 88–90, 237–238, 243–244.

66 Boehmer, Wiffen, and Wiffen, *Bibliotheca Wiffeniana*, Vol. I, 79–80.

67 Pérez, *The Spanish Inquisition*, 66–67. Roland Bainton, *Women of the Reformation: From Spain to Scandinavia* (Minneapolis, Minnesota: Augsburg, 1977). John Edwards, *The Spanish Inquisition* (Stroud, Gloucestershire, UK: Tempus, 1999), 95. Stefanie Pastore, *Una herejía española: conversos, alumbrados e Inquisición (1449-1559)* (Madrid: Marcial Pons, 2010), 165–171.

68 Pérez, *The Spanish Inquisition*, 67–68.

69 Homza, *Religious Authority in the Spanish Renaissance*, 3–5.

70 Homza, *Religious Authority in the Spanish Renaissance*, 32.

71 Longhurst, *Erasmus and the Spanish Inquisition*, 74–77.

72 Luttikhuizen, *Underground Protestantism in Sixteenth Century Spain*, 47.

73 Philippe Bénéton, *The Kingdom Suffereth Violence: The Machiavelli/Erasmus/ More Correspondence and Other Unpublished Documents*, trans. By Paul J. Archambault (South Bend, IN: St. Augustine's Press, 2012), 24, 183–184.

74 Erasmus, "Letter to Boniface Amberbach, Basel, 10 September 1535," in Bénéton, *The Kingdom Suffereth Violence*, 193.

75 Homza, *Religious Authority in the Spanish Renaissance*, xi–xii, 69. Massing, *Fatal Discord*, 677.

76 Pérez, *The Spanish Inquisition*, 72.

77 Massing, *Fatal Discord*, 711–712.

78 David Coleman, "Spain," in Pettegree, ed., *The Reformation World*, 299.

2   The Reformation in Spain, 1517–1556

The coming of the Reformation to Spain posed new problems for the Inquisition. Previously the targets had been clear: new Christians – converted Jews, and to a lesser extent, converted Muslims – and their descendants. Old Christians, those with "pure blood," had simply not been of interest, except in the rarest and most blatant forms of heresy and blasphemy, such as atheism. The ideas of Martin Luther, however, did not respect ancestry, and could be embraced by the rootless as well as the most entrenched noble families. The previous methods, such as the use of genealogical evidence to identify potential threats, were no longer valid. For the Spanish Inquisition, a new approach was essential to cope with this new threat. Any deviation from Catholic orthodoxy, whether from poor religious education or the specific embrace of Reform theology, was therefore a critical threat, as a potential opening that could crumble the ecclesiastical edifice of Spanish and imperial Catholicism.[1]

Martin Luther and his theological and spiritual imperatives initially had little direct impact in Spain. With printing presses and literacy less widespread in Iberia than in the Low Countries, the urban areas of France, or much of the Holy Roman Empire, there were fewer eyes to read Luther's books, especially in their initial German versions. As some historians have illustrated, although Martin Luther's name became well known throughout Europe after 1520, his writings spread less quickly. Their dissemination was hampered not only by censorship and Inquisitorial efforts by Catholic states, but perhaps even more by the "Germanical" tone and emphasis of the author on issues not of universal concern in Christendom. For at least the first few decades after 1517, to be a Protestant was nearly synonymous outside the Holy Roman Empire with being a German. Calvin's writings, initially in French and later in Latin, did not initially expand access to a Spanish audience either.[2] Spain remained on the periphery of the Reformation, even though the movement itself soon moved to the center of Spanish Habsburg strategic thinking under Charles V and Philip II.[3]

That Luther's works were printed primarily in the German language, which he helped to standardize, but which was not a tongue well known outside of central Europe, was also a factor hindering their dissemination. For good reason, some of the first non-Germans charged as Protestant heretics

DOI: 10.4324/9781003197676-3

were accused of translating Luther's works into their vernacular languages, whether English, French, Spanish, or Italian. The Spanish Inquisition was highly attuned to rumors of attempts to smuggle works by Luther or Calvin in any language into Spain, but with so many ports, a long coastline, and a mountainous and porous border with France, their task remained a challenging one. The creativity of smugglers, including adding false bottoms to wine casks, continued to compete against the best sleuthing efforts of the Spanish Inquisition.[4] It was not just works in the Spanish language that might catch the attention of the Inquisition and its collaborators; even unauthorized Latin Bibles could be seized and burned when found without printing and importation approval from Spanish authorities.[5] Mere possession of Lutheran books was sufficient to receive punishment from the Inquisition. Miguel de Veroiz, a merchant from the northern port city of San Sebastian, was convicted in 1567 by the tribunal of Logroño of "dealing with Lutherans and possession of forbidden books." His sentence was public penance, a reprimand, and a fine of 100 ducats.[6]

Over time, it would not be Luther as a person, or his writings in tangible form, but the justifiable fears among Spanish clergy, the monarchy, and officials of the Spanish Inquisition that Luther, and Protestantism more broadly, could pose an existential threat to the underpinnings of not just the Catholic Church, but the Spanish kingdom of Charles I (later Emperor Charles V) and Philip II. Especially after seeing the civil wars, rebellions, and monarchical upheavals that Reformation ideas brought to the Holy Roman Empire, France, and England, these two rulers vowed not to see these troubles come to Spain, pledges that overall they managed to fulfill successfully and completely.

Even so, the authority of the Spanish Inquisition did not extend outside of Spanish territories; Spanish students and teachers throughout Europe encountered the ideas of Luther and Calvin through greater access to the publications and disciples of these teachers in universities and seminaries. While most Spanish Protestants knew better than to return to Spain with these beliefs and writings, some did become significant within the small Protestant communities at home, while others engaged with the broader world in areas outside or only partially under Catholic and imperial authority, such as England, the Low Countries, and the Lutheran states within the Holy Roman Empire.

As Henry Lea, prominent historian of the Spanish Inquisition noted, Spain was hardly in danger of becoming a Protestant nation in the mid-sixteenth century, despite the true devotion of small cells of believers in Seville, Valladolid, and elsewhere. Even if one presumes that every Spaniard accused of heresy was a faithful Protestant, a claim that seems wildly unrealistic, there were nowhere near as many Lutherans and Calvinists to tip the balance away from Catholicism. Rather than seeing a mass conversion rise up from the population (as in the Netherlands), or one decreed from a monarch (as in England and some German states), or a shift enough to cause civil wars (as in France), the impact in Spain was on existing Catholic beliefs and institutions. In Spain, the Protestant Reformation did not achieve support for itself, but instead "the little band of Spanish Protestants" exerted "an enduring influence on the fortunes of the Inquisition, and on the development of the nation." Lutheranism, or more accurately the threat of Lutheranism, provided a much-needed spark to reignite the Inquisition, at the same time attracting the resources to maintain two more centuries of existence for the Holy Office.[7] Even so, absent the immediate and resolute actions of the Spanish Inquisition against hints of Protestant Reform, there was a chance that the initial cells of interest in the ideas of Luther and Calvin could have metastasized into the same wide-scale irruptions seen in the Low Countries, France, and the northern states of the Holy Roman Empire.[8]

The first serious concerns among Inquisitorial officials about this new religious direction emerged after the Diet of Worms, the failed effort by Charles V to use reason and theological argument to bring Martin Luther, the rebel Augustinian monk, back within the fold of the Church. With Luther allowed to depart in safety, thanks to an ill-conceived imperial guarantee of safe passage, his ideas began to spread initially among the German principalities and states of the Holy Roman Emperor, then to other areas within Europe. In some cases, however, the name "Luther" preceded actual knowledge of his theological ideas or deliberate embrace of heresy. Among the first few examples of men and women convicted of the new heresy were several unlikely – or unable – to have read works by "Martín Lutero," whose writings were not yet translated into Spanish. Some Inquisitors seemed equally ignorant, even at this early stage conflating as Lutheranism any ideas inconsistent with Catholic doctrine, including praise for the Ottomans.[9]

Some of the initial carriers of Protestant ideas into Spain were French and Dutch printers, usually journeymen traveling to Spain to work. The first notice by the Spanish Inquisition of the danger of Reformers came as early as the 1520s, with the first Inquisition trial of an accused Lutheran taking place in 1523.[10] In 1524 and 1525, Flemish, Venetian, and German merchant ships were found carrying illegal Lutheran writings; although their cargoes were seized and burned, and those guilty sent to tribunals in Valencia, San Sebastian, and Seville, this would not be the end of efforts to smuggle Protestant writings into Spain.[11] The foreign book trade was of particular concern in Spain, as secular and Inquisitorial officials alike saw this industry and the merchants who conveyed these wares as a potential vector for Protestant ideas. With a modest printing industry in the Iberian Peninsula, most books were imported, especially from Antwerp. This city in the Low Countries was only a major administrative and commercial hub but was also one of the most important centers for publishing in the world, with as many as 11% of all Spanish-language books produced, nearly all for export to Spain and the Spanish Empire.[12]

Indeed, many Spanish-language works were only published in this city, it being more profitable to produce them in the distant Netherlands for export to Spain, rather than to do so in cities such as Seville, Madrid, or even Alcalá de Henares, where there were few presses or qualified printers. There was even a small group of Spanish-language printers in Antwerp, including natives of the peninsula, focused on providing books for their home market and other Spanish-speaking parts of the empire. Their output included works ranging from theology to law to medieval romances. Among the more popular works published in Antwerp for the Spanish market were devotionals, histories, novels, poetry, Greek and Roman classics, and contemporary works by notables such as Erasmus translated into Spanish.[13]

In the 1530s and 1540s, Emperor Charles V granted imperial licenses to some printers in the city of Antwerp to produce Spanish-language editions, with exclusive rights for specific volumes. This was done to ensure the quality of important works, to protect the integrity, especially of religious books, and to control the black market of shoddy reproductions. In addition to assisting in making their enterprise more lucrative, these licenses also conveyed status and legitimacy for other books by the same printers, a helpful imprimatur at a time when censorship and suspicion began to limit presses and distribution. Wide-scale flouting of imperial rules on censorship continued, however; in some cases, the same presses that boasted of the emperor's imprimaturs also produced underground Protestant works.[14]

It was in the late 1540s, however, that Lutheran and Calvinist ideas began to have a significant impact in Spain, with increasing numbers of investigations launched by the Spanish Inquisition, decrees against its incursion, and public statements by state and Church warning of its dangers. The previous openness to reason and classical learning, championed by Cardinal Cisneros, ended abruptly, given the threat of Protestant ideas entering under other auspices, even previously encouraged schools of thought, such as that of Erasmus. As one historian commented, "(b)y 1538, Erasmianism was no longer welcome in Spain, liberal humanism was suspect, and Protestantism was regarded with heightened alarm and, after 1558, relentlessly investigated by the Inquisition."[15]

The alarm about the Reformation encompassed Erasmus, who had always considered himself an orthodox Catholic and corresponded with Popes, kings, cardinals, and emperors, counting among them friends and supporters.[16] While sentences against Erasmians and even *Alhumbrados* had often been modest – financial penalties, penance within the Church, and public apologies for error were quite common – the advent of the Protestant danger intensified sentences commensurate with the existential threat to the Catholic Church in Spain. Increasing numbers of those identified as heretics were no longer allowed to return to the Church; they received the maximum available sentence: death at the hands of secular authorities, after the public ritual of the *auto da fe*.[17] Some arrested by the Inquisition were accused of being simultaneously *Alhumbrados* and Lutherans, as was the case with Maria de Cazalla, arrested in 1531. Despite two years of investigations, the compilation of a massive file of testimony, and multiple interrogations about her views on mysticism and Luther, in the end she was allowed to reconcile to the Church. She was not proven to be either a Protestant or an *Alumbrada*, but presumably the two years she spent detained in the prison of the Holy Office was sufficient punishment to serve as a warning.[18]

Other Protestants were sentenced to a term of service as oarsmen in Spanish galleys, a harsh sentence that often resulted in death or, if not, long-term illness and injuries from the harsh conditions, poor food, and other risks accompanying naval warfare. For example, six French subjects and a Catalan, all convicted of Protestant heresies, were sent to row in the Spanish navy by the Barcelona tribunal of the Inquisition in 1552. Of the 2,232 sentenced to galley service from the Aragon tribunals of the Inquisition between 1560 and 1640, 395, or just under 18%, were Protestants. These were overwhelmingly foreigners, with only 37, or just over 9%, being Spanish subjects. While these numbers of Protestants were small compared to the thousands of *Moriscos*, bigamists, and others sentenced to the galleys, they were nonetheless an example of one method used by the Inquisition to punish heretics who were guilty, but of lesser affiliation to or knowledge of Protestantism than open adherents.[19]

At times, a sentence to the galleys could be extended due to a lack of paperwork granting the end of the punishment. For example, Pierres de Ribera of Rouen (France) was convicted by the tribunal of Toledo of being a Lutheran, having lived in Geneva and practiced as a Calvinist there for eight months, part of a seven-year period during which he was a convinced Protestant. As with other cases, the Inquisitors used the label *"luterano"* indiscriminately for all Protestants. After Ribera's confession and confirmation by witnesses, he was sentenced on 20 July 1570, to confiscation of his property, abjuration in the church of San Pedro Mártir, and four years of service on the king's galleys. On 21 June 1575, his wife reported that she needed a certificate showing completion of his penalty; the navy would not release her husband, despite the end of his sentence. The tribunal provided the document and he was released.[20]

There were small numbers of Protestants convicted by the Spanish Inquisition during the 1520s and 1530s. One of the first to be tried in Spain was Diego de Uceda, arrested in 1528, and accused "as a Lutheran" and "a great heretic." An employee of the Treasurer of Calatrava, working in the service of Emperor Charles V at Burgos, Uceda had been overheard at a tavern dismissing the value of religious images and saying that Luther was right that priests and bishops should be poor. He was denounced to the Inquisition and arrested in Cordoba, where he was visiting relatives. In his case, as well as others from the same time, the records include detailed genealogies, likely a holdover from the investigations of *conversos*. During former trials of converted Jews and their descendants, a high percentage of "Old Christians" among one's ancestors could be a major point in favor of the accused. While this argument was far less relevant with the new Protestant heresy, the practice of noting genealogical information continued at least until the 1540s.[21]

His case was initially dismissed in Cordoba, based on his insistence that he had been misheard. His lineage as an Old Christian and his role in the imperial court were also factors in this initial decision, but it was not the end of his travails. He was transferred to Toledo, where the proceedings restarted.

The Inquisitors presented witnesses and extracted from Uceda a confession that corroborated many statements from him praising Erasmus, encouraging others to read the scholar's work, and expressing doubts about the sacraments and other elements of Catholic doctrine. He had initially resisted the questioning, attesting that he had always been completely faithful to the Church, but after enduring the pain of torture, cried out: "Stop it, I'll tell; I'm dying; stop it, I'll tell."[22] Although he would later attempt to clarify his statements once he was no longer under torture, in the end his frequent praise of Erasmus and refusal to denounce Luther, even while proclaiming he was a faithful Catholic, gained him a conviction. Fortunately for Uceda, he was not convicted of being a Protestant, but instead was allowed to return to the Church. His sentence resembled that of many others found guilty of errors, rather than open defiance of Catholic doctrine:

> On the morning of July 22, 1529 – seventeen months after he had been denounced by Rodrigo Duran – Diego de Uceda, bare-footed and bare-headed, with wax candle in hand, abjured his heresy at an auto de fe in the public square of Toledo. He was required to make seven Saturday pilgrimages to a shrine of his choice, there to recite the Pater Noster and the Ave Maria fifteen times each. On any three Fridays he was to fast on a Lenten diet. He was to confess and take Communion on the next three major Church festivals of Whitsuntide, Christmas and Easter, and was required to submit evidence of having done so. He was also fined sixty ducats.[23]

Among the early executions was that of John Tack, an English subject of Flemish origin, whose death sentence for relapsing into Lutheranism was carried out in Bilbao in 1539. He may have been the first foreigner killed at the orders of the Spanish Inquisition for the Protestant heresy.[24] Tack represented an early example of the shift of Inquisition trials from persecution of *conversos* to that of Protestants; by the mid-1540s, Lutherans and Calvinists eclipsed those accused of being false Jewish converts to Catholicism. By the 1550s, Spanish subjects convicted for Protestantism also exceeded in many tribunals the numbers of those accused of false conversions from Islam to Christianity, an ongoing challenge from the previous century.[25]

At times the Inquisition showed mercy, especially on those for whom there were mitigating factors. On 3 August 1548, Pedro Pul, a German native who had moved to Spain at a young age, was denounced to the tribunal in Toledo. After extensive questioning of Pul and witnesses, they concluded that although he had praised Luther as "a good man" and stated that "Lutherans were better than Spaniards," these errors were made out of ignorance, not deliberate heresy. Pul had been raised in Germany without a proper Catholic background. His parents had died when he was a child and he had come under the influence of Lutherans in the area, with whom he had attended Protestant services three or four times. In view of his youth – he was not yet 20 at the time – his ignorance, and repentance, he was recommended for reconciliation to the Church. He was ordered to participate in a public *auto da fe* "with a lit wax candle in his hands, to purely confess his errors and be pre-emptively absolved" in case of any sins he might have committed out of his ignorance. He promised to be faithful "and obedient to the Holy Mother Catholic Church" from now on "as a true Catholic."[26]

The goals of the Inquisition to find the truth, to punish heresy, and to reconcile the lost to the Church could also intersect in complicated ways. Ignorance, true penitence, and positive witnesses attesting to the character of an accused could moderate the sentence, but these mercies became increasingly rare after the 1540s for those suspected of Protestantism. The absolution and suspension of excommunication for Hernán Rodriguez, arrested in 1547 and convicted in 1548, also included the seizure of his assets, a harsher sentence than what Pul received, but clearly still an example of "extending mercy" to the "truly penitent."[27] Others were found unable to be convicted because they lacked a sound mind, such as Francisco García de Consuegra, accused in 1573 of being Lutheran, who after being interviewed was found to be "crazy and a drunken fool," which explained his comments about being exempt from confession. He was allowed to repent his errors and be reconciled to the Church.[28]

While the majority of accused Spanish Protestants were men, there were women among the cases brought to the Inquisition. Rarely, these resulted from self-reporting of possible heresy. Sister María de San Jerónimo, a nun from Madrid, denounced herself to the Spanish Inquisition in 1581. Over the next 15 years, she participated in a voluntary investigation of her beliefs and behavior. Wracked by guilt over her own sins, she confessed to many failings of spirit and action. Faced with a lack of interest by the tribunal, she wrote an extensive confession and was reconciled. In her apology, she revealed "great fear and shame" about the doubts she had about the Catholic faith. "I humbly ask for mercy," she noted to the Inquisition. Her confession of sins included eating meat at times when it was forbidden and not consistently holding vigils on holy days. At times, she did not treat the cross with proper respect. With multiple witnesses in her favor, attesting to her Catholic orthodoxy, obsession with being a faithful Catholic, and good deeds, she was granted absolution in 1596.[29]

Most accused Protestants were not so fortunate. Francisco del Rio, arrested in 1545, was denounced to the Inquisition for having spoken publicly in favor of Luther and against the Catholic Church. According to testimony presented to the Spanish Inquisition, he spoke "heretical and scandalous words and propositions." In his conviction, the judges noted that del Rio was "affirmed as a Lutheran heretic and in errors and ideas against the Holy Office and determinations of the Catholic Church." Based on his many heresies, he would be excommunicated and "released to the secular authorities" (executed) in public. While his embrace of Lutheranism was so substantial that he could not avoid execution, if he made no more heretical comments and asked to be reconciled to the Church, he could be absolved as a penitent before his death, thus sparing him from an eternity of torment.[30]

More common was the experience of Juan Rosel, a folk healer arrested in 1561 after a two-year investigation. Of French origin, he was 36 when arrested, described as "a small man." Witnesses testified that he had traveled to Germany and brought back Lutheran books. He admitted that he did not respect holy days, since these decisions were made by men and not God, and he believed he had the right to work whenever he wanted. At the time of his arrest, he confessed that he had not been to Mass in three years since God never commanded people to attend this rite. Not especially repentant, he was judged a heretic, Lutheran, and apostate. Posel's sentence was to be excommunicated, have his assets seized, and to be executed by the "secular arm."[31]

This era of heightened concern about Protestantism increased, and to some extent was led by, the Grand Inquisitor Fernando de Valdés, who served in this leadership role from 1547 to 1566. An experienced bishop and Church office holder, he expressed great concern about the threat of heresies within the Church. Unlike many of his colleagues and predecessors, he regarded Erasmus as heterodox, conflating the Catholic humanist with the Protestant threat. An enemy of Archbishop Bartolomé Carranza, who had closer ties to both Charles V and Phillip II, Valdés was upset when Carranza was named Primate of Spain in 1557. Despite provisions that were supposed to protect bishops against the tribunal, Cardinal Valdés would later use the Spanish Inquisition against this rival. Although there were tensions between Philip II and Fernando de Valdés, the increased Protestant threat in the 1550s enabled the Grand Inquisitor to use alarm over this danger to minimize these tensions and encourage the king and court to focus on Luther and Calvin. The king supported this focus, even at the expense of expanding the definition of Lutheran to include a wide range of beliefs and practices.[32]

Valdés also gained major concessions from Pope Paul IV, arguing in a memorandum of September 1558 to the Pope that the threat of the Protestant Reformation required the strength of the Spanish Inquisition to be reinforced. The impact of Luther's campaign had brought a new threat to Spain, with the heresy of Reformist ideas replacing *conversos*, *Moriscos*, and other heresies as the primary danger facing the Catholic Church. Although thus far, the document argued, Spain has remained "freest of this stain" among the nations of the world, this was due to the activity of the Spanish Inquisition, which needed to be reinforced and resourced effectively for the challenges ahead. In January 1559, the Pope agreed to the demands of the Spanish Inquisition. Among the new concessions was a key financial one – to allow the Holy Office to receive dedicated revenues from every cathedral. There was also an exemption, waiving for the Grand Inquisitor and members of the Suprema the requirement after the Council of Trent that bishops reside in their ecclesiastical seat. Finally, in regard to allowable punishments for heretics of this new strain, the Inquisition received papal authorization to execute penitent Protestants under certain circumstances, such as high societal status or the impact of the individual's actions leading others into heresy.[33]

Previously, only unrepentant heretics, or those that had relapsed after initial repentance would normally receive this most severe of punishments from the Spanish Inquisition. It was a mark of the fear of Valdés, Philip, and even the Pope, that the Protestant Reformation was the greatest threat to Catholicism, at least since the division of the Church between Catholicism and Eastern Orthodoxy in the eleventh century. While prior to 1558, Philip had at times followed his father's example, exercising occasional magnanimity toward Protestants and especially repentant former Protestants, this ended in the midst of the rising strength of Calvinism, Lutheranism, and Anglicanism on all fronts. He indeed felt increasingly beleaguered, responding favorably to the Grand Inquisitor's hard line, even against priests and notables who were not only known to the king or close to his father, but had previously been within Philip's inner circle.[34]

The ascension of Philip II also augured an intensified campaign against the Protestant heresy within Spain. Gone were the days of imperial licenses to publishers in Antwerp; in 1558, Philip II issued a decree banning the import, sale, or possession of any Spanish-language book published outside Spain, upon penalty of death for violations. This order effectively destroyed the legal market for publishers from the Netherlands. The king also reinforced the requirement for prior censorship for all books to be published in Spain. While there were eventually some exceptions made, especially for presses that held valid licenses, these restrictions reduced the availability of books in the Spanish market, as domestic producers were unable to match the mass-production capacity, distribution network, and reputation for quality of Antwerp's presses.[35]

Although Philip II's decree did result in an increase in printing in Spain, the modest gains by Spanish presses were weak compared to the explosion of book publishing across Europe in the last half of the sixteenth century. While the target of Philip II's decree was Protestantism and its heresies, he also effectively wounded learning and literacy in general, with Spain a bystander in the dramatic spread of reading and publishing in the sixteenth century across Europe. Similarly, Spain's literacy rates remained much lower than elsewhere in Europe, close to 4% in the sixteenth century, compared with 12% in the Netherlands, 16% in Great Britain, and 19% in France.[36]

The reaction by Philip and his censors was not excessive, but a legitimate response to an active enemy. Protestant writers and printers in the Low Countries, Germany, and Geneva specifically targeted Spanish audiences with translated works. Spanish exiles organized printings and shipments of works by their own authors, as well as Bible translations and Spanish-language works by Luther and Calvin.[37] As early as the 1520s, there were initial Spanish translations of some of Luther's works, with some making their way as far as Spain.[38] Not only books, but clandestine missionaries attempted to spread the ideas of John Calvin throughout Europe, including into Habsburg lands. As much as Philip II rejected compromise with what he and the Holy Office regarded as heresy, so too did militant Calvinists refuse to accept coexistence with, or rule by, Catholic kings and emperors. The lines had hardened by the 1550s and would remain so across Europe for the greater part of a century.[39]

The fears of Charles V, Philip II, and the Spanish Inquisition did come to fruition; there were Spanish Protestants, especially in the 1550s. Although they were fewer in number than in France or the Low Countries, and clearly did not have support from princes as in the Holy Roman Empire, England, and Scandinavia, they were real, devout, and committed to the new doctrines espoused by Luther and Calvin. In two cities, Seville and Valladolid, there were organized cells of Protestants who read, prayed, and worshipped together, although not in large enough numbers at the same times to be considered congregations or churches. While over eight hundred Spaniards and foreigners were tried by the Spanish Inquisition in the 1550s on charges of Protestantism, this was a relatively small number out of perhaps 7.5 million residents in Spain at this time.[40]

It was primarily in ports and major cities where small groups of Protestants were found. Seville was host to a relatively large and prominent community. The Andalucian city, with approximately 120,000 people in the mid-sixteenth century was probably the richest in Spain at the time, as most of the resource and metal wealth of the Indies passed through the port, before being distributed throughout Spain and the empire. As a major commercial center with a cosmopolitan population of English, Italian, French, Flemish, and German merchants, there were also ample opportunities to smuggle in Protestant works, to engage in discussions with foreigners, and to travel internationally: three practices that were inherently suspect from the perspective of the Spanish Inquisition. Indeed, some of the most famous Protestants, and prosecutions of them, were associated with Seville and the surrounding area.[41]

At one point in 1559, there were so many arrests of alleged Protestants in the city and surrounding area that the main headquarters of the Inquisition, Castillo San Jorge, ran out of detention cells and the Holy Office had to contract with nearby houses for additional rooms.[42] So overwhelming did the initial discoveries of Protestants seem, that one anonymous clerk of the Inquisition in Seville wrote: "This city is lost and full of Lutherans."[43] To the Inquisition, the threat was clear, as were the questions: was this just a small element, isolated and easily managed by the local tribunal of the Inquisition, or was this just the first part of a broader and deeper Protestant community within Spain? Could this be managed efficiently at the local level, or would this expose a broader threat which posed a danger to the entire Spanish monarchy and Church?[44]

Among the most prominent Spanish religious teachers and leaders accused by the Spanish Inquisition of Protestant beliefs were Dr Agustín de Cazalla, Juan Gil, and Dr Constantino Ponce de la Fuente.[45] Cazalla, former chaplain and preacher to Charles V, was canon of the cathedral of Salamanca, and a well-known religious teacher. He and his brother, Francisco de Vivero, a parish priest, and their sister, Beatriz de Vivero, were among 14 accused Protestants executed in Valladolid on 21 May 1559. Cazalla no doubt added to the concern of his Inquisitors about the growing Protestant threat within Spain when he noted during his investigation that had the Spanish Inquisition delayed his arrest by four months, there would equal numbers of Protestants and Catholics in Spain. With two more months beyond that, it would be the Protestants arresting the Catholics. While this bombast was a serious exaggeration, it must have been a startling retort to hear, especially delivered to an institution already intently focused on rooting out this heresy in Spain. His promise "to do to them what they do to us" would also have been alarming to the men of the Holy Office, given their use of torture and executions, the latter through the secular state.[46] Some Inquisition leaders also noted the same concern about the potential explosive growth of Protestantism, having seen this pattern elsewhere in Europe.[47]

Cazalla and his two siblings were strangled before their bodies were burned; a mercy, given their full and detailed confessions prior to the day of their execution. The body of their mother, Leonor de Rivero, who had died before their trials, was exhumed, and burned alongside those of her children. Only one of those convicted refused to recant their heretical beliefs and practices; Antonio de Herreruelo, an attorney who rejected the pleadings of his fellow prisoners to renounce his beliefs, was burned alive at the stake before the gathered crowds.[48] The convictions for these individuals were based on possessing Reformed texts, participating in worship or prayer with like-minded Spaniards "outside the official devotional framework of the Catholic Church," and discussing these ideas with others, whether actively proselytizing or not.[49]

Trials of suspected Protestants followed a set process, like other prosecutions by the Spanish Inquisition, with defined roles, procedures, and possible outcomes dependent on the participations of witnesses, attorneys, court officials, and the accused. The example of Pedro de Cazalla, priest and the brother of Agustín de Cazalla, illuminates a typical case. Father Cazalla, a parish priest in the small town of Pedrosa, west of Valladolid, came to trial in spring 1558. The Inquisitorial prosecutor called 33 witnesses to testify, among them Catalina Romana, who had learned from Father Cazalla. She had read the four Gospels and Epistles of St. Paul and, as with others in their group, had come to believe that justification by faith alone, rather than with works, led to salvation in Christ:

> We already have glory in the hope of glory, and not only this, but in suffering we have glory, knowing that in suffering patience works and hopes, and that hope does not cause confusion, because it is the gift of God poured into our hearts by the Holy Spirit that was given to us.[50]

She learned these beliefs from Father Pedro de Cazalla. From him she came to disbelieve in the idea of purgatory, having found no mention of it in the Bible. In a quote that could have come directly from Luther, she cited James 2:17: "faith without works is dead." Romana, also under investigation by the Inquisition, was executed for her beliefs on 21 May 1559, at the first *auto da fe* in Valladolid focused on Spanish Protestants. Philip II's younger sister, Juana, presided over the event, as did the king's son, Don Carlos, crown prince of Spain.[51] Both swore oaths as magistrates, despite their youth: she was 21 and he was a mere 14. Philip II and other member of the royal family would attend other *autos* over the next few years, by their presence showing the monarchy's endorsement of the actions of the Spanish Inquisition.[52]

Faced with significant evidence against him from witnesses such as Romana, and devoted to these beliefs, Father Cazalla confessed on 4 May 1558. He recounted how he had been influenced by sermons by Archbishop Carranza – at the time also under investigation by the Inquisition and soon to be arrested. Cazalla indicated that Carranza had mentioned "some doctors (of theology) from Germany," an allusion to Lutheran teachers, and insisted that since salvation comes from Christ alone, there is no need for purgatory. Cazalla's confession yielded a sentence of guilt as an "apostate heretic Lutheran" who had committed "notorious heresies and errors against our holy Catholic faith and evangelical law and against that which is the holy Roman and apostolic Mother church, ruled and governed by the Holy Spirit." Among his admitted heretical beliefs were that there were only two valid sacraments in the Church: baptism and Communion, the latter as only commemoration of the Last Supper, not as a moment of transubstantiation into the body and blood of Christ. His sentence was to be stripped of his priestly orders, have all his earthly assets confiscated, and to be released to the secular authorities for execution. This sentence was carried out at the *auto da fe* in Valladolid on 8 October 1559, attended by Philip II and Don Carlos. This followed the execution of Pedro's brother Agustín and other family members in May 1559.[53]

There were a variety of beliefs among accused Spanish Protestants, but common to them, as with Reformers throughout Europe, was the tripartite faith in Scripture alone as the way to understand the way of Christ, grace alone as God's intended way to salvation, and faith alone as the human effort needed to receive salvation.[54] The Inquisition was determined to punish those who held these beliefs, whether or not they were available for trials and *autos da fe*. Exhumations and burning in effigy of those convicted were not unusual. For those who had died, the ceremony nonetheless allowed the Inquisition to seize their assets from their estate or heirs. For those on the run, in exile, or otherwise outside the jurisdiction of the Spanish Inquisition, the process allowed the same confiscation of property, as well as alerting other tribunals and government officials to be on the alert for any attempted return to Spanish territory. It also punished the family members or other prospective heirs. In some cases, the prospect of these losses convinced the accused to stay to defend themselves, although this could be a dangerous option, depending on the severity of their alleged heresy. Even when someone convicted and burned in effigy had no resources, or was deceased, the public spectacle was popular and "and provided an extremely satisfying catharsis" to public demands for justice against heretics.[55]

Indeed, the January 1559 concession by Pope Paul IV to the Spanish Inquisition doomed these and other Protestants; prior to this change, their acts of repentance likely would have led to less serious punishments. The belief of both the Grand Inquisitor and Philip II that this extreme danger required extreme efforts, however, led to widespread death sentences against those convicted of the Protestant heresy. There was therefore little incentive to recant, other than to receive the more merciful death of strangulation, rather than meeting the end of life awake and alert to the flames of the burning stake.[56]

Juan Gil, also known as Doctor Egido (or Aegidius), the cathedral preacher of Seville, was first arrested in 1550. He quickly recanted his heretical views and, also receiving a letter of support from Emperor Charles V, was surprisingly not executed. He never claimed to be a Protestant, identifying as an Erasmian Christian humanist and showing some sympathies for the *Alhumbrados*. While others he taught became openly Protestant, he remained a reformist within the Catholic Church.[57] As the lead preacher of the largest cathedral in Spain, he influenced a large audience of lay and clergy, also taking on the role of inspector for parishes within the diocese, disseminating his teachings even more broadly. His messages included admonitions to take care of the needy, to focus on the example of Christ, and to disregard traditional devotions to saints and relics and distractions from salvation through Jesus. After a two-year process, and a detailed investigation of his sermons and writings, in 1552, Gil received his sentence at an *auto da fe* in Seville. Instead of being executed, the tribunal found him mistaken, but not a heretic. After confessing his errors, he received a three-year prison sentence and was forbidden to preach or write theology. Some historians argue that support from the emperor and Gil's popularity mitigated against a more severe sentence, as had his persistent claims that he was a devoted Catholic. Shortly after completing his sentence, he died in 1555. On 20 December 1560, with the mood having shifted toward more severe sentences, Gil was convicted in Seville, and his body exhumed for burning.[58]

Dr Constantino Ponce de la Fuente died before his death sentence could be executed, perhaps by his own hand. Even so, he was burned in effigy on 22 December 1560; two years later his body was exhumed and burned.[59] Born in 1502 near Cuenca, he studied at the University of Alcalá, and arrived in Seville to become a preacher in the cathedral. He was ordained a priest and completed his theological studies at the university in Seville, afterwards therefore being known as "Doctor Constantino."[60] Becoming known for his teaching and preaching, he was invited to deliver the funeral oration for Empress Consort Isabella of Portugal, wife of Charles V. Her death devasted Charles V, who never remarried and wore black for the rest of his life; being chosen to preside over this solemn event was a mark of Ponce de la Fuente's reputation.[61]

During the 1540s, Ponce de la Fuente completed several works of theology and Christian discipline, which he published at his own expense in Seville. Among them were his "Confession of a Sinner," "Summary of Christian Doctrine," and "Exposition of the First Psalm of David."[62] His first work, among his most popular, was an exposition of Jesus' Sermon on the Mount. His works remained focused on Scripture, with little or no mention of the Catholic Church, the role of the Pope or bishops, or any of the contentious issues of theology raised by Luther or Calvin. Summoned by Charles V to serve as the emperor's personal confessor and court chaplain, he left Seville in late 1548, accompanying Prince Philip through Habsburg lands in the Italian peninsula and the Holy Roman Empire until arriving at the imperial court in the Low Countries the next spring. Over the next several years, he accompanied Charles V and Prince Philip on their travels, visiting the Council of Trent and spending time in England during Philip's time as king consort to Queen Mary. He returned to Seville in 1555, his service to the royal court complete.[63]

Appointed canon of Seville Cathedral in 1556, after defeating false accusations that he was married with children, he taught extensively in the city, including in schools. He attracted the negative attention of the Jesuits, who suspected him of heresy, but were initially unable to catch him preaching or writing anything unorthodox. He was even questioned by the Holy Office but was careful not to answer in anything but respectful expressions of Church doctrine. It was only in the summer of 1557, in the midst of arrests of more than one hundred other Protestants, that Inquisitors found documents, written in Ponce de la Fuente's hand, that denounced the Pope as the Antichrist and espoused full-throated identification with the ideas of Martin Luther. Charles V was surprised and disappointed by the news of the Spanish Inquisition's case against his former chaplain, allegedly noting: "if Constantino is a heretic, then he is a great one."[64]

Arrested and interrogated by the Spanish Inquisition, after some initial resistance, he confessed to his Protestant beliefs, refused to recant, and gave himself up for whatever the tribunal thought was fair justice. Never in particularly robust health, his condition deteriorated in the prison of the Inquisition and, before he could be paraded through an *auto da fe* to his execution, he died in his cell. His published works, in which the Spanish Inquisition had failed to find any hints of heresy, were banned in 1559, guilty by reason of authorship, if not content. Ponce de la Fuente's passing in summer 1560 was not the end of his time with the Spanish Inquisition; his body was exhumed on 22 December of that year and burned.[65]

It was challenging to purchase and possess Protestant works within Spain, given the attentiveness of the Spanish Inquisition to illegally imported works. Possessing works was risky, but it was even more dangerous to profess these ideas within earshot of potential informers of the Spanish Inquisition, who could gain financial rewards or social prestige from reporting Protestants. These dangers were much less apparent for Spaniards living and studying elsewhere in Europe so directly. While some Spanish students and scholars had left prior to the enhanced anti-Protestant efforts of the Inquisition, others fled in reaction to fears of their fate at the hands of the tribunal. The loss of intellectuals and scholars certainly weakened Spain's universities and religious institutions. So effective was the Holy Office at discovering Protestants in Spain and deterring those initially open to the ideas of Calvin and Luther that, after 1560, almost all those investigated and tried for these heresies were foreigners – primarily French, Flemish, Dutch, English, or German.[66] The penalties for foreigners were often harsher than those imposed on Spaniards.[67]

Another group of Spanish Protestants clustered around the monastery of San Isidoro del Campo, near Seville. Some of the Hieronymite monks who lived at this location in the early sixteenth century began to read with interest the writings of Luther and other Protestant writers, smuggled from Germany or Geneva into Spain. Among the monks who began to embrace the new religious perspective were Antonio del Corro and Cipriano de Valera. They and 20 other monks out of the 40 in residence at the monastery became Protestants around the year 1556. They shared works, ideas, and discussions about theology and the implications for their faith and the Church of these new ideas. Putting aside what had been the rituals of their monastic order, they embraced the new ideas. Fearing the Spanish Inquisition, Corro, Valera, and ten other monks in their order fled Spain for Geneva in 1557.[68]

Antonio del Corro, a brother in the Hieronymite order, had perhaps become acquainted with Protestant ideas and writings through an older uncle, a senior Inquisitor in Seville, who seems to have shared some heretical works with him. Seeing the progress of the Inquisition in the region, and likely with advance word from his relative about what awaited him if he remained, Corro left Seville. Along with many of his colleagues, he was convicted in absentia and burned in effigy at a Seville *auto da fe* on 26 April 1562. By this time Corro had left Geneva, after arguing with Calvin, traveling to Lausanne to study under the Calvinist theologian Theodore Beza, who would later be named successor to Calvin. In 1559, Corro left Lausanne for Navarre, the Huguenot kingdom in the Pyrenees, under Queen Jeanne, a devout Protestant. At the recommendation of Calvin, the Spaniard became the tutor to Prince Henry of Navarre, who would later become King Henry IV of France.[69] Although the two had argued, at one point over Miguel Servetus, another Spanish Protestant, Calvin thought well enough of Corro to endorse his role as Henry's teacher. Corro was also encouraged to come by the Queen, who promised to allow him to set up a press to produce his works of theology.[70]

In 1566, Corro accepted an invitation to come to Antwerp to preach for the Spanish community there, even while realizing the danger of coming back to the lands controlled by Philip II. At the time, there was hope, perhaps misplaced, that the king would extend the principle of the Augsburg Confession to the Netherlands, allowing the local population to practice Calvinism, provided they pledged loyalty to Philip II. This proved a mistake. In the Netherlands, he was cautioned not to publish writings or preach sermons that would provoke Margaret of Parma, regent of the Netherlands and half-sister to the king. Realizing that to accede to these demands would be a betrayal of his beliefs, he expressed these concerns in a letter to Philip II. This letter from March 1567 was an earnest plea for religious tolerance, noting that the Pope allows the Jews to worship in Rome and that in Istanbul, three religions are allowed. His letter found no echo and so, faced with a tightening circle of denunciations and the possibility of being arrested, in April 1567 he fled to England.[71]

Continuing his life as an exile in England, Corro found a small expatriate community of Spanish Protestants and, although he participated in many theological arguments, enjoyed far greater freedom than he had found elsewhere throughout his travels. For the next two decades, he would serve in a variety of positions from preacher at Temple Church in London to university educator at Oxford to canon at St Paul's Cathedral in London. He continued to write, completing works on theology, Bible commentary, and the French and Spanish languages.[72] His most famous work, *The Spanish Grammar*, is likely the first such work on Spanish. It was initially published in 1586 and translated into English in 1591. Antonio del Corro died in 1591.[73]

Cipriano Valera was younger than many more prominent Spanish Protestant leaders. In Seville, he had learned from Constantino Ponce de la Fuente and Juan Gil, and, as a fellow friar at San Isidro, also knew Cassidoro de Reina and Juan Perez, fleeing Seville for Geneva in 1557 along with other Hieronymite monks from the same community.[74] Valera was burned in effigy by the Spanish Inquisition in Seville in 1562, along with other Spaniards that had fled from the tribunal.[75] He and other Spanish monks from their exile group found Calvin's city in some ways just as confining as Spain, and did not stay long.[76] From Geneva, he made his way to England, where in 1560 he was admitted to Cambridge University to earn his bachelor's degree. By 1563, he had also completed his master's degree at the same institution. In 1565, he became a tutor at Oxford University, but by 1573 he had moved to London to work with fellow Spanish Protestants on translations into Spanish of the Bible and Protestant works. His writings included denunciations of the papacy, exhortations toward Spanish prisoners of the Barbary states to hold fast against both Islam and Catholicism, and a translation in Spanish of Calvin's *Catechism* and *Institutes*. His greatest work was his 1602 edition of the Bible in Spanish, a collaborative work that built on previous translations by Cassidoro de Reina, as well as the initiative of Cardinal Ximenez de Cisneros earlier in the century at Alcalá de Henares.[77]

Reina, who would also write commentaries on the Gospels of John and Matthew, was also possibly the author of the first critical account of the Spanish Inquisition.[78] He also wrote a history of the Popes, through 1588, recounting their sins, vices, and cruelties to show their illegitimacy to rule Christendom. His description of the Pope as "a man of sin, and the son of perdition, of the Antichrist, who is seated in the Temple of God as God" was consistent with the portrayal of the papacy by other Protestant writers. In addition to criticizing both individual Popes and the leadership of the Catholic Church as immoral and in league with Satan, Reina complained about the ban on Spanish vernacular Bibles: "Why do other nations, and not the Spanish, have the ability to read and hear in their own language the word of God, as is written in the Holy Bible?"[79]

Spaniards abroad, especially in Paris, the Lutheran-influenced states of the Holy Roman Empire and the Low Countries, had significantly more opportunities to learn about Protestant ideas, as well as to hold them in relative safety. One example of a Spaniard who embraced Lutheran ideas while abroad was Francisco de Enzinas, who as a teenager studied in the Catholic university in Louvain, but later attended the University of Wittenberg as a student of the Lutheran theologian Philip Melanchthon. At Wittenberg, in addition to collaborating with Melanchthon and other Lutheran scholars, Enzinas dedicated himself to the translation of the Greek New Testament into Spanish, a project in keeping with the Protestant embrace of vernacular languages for worship and reading of the Bible.[80] Some scholars consider him to be the first genuine convert to Lutheranism among Spaniards; certainly in his accomplishments and prestige he was among the most famous of early adopters of the faith.[81]

Having completed this work in 1543, after spending some months in Rome visiting with fellow scholars and Protestants, Enzinas traveled to the Netherlands to supervise the printing of his Spanish translation of the New Testament in Antwerp. The Low Countries was at this time seeing trials and executions of Lutherans, but Enzinas seems not to have been especially concerned. At the encouragement of friends, he was introduced to Emperor Charles V, before who the Spaniard argued for imperial permission to print his Spanish New Testament. The emperor seemed initially favorable to the Spaniard's request, asking him a series of questions to ascertain his religious intent and the scope of his scholarly work. The emperor and his advisors must not have liked the answers provided, however, as three weeks later, on 13 December 1542, Enzinas was arrested.[82]

His case came before the Privy Council in Brussels, which to his friends seemed fortunate, since had the arrest been in Spain or Rome, he would have been before an Inquisitorial tribunal. Even so, the time Enzinas spent at Wittenberg did him great harm, as his interrogation over several months focused on his study under Melanchthon, an avowed Lutheran and "notorious excommunicated heretic" in the eyes of the Catholic Church. Refusing to denounce Melanchthon, and taking a theologically combative position against his accusers, Enzinas found himself in August 1544 not only under investigation, but indicted for heresy, at the direct order of the emperor to whom he had naively brought his initial publishing request. His arguments that "justification by faith alone" was a doctrine that came from the apostle Paul, and not from Luther, if anything made his situation worse.[83] Taking advantage of inadvertently unlocked doors and realizing he could not win his theological and legal case, in early February, Enzinas escaped from Brussels, making his way back to Wittenberg with the assistance of several friends.[84]

He remained vulnerable, however, given that his family remained in Spain and his travels could not help but take him through lands loyal to the Catholic Church and the emperor. Given his flight from justice, an imperial order for his arrest was pending, making him vulnerable to being seized at any time. He initially settled in Basel, Switzerland, beyond the imperial reach. Earning limited income as a teacher and translator, he depended on support from family and friends. Concerned about the possibility of being kidnapped by imperial agents, Enzinas even considered seeking refuge in the Ottoman Empire, having heard from Melanchthon and others of the sultan's religious tolerance; although an Islamic monarchy, Jews and Christians were allowed to practice their faiths relatively unmolested. The burning for heresy in 1547 of his brother, Diego Enzinas, was a terrible blow. This action by the Roman Inquisition weighed heavily on his mind and was a reminder of his vulnerability to the power of the Holy Roman Empire, the Catholic Church, and the Spanish Inquisition. There were few places of true refuge for a Spaniard in his situation, and even fewer for someone so openly identified with Luther; Calvin's Geneva, the Low Countries, and Scotland, all welcoming to Calvinists, were not so accommodating of those following the ideas of Luther.[85] During his time in Geneva, Enzinas wrote to both Charles V and Prince Philip, urging them to restrict the power of the Spanish Inquisition, which was bringing so much suffering into the world, as well as to stand up to the Pope in defense of Spanish freedom. Enzinas implored Charles and Philip to "return to the honor of the Redeeming Son and Our Lord, and do not consent that so many innocents should die" at the hands of "the blind and tyrannical Inquisition," and its partners in Rome, this "dirty and Epicurean multitude of men given to hatred, cruelty and dissolution."[86]

With his message ignored by the Habsburgs, and perhaps to escape the reach of these institutions, in 1548 Enzinas instead accepted a teaching position at Cambridge University, grateful for the invitation from Archbishop Thomas Cranmer. Unsettled in England, and unable to make progress towards publishing his works, he returned to the continent in late 1549, living with his family in Basel and Strasbourg, two towns friendly toward Protestants. In 1552, Enzinas met with Calvin at Geneva, recommended to the Protestant leader by Melanchthon. On 30 December of that year, Enzinas died of the plague in Strasbourg, followed shortly thereafter by his wife.[87] His translations of works by Luther and Calvin, and especially of the New Testament from Greek into Castilian Spanish, and his other scholarly writings based on his command of Greek and Latin, were significant accomplishments. He was one of the few prominent Spaniards to remain aligned with Lutheranism, rather than Calvinism.[88]

Another Spaniard, Juan Díaz, born around 1515 in Cuenca, also became a Protestant through study abroad and travels throughout Europe. He began his university studies at Alcalá de Henares, leaving around the same time as did Juan de Valdés, who fled the inquiries of the Spanish Inquisition. Arriving at the University of Paris in 1532, he found there the intellectual freedom that was gradually fading from his home country. Díaz stayed in Paris for 13 years, learning and becoming an expert in Hebrew, becoming known thereafter for his translations. Through colleagues at the university, likely Huguenots, he also became familiar with and conversant in the writings of Erasmus and Luther.[89]

In 1543, Juan Díaz traveled to Rome, there meeting with Francisco de Enzinas, who likely introduced him to Protestant ideas in a comprehensive way. Two years later, Díaz left Paris for Geneva, where he met and engaged directly with John Calvin, who was favorably impressed by the Spaniard. Moving from there to Strasbourg, Díaz continued to teach and write, now as a committed Protestant. He completed several works in theology and Christian practice, such as *Annotations theologicae*, no longer extant. Because of his understanding and renown as a scholar and teacher, Díaz was subsequently nominated by his fellow Protestants to represent them at the Diet of Ratisbon in 1546. This meeting was convened by the emperor as a last attempt to reconcile Catholics and Protestants under the mantle of Charles V and the Catholic Church, with the monarch hoping for more success in reconciling and reconsolidating the erstwhile theological rebels than was achieved at the Diet of Worms.

The emperor, hoping to attract maximum participation from all theological camps, guaranteed safe passage for all participants, whether Catholic or Protestant. At the imperial meeting, Díaz stood out, as a rare Spaniard among mostly German Protestants. The Spanish delegates on the Catholic side were offended that one of their nationality was arguing for the ideas of Luther and Calvin. Single-handedly, Díaz was undermining the image of Spain as the loyal Catholic champion of Rome not only at this meeting, but at the Council of Trent. Spaniards had been highly prominent at this official Church council, which had begun its theological and organizational work the previous year, focused on strengthening the Catholic Church and equipping believers with the means to combat the Protestant threat.[90]

Drawn into multiple doctrinal debates with a Spanish priest, the Dominican friar Pedro de Malvenda, Juan Díaz ignored warnings from friends to be cautious so close to the power of the emperor and his Catholic allies. Friar Malvenda was a representative of orthodox Catholicism and hoped to persuade Díaz through discussion. Unable to convince Díaz through theological or practical arguments, the friar tried to use warnings about the certainties of imperial justice and even the Spanish Inquisition to persuade his fellow countryman to renounce the Reformation, without success on either front. In the end, it would be a family member whose betrayal would seal his fate. Juan's brother, Alonso Díaz, a lawyer working for the Catholic Church in Rome, made it a personal mission to induce Juan to renounce Protestantism and return to the Church. If this failed, he hoped at least to persuade Juan to accompany him back to Rome but was unsuccessful in this alternative proposal. Alonso was already at work resolving to put an end to heresy by his brother, one way or another. Deciding on the most extreme solution to his brotherly quandary, Alonso secured the assistance of an Italian assassin and plotted Juan's murder. Through the ruse of a letter warning him to beware of danger from Friar Malvenda, Alonso lured Juan to his death in March 1546, after the conclusion of the conciliar meeting in Ratisbon.[91] Although initially convinced of the justice of his actions against heresy, Alonso eventually felt guilt for his actions against his own brother and, wracked by regret, committed suicide in Trent five years later.[92]

Other than during the 1550s and early 1560s, when the Spanish Inquisition found multiple prominent Protestants, and accused even more of heresy, the beliefs of Calvin and Luther did not find much fertile ground in Spain. The small corps of Spanish Protestants, perhaps 1000 or so, were reduced by the fires of the Inquisition or fled into exile.[93] Although in reduced numbers, there continued to be dozens of Protestants brought before tribunals in Aragon in the 1570s, even as those in Castile found fewer Protestant suspects. The Aragonese Inquisition during this period primarily targeted foreigners or those engaged in commerce or other connections to foreign influences, but even with these groups the number of cases and *autos da fe* fell to almost nothing by the end of the decade.[94] The Inquisition would often take months, even years, to gather evidence and witnesses for potential cases to gather more incriminating materials, so there was a lag in processes.[95] Even so, the decline was real over time, as the attraction toward the ideas of Luther and Calvin in Spain had subsided. While Protestant heretics made up fewer than 20% of those tried, convicted, and executed by Inquisition tribunals in Castile, 1570–1625, they were an even smaller percentage, only 10% of those facing a similar fate among the tribunals of the Spanish Inquisition in Aragon.[96]

As some historians have noted, Spain's geographic distance from Germany and Geneva, previous reforms within Spanish Catholicism, and the displacement of potentially Protestant dissent into the *Alhumbrado* movement were factors that mitigated against religious insurgency. Spain was not the Holy Roman Empire, with distinct states and monarchs jealous of their local prerogatives, nor was it the Low Countries or France, with highly developed and prosperous middle classes and upper nobility susceptible to a theology that identified wealth as a sign of God's favor. The effectiveness of the Spanish Inquisition and the uncompromising position of Philip II were the final factors that crushed the tentative and limited efforts by Protestants to bring their beliefs to Spain. While the Protestant Reformation did not take hold in the Iberian Peninsula through mass conversion to the ideas of Luther or Calvin, the new forms of Christianity would remain an external threat to the Habsburgs and their domains for the rest of the sixteenth century.[97]

Notes

1 José Ignacio de la Torre, *Breve Historia de la Inquisición* (Madrid: Nowtilus, 2014), 108–109.
2 Marshall and Ryrie, eds. *The Beginnings of English Protestantism*, 5.
3 David Coleman, "Spain," in Pettegree, ed., *The Reformation World*, 296.
4 On the German-centric interpretation of Luther's theology and success, see Andrew Pettegree, *Brand Luther* (New York: Penguin, 2016), 332–334. No Author, *Protestantism in Spain, Its Progress and Its Extinction by the Inquisition*, 26.
5 Luttikhuizen, *Underground Protestantism in Sixteenth Century Spain*, 171.
6 Archivo Histórico Nacional (AHN), Inquisición, lib. 833, in Schäfer, *Protestantismo Español e Inquisición en el Siglo XVI*, Vol. 2, 20. The financial equivalent in 2022 would be approximately $15,000.
7 Lea, *A History of the Inquisition of Spain and the Inquisition in the Spanish Dependencies*, Vol. III, 411. David Coleman, "Spain," in Pettegree, ed., *The Reformation World*, 298.

8 David Coleman, "Spain," in Pettegree, ed., *The Reformation World*, 297.

9 Pérez, *The Spanish Inquisition*, 62.

10 Lea, *A History of the Inquisition of Spain and the Inquisition in the Spanish Dependencies*, 413.

11 Pérez, *The Spanish Inquisition*, 61.

12 Alexander S. Wilkinson, *Iberian Books: Books Published in Spanish or Portuguese or on the Iberian Peninsula before 1601* (Leiden, Netherlands: Brill, 2010), xvii.

13 César Manrique Figueroa, "Sixteenth Century Spanish Editions Printed in Antwerp Facing Censorship in the Hispanic World: The Case of the Antwerp Printers Nutius and Steelsius," in Violet Soen, Dries Vanysacker and Wim François, eds, *Church, Censorship and Reform in the Early Modern Netherlands* (Turnhout, Belgium: Brepols, 2017), 108–113.

14 Manrique Figueroa, "Sixteenth Century Spanish Editions Printed in Antwerp Facing Censorship in the Hispanic World," 115–116.

15 Mary E. Giles, ed., *Women in the Inquisition: Spain and the New World* (Baltimore: Johns Hopkins University Press, 1999), 5.

16 Homza, *Religious Authority in the Spanish Renaissance*, xix. Lea, *A History of the Inquisition of Spain and the Inquisition in the Spanish Dependencies*, 414–416.

17 Pérez, *The Spanish Inquisition*, 69–70.

18 AHN, Inquisición, Legajo 110, Exp. 6. Inquisición, Toledo, 1531–1535. Maria de Cazalla.

19 Monter, *Frontiers of Heresy*, 33–35, 328. These figures exclude the tribunal in Sicily which, although organizationally part of the Aragonese Secretariat of the Spanish Inquisition, was outside Spain.

20 Schäfer, *Protestantismo Español e Inquisición en el Siglo XVI*, Vol. 2, 237–238. AHN, Inquisición de Toledo, leg. 112, N. 8.

21 AHN, Inquisición, Legajo 112, Expediente 22. Ignacio, *Breve Historia de la Inquisición*, 109.

22 John Longhurst, *Luther's Ghost in Spain (1517-1546)* (Lawrence, Kansas: Coronado Press, 1969), 130.

23 Longhurst, *Luther's Ghost in Spain*, 133.

24 Monter, *Frontiers of Heresy*, 37.

25 Monter, *Frontiers of Heresy*, 38–39.

26 AHN, Inquisición, Legajo 112, Exp. 4. Inquisición, Toledo, 1548–51, Pul, Pedro.

27 AHN, Inquisición, Legajo 112, Exp. 11. Inquisición, Toledo, 1547–1548, Rodriguez, Hernán.

28 AHN, Inquisición, Legajo 110, Exp. 11. Inquisición, Toledo, 1573–1574, García de Consuegra, Francisco.

29 AHN, Inquisición, Legajo 110, Exp. 12. Inquisición, Toledo, 1581–1596, San Jerónimo, María de.

30 AHN, Inquisición, Legajo 112, Exp. 7. Inquisición, Toledo, 1545–1550, Rio, Francisco del.

31 AHN, Inquisición, Legajo 112, Exp. 13. Inquisición, Toledo, 1561, Rosel, Juan.

32 Pérez, *The Spanish Inquisition*, 106–107.

33 Monter, *Frontiers of Heresy*, 40–42. Bataillon, *Erasmo y España*, 709.

34 Edwards, *The Spanish Inquisition Refashioned*, 47–48.

35 Manrique Figueroa, "Sixteenth Century Spanish Editions Printed in Antwerp Facing Censorship in the Hispanic World," 117–120.

36 Eltjo Buringh and Jan Luiten Van Zanden, "Charting the 'Rise of the West': Manuscripts and Printed Books in Europe, a Long-Term Perspective from the Sixth through Eighteenth Centuries," *Journal of Economic History*, June 2009, Vol. 69, No. 2, 417, 421, 434.

37 Boehmer, Wiffen, and Wiffen, *Bibliotheca Wiffeniana*, Vol. II, 65.

38 Alonso Burgos, *El luteranismo en Castilla durante el siglo XVI*, 52. Nieto, *Juan de Valdés y los orígenes de la Reforma en España e Italia*, 546–549.
39 Lynch, *Spain 1516-1598*, 343.
40 Lynch, *Spain 1516-1598*, 347. Jan de Vries, "Population," in Thomas A. Brady, Heiko A. Oberman, and James D. Tracy, eds., *Handbook of European History, 1400-1600* (Leiden, Netherlands: Brill, 1994), 13.
41 Gabino Fernández Campos, *Reforma y contrarreforma en Andalucía* (Seville: Editorial MAD, 2006), 19. López Muñoz, *La Reforma en la Sevilla del XVI*, Vol. I, 20, 22, 30–31, 44.
42 Luttikhuizen, *Underground Protestantism in Sixteenth Century Spain*, 221.
43 "Estaba esta ciudad perdida y llena de luteranos." Schäfer, *Protestantismo Español e Inquisición en el Siglo XVI*, Vol. 1, 370.
44 López Muñoz, *La Reforma en la Sevilla del XVI*, Vol. I, 9.
45 Lynch, *Spain 1516-1598*, 345–347. Fernández Campos, *Reforma y contrarreforma en Andalucía*, 23.
46 Enric Balasch Blanch and Yolanda Ruiz Arranz, *Atlas Ilustrado: La Inquisición en España* (Madrid: Susaeta, 2014), 147.
47 Fernández Campos, *Reforma y contrarreforma en Andalucía*, 24. Adolfo de Castro, *The Spanish Protestants and Their Persecution by Philip*, trans. by Thomas Parker (London: Charles Gilpin, 1851), 15.
48 Pérez, *The Spanish Inquisition*, 69–70.
49 Edwards, *The Spanish Inquisition Refashioned*, 43.
50 "Proceso criminal del Fiscal de Este Santo Oficio contra Pedro de Catalla, clerigo, cura de Pedrosa, natural de esta villa de Valladolid, hermano de doctor Cazalla," Valladolid, 1558. *Procesos de protestantes españoles en el siglo XVI* (Madrid: Revista de Archivos, Bibliotecas, y Museos, 1910), Microfilm. Biblioteca Nacional, Madrid: Archivo de Simancas, 72–73. No Author, *Protestantism in Spain, its Progress and its Extinction by the Inquisition*, 40.
51 Luttikhuizen, *Underground Protestantism in Sixteenth Century Spain*, 116.
52 "Proceso criminal del Fiscal de Este Santo Oficio contra Pedro de Catalla," 73.
53 "Proceso criminal del Fiscal de Este Santo Oficio contra Pedro de Catalla," 96–97, 107, 192. No Author, *Protestantism in Spain, Its Progress and Its Extinction by the Inquisition*, 43–51.
54 Fernández Campos, *Reforma y contrarreforma en Andalucía*, 45.
55 Monter, *Frontiers of Heresy*, 21, 331.
56 Monter, *Frontiers of Heresy*, 42–43.
57 Robert C. Spach, "Juan Gil and Sixteenth-Century Spanish Protestantism," *The Sixteenth Century Journal*, 1995, Vol. 26, No. 4, 858. https://doi.org/10.2307/2543791.
58 Pérez, *The Spanish Inquisition*, 71. No Author, *Protestantism in Spain, Its Progress and Its Extinction by the Inquisition*, 16–17, 23–25.
59 Pérez, *The Spanish Inquisition*, 70.
60 Boehmer, Wiffen, and Wiffen, *Bibliotheca Wiffeniana*, Vol. II, 4–5.
61 Boehmer, Wiffen, and Wiffen, *Bibliotheca Wiffeniana*, Vol. II, 7–8.
62 Constantino Ponce de la Fuente, "Exposición del Primer Salmo de David, Confesión de un Pecador," in Emilio Monjo Bellido, ed., *Obras de los Reformadores Españoles del Siglo XVI* (Seville: Editorial MAD, 2009), 28–36.
63 Boehmer, Wiffen, and Wiffen, *Bibliotheca Wiffeniana*, Vol. II, 10–12.
64 Boehmer, Wiffen, and Wiffen, *Bibliotheca Wiffeniana*, Vol. II, 17.
65 Boehmer, Wiffen, and Wiffen, *Bibliotheca Wiffeniana*, Vol. II, 17–18, 33–34.
66 Pérez, *The Spanish Inquisition*, 71.
67 Schäfer, *Protestantismo Español e Inquisición en el Siglo XVI*; AHN, Inquisición, lib. 834, fol. 74, 32.

68 Boehmer, Wiffen, and Wiffen, *Bibliotheca Wiffeniana*, Vol. III, 3.
69 Boehmer, Wiffen, and Wiffen, *Bibliotheca Wiffeniana*, Vol. III, 6–9.
70 Boehmer, Wiffen, and Wiffen, *Bibliotheca Wiffeniana*, Vol. III, 10–11.
71 Boehmer, Wiffen, and Wiffen, *Bibliotheca Wiffeniana*, Vol. III, 25–28. Antonio del Corro, "Carta a los Pastores Luteranos de Amberes, Carta a Felipe II, Carta a Casiodoro de Reina, Exposición de la Obra de Dios," in Monjo Bellido, ed., *Obras de los Reformadores Españoles del Siglo XVI*.
72 Antonio del Corro, "Comentario Dialogado de la Carta a los Romanos," in Francisco Ruiz de Pablos, ed., *Obras de los Reformadores Españoles del Siglo XVI* (Seville: Editorial MAD, 2010).
73 Boehmer, Wiffen, and Wiffen, *Bibliotheca Wiffeniana*, Vol. III, 28–77.
74 Fernández Campos, *Reforma y contrarreforma en Andalucía*, 55–56. Luttikhuizen, *Underground Protestantism in Sixteenth Century Spain*, 280–293.
75 Boehmer, Wiffen, and Wiffen, *Bibliotheca Wiffeniana*, Vol. III, 149–150.
76 López Muñoz, *La Reforma en la Sevilla del XVI*, Vol. I, 147–148.
77 Boehmer, Wiffen, and Wiffen, *Bibliotheca Wiffeniana*, Vol. III, 151–157.
78 Casiodoro de Reina, "Comentario al Evangelio de Juan," in Francisco Ruiz de Pablos, ed., *Obras de los Reformadores Españoles del Siglo XVI* (Seville: Editorial MAD, 2009), 16–18. The work in question, *Sanctae inquisitionis Hispanicae artes aliquot detectae*, (*Some Arts of the Spanish Inquisition*), is examined in Chapter 3.
79 *Reformistas antiguos españoles*, Vol. 6, "Dos Tratados: El Papa i de sus autoridad, colejido de su vida I dotrina" and "De la misa: el uno i el otro recopilado de lo que los doctors y gonzilios antiguos, i la sagrada escritura enseñan," ix, x.
80 "Enzinas, Diego de," Real Academia de la Historia," accessed 17 February 2022, https://dbe.rah.es/biografias/64865/diego-de-enzinas. Els Agten, "Traveling Scholars and Circulating Ideas in Early Modern Europe. The Case of Francisco Enzinas," in Borreguero Beltrán and Retortillo Atienza, *La memoria de un hombre*, 248–249.
81 Pérez, *The Spanish Inquisition*, 63–64.
82 Boehmer, Wiffen, and Wiffen, *Bibliotheca Wiffeniana*, Vol. I, 135–140.
83 Boehmer, Wiffen, and Wiffen, *Bibliotheca Wiffeniana*, Vol. I, 140–143.
84 Boehmer, Wiffen, and Wiffen, *Bibliotheca Wiffeniana*, Vol. I, 143–144. Els Agten, "Traveling Scholars and Circulating Ideas in Early Modern Europe. The Case of Francisco Enzinas," in Borreguero Beltrán and Retortillo Atienza, *La memoria de un hombre*, 250–251.
85 "Enzinas, Diego de," Real Academia de la Historia, accessed 17 February 2022, https://dbe.rah.es/biografias/64865/diego-de-enzinas; Els Agten, "Traveling Scholars and Circulating Ideas in Early Modern Europe. The Case of Francisco Enzinas," in Borreguero Beltrán and Retortillo Atienza, *La memoria de un hombre*, 252–253.
86 *Reformistas antiguos españoles*, Vol. 12, "Dos Informaziones: una dirigida al Emperador Carlos V, i otra, a los Estados del Imperio, obra, al parezer, de Franzisco de Enzinas. Prezede una Suplicazion a D. Felipe II, obra, al parezer, del Dr. Juan Perez. 1857," 35, 187, 189.
87 Boehmer, Wiffen, and Wiffen, *Bibliotheca Wiffeniana*, Vol. I, 149–155. Els Agten, "Traveling Scholars and Circulating Ideas in Early Modern Europe. The Case of Francisco Enzinas," in Borreguero Beltrán and Retortillo Atienza, *La memoria de un hombre*, 253–254, 259–260.
88 "Enzinas, Francisco de," *Real Academia de la Historia*, accessed 17 February 2022, https://dbe.rah.es/biografias/6721/francisco-de-enzinas.
89 Boehmer, Wiffen, and Wiffen, *Bibliotheca Wiffeniana*, Vol. I, 187.
90 Boehmer, Wiffen, and Wiffen, *Bibliotheca Wiffeniana*, 187–190, 199.
91 "Díaz, Juan," Real Academia de la Historia, accessed 17 February 2022, https://dbe.rah.es/biografias/64861/juan-diaz; Boehmer, Wiffen, and Wiffen, *Bibliotheca Wiffeniana*, 191–195.

92 Boehmer, Wiffen, and Wiffen, *Bibliotheca Wiffeniana*, Vol. I, 198.
93 David Coleman, "Spain," in Pettegree, ed., *The Reformation World*, 301–305.
94 Monter, *Frontiers of Heresy*, 44–45.
95 No Author, *Protestantism in Spain, Its Progress and Its Extinction by the Inquisition*, 27–28.
96 Monter, *Frontiers of Heresy*, 48–49.
97 Pérez, *The Spanish Inquisition*, 71–72.

3 Charles V, Martin Luther, and the Habsburg Empire

The Protestant Reformation within Spain had, despite some initial concerns about its threat to the monarchy, Church, and society, limited long-term impact in terms of religious affiliation: no permanent Protestant Church emerged on Spanish soil. However, just as these new religious movements could lead to internal concerns and an intensified focus from the Spanish Inquisition, so the broader challenge of the ideas of Luther, Calvin, and other Reformers imposed costs and questions on Habsburg domains elsewhere. Holy Roman Emperor Charles V and his son, King Philip II, were the leading monarchs of the western branch of the Habsburg monarchy, a ruling dynasty that reigned over Spain, much of Italy, modern-day Belgium and the Netherlands, most of the western hemisphere and other territories on three continents. For much of this period, beginning in the late sixteenth century and into the early seventeenth century, Philip II and his heirs also controlled Portugal and the Portuguese empire in Brazil, South Asia, and littoral southern Africa.

For good reason the Habsburg realms enabled their monarchs to nurture ambitions to lead a universal empire, ruling all Catholic Christendom in Europe and the wider world. While in the end they failed to establish this global state, that they could realistically imagine doing so, and strike fear into their enemies over the prospect, gives a clear indication of their secular power and imperial potential. Not powerful enough to defeat all their enemies at once, but too strong to be defeated decisively by any of their rivals, Charles V and Philip II, successively, were mighty enough to imagine a final victory, but not powerful enough to bring this dream to fruition. For both men, it was "the religious question" that was central to their decision-making. Their primary endeavors focused on promoting the unity of their realms through ardent support to Catholicism, the Catholic Church as an institution and, in the case of Spanish territory, the Spanish Inquisition.[1]

While Charles V had initially set limits on the actions of the Spanish Inquisition, making clear that he supported Erasmus and would brook no inquiry of the writer, the travels of the emperor kept him away from Spain for many years at a time, allowing the Holy Office a great deal of autonomy. Absent the protection of the emperor, many Erasmians, even devout Catholics and those close to the monarch, found themselves under the watchful eye of

DOI: 10.4324/9781003197676-4

the Inquisition. This hesitation and desire to protect some of his subjects did not extend to the emperor's son, Philip, who empowered the Holy Office to proceed in all cases of suspected heresy, even against those in the king's inner circle of advisors, clerics, and family members.[2] Although in individual cases the emperor at times proposed moderation on the part of the Spanish Inquisition, and did seem more willing to consider compromises with Protestants than did his son, Charles V was nonetheless an ardent enemy of the Reformation, hoped to drive it from his lands and all of Europe, and only hesitated when confronted by insurmountable odds, when his resources were exhausted, or when he hoped to draw Protestants back into the Catholic Church through a temporarily moderate approach.[3]

Philip II, despite his wars against England, France, the Ottoman Empire, and Dutch, Portuguese, and Italian rebels, was without question the most powerful man of his age. The list of his royal and princely titles gives a sense of the scale of his secular and spiritual authority, but also his obligations and entanglements. He was King of Castile, of Aragon, of Portugal, of the Two Sicilies, of Gibraltar, of the Canary Islands, of the Indies, the Islands and Mainland of the Ocean Sea; Count of Barcelona; Duke of Milan and Burgundy; Archduke of Austria; Lord of the Netherlands, and Prince of Swabia. For four years, while married to Mary Tudor, he was also *de facto* King of England, France, and Ireland, although he endured the humiliation of never being formally crowned with this title. Finally, in an expression of Spain's ongoing crusading fervor and desire to return to the Holy Land, Philip II remained one of several pretenders for the Kingdom of Jerusalem, a distant land, but still within the king's vision for his empire.

The challenge the Protestant Reformation posed to Philip II, "The Most Catholic King," was not just in these many far-flung domains and on the battlefields of Europe, but to the temporal and spiritual legitimacy of the Catholic monarchy itself. Philip's Protestant enemies offered him multiple false choices, including demands for religious tolerance, a permanent truce, or conversion to Lutheranism or Calvinism. However, Philip II's only real strategic option was unremitting external warfare paralleled by internal persecution of these new faiths. In this context, the revival and strengthening of the Spanish Inquisition, the unremitting search for Protestant elements within Spain, and the constant campaigns to defend the limits of Catholicism in Europe were legitimate responses to the only existential threat to the largest empire of the sixteenth century. More of a strategist than his father, Philip II saw Castile as the center of his empire, unlike Charles V, whose peripatetic imperial style reduced his capacity to focus on one threat, such as France, the Ottomans, or Martin Luther.[4]

The Protestant Reformation was not the only danger. Spain faced the powerful kingdom of France on its northern border, a rival Catholic power that caused no end of problems for Spain in Italy, in relations with the Vatican, and even dared to ally with the other great temporal threat, the Ottoman Empire. To the East, the Ottoman Empire was an expansive and militant Muslim state, led by Turkish sultans devoted to *jihad* against the West.

Ottoman and Spanish navies clashed repeatedly in the Mediterranean, most famously in the apocalyptic sea battle of Lepanto of 1571. While the English were no real rival, despite their 1588 defeat of the Spanish Armada, they continued to be a peripheral threat to Spanish shipping and colonies, as well as a supporter of Dutch Calvinist rebels against Philip in the Netherlands. Although Protestant England was fiercely anti-Spanish, blaming Philip and Mary for their persecution of Protestants through the English Inquisition, the English were unable to fund or field sufficient forces to threaten the heart of the Spanish empire. The French, Ottomans, and English on their own were relatively conventional threats, which Spain was able to counter through armies and navies. Moreover, these were external dangers; Philip II did not fear large numbers of his subjects suddenly converting to Islam to enlist in the Ottoman armed forces or rushing to the French border to ally with King Francis I in Paris.

As the German princes could and did warn Philip, however, the theological earthquake of the Protestant Reformation could transform populations in a matter of months, overturning centuries of Catholic faith, expelling priests, and desecrating what had been holy. This was what Philip feared, more than Ottoman galleys disgorging Turks near Barcelona, French soldiers pouring across the Pyrenees, or England's pirates sailing up the Guadalquivir to sack Seville's cathedral. Devotion to the Roman Catholic Church, and the indissoluble tie between monarchy and faith, was the essential buttress for kingship. Questioning either Church or state, so intertwined that the withering of one could cause the death of the other, was a mortal threat to Philip II's reign, indeed, to the entire ideological and theological justification for the Habsburg state. While enemies abounded for both Philip and Charles, only the Protestant Reformation and its ardent believers "menaced the destruction of the spiritual unity of the empire."[5]

At the time of his coronation as Holy Roman Emperor in 1519, Charles V did not intend to engage in religious warfare within his European territories. Looking to safeguard his inherited domains, he also hoped to marry well, seeking for several years a bride who would bring additional territory and resources, diplomatic advantages, and be likely to produce an heir. After considering French, English, and German prospects, he eventually chose a Portuguese princess, Isabel, who in addition to a sizable dowry could be expected to buttress his rule in Spain and act as queen regent in his absence for what he expected would be extended campaigns against Islam.[6] Indeed, his preferred enemy was the vast Ottoman Empire, which loomed large and threatening in the Eastern Mediterranean and south-eastern Europe. Although not himself a Spaniard, he embraced the Crusading vision of previous Spanish kings and queens, who dreamed of following the anticipated conquest of North Africa by proceeding along the Mediterranean coast to liberate Jerusalem from Islam. This hoped-for route of campaign became known as the Spanish Road. Crusading popes had in earlier centuries mandated that Spanish knights and other warriors consecrated to the fight for the Holy Land confine their fighting against Muslims initially to the Iberian

Peninsula until the Reconquista was won. The road to the Church of the Holy Sepulcher, where Jesus walked and pilgrims prayed to follow passed not through the Levant, but across the straits of Gibraltar and through the North African littoral.

The first news of Martin Luther's declarations against the Church came to the imperial court soon after 1517, when the Augustinian monk nailed his *Ninety-five Theses* to the church door. His arguments for justification through faith and against corruption within the Catholic Church resonated across Europe, building on previous criticisms by Erasmus and other authors of corruption and doctrinal failings within the Christian traditions. Redemption through Christ alone, rather than mediated through the institutions, rituals, and sacraments of the Church, Luther argued, was the route to salvation. Luther provoked the ecclesiastical hierarchy and the papacy, given his harsh criticisms of practices such as indulgences, the selling of Church offices, stacking the income and privileges of multiple Church sinecures, and abject moral failures within the Church, including widespread bribery and excesses within the Vatican itself.[7] Through sermons and publications such as "To The Christian Nobility of the German Nation" and "Of The Liberty of a Christian Man," Luther presented a strong case for resisting the directives of a corrupt Catholic Church, accepting that grace came directly from God, and that works were empty of salvatory value.[8]

Emperor Charles V, hearing of the increasing popularity of Luther, even among some priests and bishops, resolved to confront the monk directly, urging him to recant for the good of Christendom. Promising safe conduct, he invited Luther to defend himself before the Church's leading theologians. At the Diet of Worms, Charles V intended to convince Luther to admit to his errors, hoping by this anticipated return to the faith he could pre-empt the spread of dissent within the Church. Many of his key advisors tried to dissuade the emperor from this public display, realizing the noted rhetorical skills of Luther, as well as his fierce determination not to back down in the face of pressure. The Franciscan Jean Glapion, the emperor's counselor and confessor, tried to convince him to leave debating Luther to Erasmus, rather than elevating the Augustinian monk to a position of equal status. Perhaps this approach might have kept Luther within the Church, or at least minimized his international celebrity.[9] In the event, the confrontation went badly for Charles V. Emboldened by the imperial safe conduct, Luther took advantage of the opportunity to push his case for reform, either within the Catholic Church or outside of it. Charles would spend the next 37 years, until his death at the age of 58, confounded by the Reformation. Unable to persuade its ending, he also lacked the will and resources to prosecute a war of elimination against this disruption in the unity of Christendom.[10]

The emperor missed a key opportunity to stop Luther before one monk became a movement. Some of Charles' ministers suggested he reverse his promise of safe conduct and arrest Luther, or at least dispatch agents after the Diet to arrest him away from the city. Indeed, it seems as if the emperor was resigned to tolerate Luther within Catholicism; after the Diet he transferred most of his imperial lands to his brother, Frederick, naming him regent over the Holy Roman Empire and leaving Luther as an unmet challenge.[11] The emperor did condemn Luther strongly after the conclusion of the Diet as a "notorious heretic," calling upon the princes of the Holy Roman Empire to join him in crushing the upstart monk. With imperial states already seeing widespread conversions to Luther's ideas, and the former monk receiving promises of protection against imperial forces, the unity desired by Charles V was not to be.[12]

In his written response to Luther, issued after the Diet, Charles V made additional mistakes. The first error was responding in French, given that Luther was German, as were nearly all the princes of the Holy Roman Empire, as well as the initial audiences for Luther's messages. The emperor never did learn German, which would be a challenge for him in this role.[13] In his letter, the emperor did not directly address the theological claims of Luther, losing a key opportunity.[14] The emperor would later express deep regret over not having seized and executed Luther at Worms. The emperor's inability to convince the Pope to convene a Church council, or to accommodate any of the complaints of Luther within the Church, also came as a defeat to Charles, who for many years persisted in the hope of a reconciliation within Christendom.[15]

The emperor and his allies in a sense failed in both directions, being neither harsh enough to crush Luther, nor welcoming enough to maintain him within Catholicism. On the side of a harsh response, the time for this could have been immediately after Worms. Seeing the enormity of Luther's heresy as a mortal sin against God, Charles could have justified not honoring the safe conduct he had granted to the monk in the name of saving the Church and Empire; few would have questioned the most powerful man in the world, backed by the spiritual authority of the Pope, in repressing one lone heretic. With the failure of Charles V's attempt at accommodation from the 1520s to the 1540s, and his parallel unwillingness to use every means at his disposal against Luther and his supporters, "a century of religious wars would commence across Europe."[16]

Although it would be too much to describe Martin Luther as an ally of the Ottoman Turks, each contributed to opportunities for the other. Charles V needed the military support of German, Hungarian, and other princes against the Turks in central Europe, and so hesitated to unleash a campaign against areas that sympathized with Luther. Similarly, the ongoing internal threat of Luther's ideas to the unity of the Holy Roman Empire and indeed all of Christendom, hindered efforts to rally an already divided Europe against Islam. There is even some evidence that the rise of indulgences, payments to the Church to reduce the time in purgatory for the deceased, originated as a medieval practice to raise funds for Crusading. In this sense, the threat of the Ottomans provided the indirect cause for Luther's protests against Church corruption.[17] Similarly, Luther denounced Pope Leo's ineffective calls for a new Crusade as not only a theological error, but another example of the Church's focus on the secular manifestations of power and authority, rather than the gains from a devotion to a spiritual connection of each believer with God.

Luther even saw admirable elements within Islam: its abjuration of idolatry, lack of an established ecclesiastical order, focus on personal piety among both rulers and ruled, and the responsibility within both Islam and Protestantism of each believer for their own path to God, rather than dependence on a priestly class. While he nonetheless saw Islam as an evil, in the context of his campaign against the corruption of the Catholic Church and its focus on its own institutional wealth and prerogatives, certainly he would have judged the empire of the Turks as a necessary evil in its challenge to Catholicism. He also noted the tolerance by the Ottoman Empire for Christian minorities, although the legal and religious subordination of these groups was not a status he would have welcomed for Lutheran minorities under Catholic rule in Europe.[18]

One of the first non-German territories to see the widespread dissemination of Luther's ideas and writings was the Netherlands. These Habsburg lands, whose prosperity came from textiles, trade, merchant fleets, banking, and shipbuilding, were a receptive audience for criticisms of the distant Catholic Church in Rome, arguments for the role of free will in salvation, and the appeal to a literate population of reading the Bible and other religious works in Dutch and other vernacular languages. Similarly, it was in the Netherlands that Charles V, through his regent Margaret of Austria, as early as 1520 made the first significant efforts in collaboration with the Catholic Church to ban Luther's writings, strengthen laws against heresy, and order the burning of Protestant works.[19] Resentment against Habsburg rule in general, and Spain in particular, was already high; seeing a viable option that justified resistance to Roman Catholicism in its Spanish form therefore found an audience in the Low Countries receptive on multiple counts.[20]

The excommunication of Martin Luther by Pope Leo X in 1521 led to additional condemnations by the emperor, including an imperial edict in May of that year, subsequently read in public and otherwise disseminated throughout the far-flung territories of Charles. This decree banned not just owning Martin Luther's books and other published materials, in whole or in part, but the printing, preaching, or discussing of any of the theologian's ideas, the possession of any images or written words mocking or deriding the Church or the Pope, or the printing of any books of any kind without prior approval by the emperor or designated secular or ecclesiastical authorities, depending on the location of the press. Printers and publishers had to submit any works under consideration to the nearest authorized university for prior censorship, with images to be reviewed by episcopal offices prior to publication as well. Failure to do so would lead to harsh penalties, including at a minimum the burning of any unapproved printings. In several examples from the early 1520s, those printing, disseminating, or possessing Luther's works were burned along with their volumes.[21]

The imperial edict faced more resistance in the Netherlands than in any other Habsburg territories. Compared to Spain, for example, literacy was higher, the book industry was more widespread and a key part of the economy of the Low Countries, and there was justifiable concern that the initial campaign against Luther could spread to works by other authors, including the Dutch intellectual Erasmus. The uneven application of the decree, as well as other mandates against Protestant ideas, also encouraged resistance. Sympathetic officials in northern regions such as Holland tended to ignore violations of the edict, unlike their harsher compatriots in Flanders, to the south, where Calvinism was weaker and loyalties to the Catholic Church more pervasive.[22]

Over time, the pre-approval process led to issuance by imperial and episcopal authorities of lists of banned books and authors, and less frequently, of approved ones. Printers still had to receive permission to issue editions of approved works, given the possibility for heresies to creep in due to error, or for previously acceptable authors to find themselves newly considered as heretics, but the list of approved authors at least gave some protection to readers, booksellers, and those with private libraries. While these lists changed over time, the presence of a book on an approved episcopal list was a strong defense for those brought before Inquisitorial tribunals or other bodies charged with enforcing heresy laws.[23] The lists of forbidden books, issued by Charles V, Philip II, and Inquisitorial and ecclesiastical authorities in Rome, Antwerp, and elsewhere, continued to add titles throughout the sixteenth century. With the continued rise of Protestantism and the widespread availability of printed works by Luther, Calvin, and others, these efforts to stifle heresy expanded to include more authors, some of whom had previously been considered orthodox.[24]

As some historians have noted, there was initially widespread support in the Netherlands for these campaigns against Protestant Reform. While the application of censorship was uneven, and there were nuclei of Protestants in the territory as early as the 1520s, the Netherlands remained essentially Catholic well into the 1540s, with Luther's ideas never becoming as widespread or as popular there as in northern Germany or Scandinavia. Local Dutch and Flemish religious and state officials in the Habsburg Netherlands collaborated with imperial ones, and later Spanish episcopal and military officials, in initially rooting out Lutheranism. Over the decades that followed, Church officials and local nobles applied the same tools of censorship, Inquisitorial tribunals, and social pressures later against Anabaptist, Lutheran, and Calvinist ideas, until the latter reached critical mass in the 1570s, at least in the northern provinces of Holland and Zeeland.[25] Parish priests, even those nominally still serving within the Catholic Church, were among the primary sources for the new religious teachings, especially in in small towns and rural areas more distant from the centers of Habsburg secular and religious authority.[26]

As in Spain, local privileges and rights of nobles were also an obstacle to the edicts of the emperor. Even Castile, source of so many loyal soldiers and much needed capital, itself saw a tax rebellion against Charles V in 1520.[27] In the Netherlands, fiscal and theological resentments converged, with enforcement of taxes and religious conformity left by tradition and law in the hands of some with sympathies more with Reform than Catholicism. At times, indifference could be as much of a hindrance in fighting heresy as actual enthusiasm for the teachings of Luther and Calvin. Although in theory Charles V ruled the Netherlands through several hereditary titles including Count of Holland and Lord of the Netherlands, in practice his edicts were in the hands of nobles, his regent, and bodies such as the Council of Holland and the Council of Flanders, with wide judicial authority and latitude in implementation and appeals from lower courts in their respective regions, including on issues of heresy.[28] City councils also had a role through local ordinances against heresy. At the highest level in the Netherlands was the Council of State in Brussels. These judicial and municipal councils often softened penalties based on mitigating factors, with women and youths often being excused based on their susceptibility to influence. Those expressing contrition, even after embracing Lutheranism, Anabaptism, or Calvinism, were frequently pardoned or given lighter sentences, such as exile, fines, or penance within the Church. Similar behavior in Spain, brought before the Spanish Inquisition, would likely have earned death.[29]

Although not now considered a region where the Protestant Reformation took hold, initially there seemed quite positive receptivity in some of the Italian kingdoms, principalities, and cities, with the obvious exception of the Papal States. The plethora of Italian states, similar to conditions in the Holy Roman Empire, initially provided more opportunities for a diversity of approaches to the Reformation. In some Italian states, Protestants found refuge, in others, persecution. With higher levels of literacy and publishing, the presence of a strong middle class in its cities, and more interest in new ideas than in many other European regions, northern Italy especially was susceptible to the ideas of Luther and Calvin.

The 1520s were a decade of European catastrophes. While the failure of Charles V to persuade Martin Luther at the Diet of Worms would later seem disastrous, there were more proximate nightmares confronting the emperor and all the continent in the following years:

> Christian Europe tears itself apart and religious passions are unleashed. In 1524, the terrible "Peasants' War" explodes in Germany. At the same time, the two great Catholic sovereigns, Charles V and Francis I, are locked in ceaseless conflict. In 1527, Rome is sacked, burned, pillaged by imperial cohorts. Around 1533, the English schism is consummated. In the East, the Turkish armies pursue their advance, like a rising tide: Suleiman the Magnificent takes Belgrade (1520) and Rhodes (1521). He invades Hungary (1526), lays siege to Vienna (1529). A leaden sky descends over Europe.[30]

The multiplication of theological and battlefield conflicts posed an ongoing challenge to Charles V and his Habsburg allies. An empire large enough to dream of ruling all of Europe and the world beyond was also sufficiently threatening to find enemies sufficient to prevent it from doing so.

Even while Charles was unable to defeat Luther in Europe, he did achieve some gains against Islam in the Mediterranean. Concerned at the taking of Tunis in 1535 by the Barbary pirate leader Kheir-ed-Din Barbarossa, who had seized it from the emperor's Muslim ally, Moulay Hassan, Charles dispatched a fleet of 400 ships and more than 25,000 men, a force of Spaniards, Genoans, Neapolitans, and the Knights of St. John, a Crusading order to whom Charles had given Malta, retaking the city and freeing several thousand Christian slaves. The great victory against Islam was somewhat overshadowed by Barbarossa's escape and attack on Minorca, but even so across Europe many Catholics saw this as a turning point. Victory at Tunis, a key outpost in North Africa, was hailed as the beginning of a great Crusade against the Ottoman Empire and its Muslim allies.[31] Although the recapture proved to be the high-water mark of the emperor's Mediterranean campaigns against Islam, it continued to figure as a triumph to be celebrated and pointed to as an example for Europe's monarchs.

During the build-up to the emperor's attack on Tunis, and for other periods during the 1520s and 1530s, his wife, Empress Isabel, was regent of Spain. She organized resources for his campaigns in Europe and the Mediterranean and led the fight against the early incursions of Protestantism into Spain. While her time as regent was relatively quiet compared to later years, there were vibrant debates with lasting consequences on the orthodoxy of Erasmus and responses to the smuggling of Lutheran works into Spain. The empress presided over *autos da fe*, denounced Lutherans as "bad and shameless," and encouraged her husband to take a hard line against Martin Luther and his followers in the Holy Roman Empire, the Netherlands, and other Habsburg lands.[32]

In addition to embracing Catholic warfare against Islam, Charles supported efforts to fight the internal battle within the Church for reform. These efforts, which later would become known as the Counter-Reformation or the Catholic Reformation, involved new religious structures, clarification of Christian theology, and taking seriously the rooting out of corruption and sinful practices within the Church. The Council of Trent, which began in 1545, was an effort by the Catholic Church to embrace reforms, promote Christian education of both priests and parishioners, and ideally to draw Protestants back into the faith through adopting the more reasonable elements of the drive for a more ethical and spiritual church.[33] Spanish theologians played a disproportionately large role in this council, which concluded its effort in 1563, having developed a comprehensive outline of Catholic orthodoxy, resoundingly rejecting key Lutheran doctrines, and outlined reforms within the Church that would serve as the foundation for the faith for the next three hundred years. One major impact of the conciliar efforts was a significant improvement in the education levels of parish priests, who as a result were better equipped to prevent, identify, and combat heresy in their churches.[34]

Other reforms, such as creating the expectation that bishops should reside in their assigned diocese, were intended to enhance pastoral attention and care to their flocks, as well as to reduce corruption and impose discipline among those in the Catholic episcopacy. In this regard, the council was attempting to address Protestant and Catholic critiques of the Church, which had pointed to wealthy bishops living extravagant lives away from their appointments as a contributing factor to the spiritual ignorance among many Europeans. Although indulgences continued to be allowed, they were greatly constrained by the council, and thereafter were used far less as a fundraising method.[35]

Philip II followed the efforts of the Council of Trent intensely, seeking – and receiving – assurances from Pope Pius IV in 1563 that the conciliar efforts were focused on reforming the Church and would come to a successful conclusion. Encouraged by secular leaders including Philip and his uncle, Holy Roman Emperor Ferdinand, the bishops, theologians, and other religious figures at the Council of Trent finally did conclude their work, despite internal squabbles over key questions, including episcopal residence and the appointment of bishops.[36] As the council concluded its work, Philip welcomed its results, mandating that its reforms and decrees would prevail in all of his domains and realms except in cases where, as in the naming of bishops, they could conflict with his claimed rights as monarch.[37]

Another success of the Counter-Reformation, or Catholic Reformation, was the rise of the Society of Jesus, more commonly known as the Jesuits, a religious order founded by the Spanish war veteran Ignatius of Loyola. Loyola, who had been injured in a battle against the French in 1521, was reborn through the painful recovery from his wounds into a militant campaigner not for military victories, but for winning souls.[38] Known for their intellectual fervor, dedication to the Pope, and willingness to serve wherever the Church saw the greatest need, the Jesuits' promotion of education, combining scholasticism with humanism, was an antidote to the reputation of other religious orders, and at times the Spanish Inquisition, for being hostile to a broad and liberal education. Initially dominated by Spanish members, with its first three generals being of Spanish origin, under the leadership of Loyola and his immediate successor, the movement gradually expanded under the patronage of the papacy and especially Philip II, who overcame his own reluctance to allow the Jesuits into Spain. With their loyalty first and foremost to the papacy, they became emblematic of the Counter-Reformation, expanding from Europe to become a worldwide order.[39] Founding universities, educating the sons of nobles and wealthy middle classes, they played an effective role in introducing Tridentine orthodoxy to Catholic elites in Spain and elsewhere.[40]

Although no Luther, Calvin, or Zwingli emerged from Spain, one Spanish scholar did rise in the context of the Reformation, making theological arguments against the Catholic Church and even contending disastrously with John Calvin: Miguel Serveto, better known as Michael Servetus. Originally from Aragon, he left Spain in 1527 to study in Toulouse after getting into theological and personal disputes at the University of Zaragoza, where he had been studying. After completing his studies in Roman law, he worked briefly in the court of Charles V. As an anti-trinitarian, his 1531 work *Seven Books on the Errors of the Trinity* earned him enmity from Catholics and Protestants; while the two factions were at odds on many theological points, there was near unanimity on the doctrine of the trinity, that Father, Son, and Holy Ghost were one.[41]

Belated attempts by the Spanish Inquisition in Aragon to bring Servetus in for questioning in 1532 and again in 1538 for possible heresy failed, for the obvious reason that he had left the country years before and was still living openly, and quite successfully, in France.[42] While it may seem as if the Holy Office was unaware of his departure and life abroad, these inquiries could also be considered as ongoing alerts to the tribunals, familiars, and support-ers of the Spanish Inquisition. It was not unusual, if at times inexplicable, for those under investigation to return to Spain, even at risk of their lives, to face charges of heresy. Whether out of defiance, a desire to clear their names, pressure to protect their financial means, or ignorance about the risks before them, these returning expatriates were sure to face a challenging future. In the case of Servetus, he did not return to Spain, but instead faced an ending of his own unforced and entirely avoidable making.

During the 1530s and 1540s, Servetus studied and then practiced medicine in Paris and other French cities, becoming a French subject in 1549. An accomplished mapmaker and medical doctor, he made practical and schol-arly contributions in both of these professional areas, but it was over theolog-ical matters that he encountered Jean Calvin. Although Servetus and Calvin initially corresponded with each other in a civil form of disputation, John Calvin eventually ended their letters, upset at the argumentative approach and theological errors of Servetus. Disagreeing with Calvin on predestina-tion, infant baptism, and other matters, in 1553, Servetus published *The Restitution of Christianity* as a direct refutation of these essential points of theology. At this point, Calvin made clear to his colleagues and to Servetus that, should their paths cross again, especially in Calvin's Geneva, it would not go well for Servetus. Surprisingly, despite his own recent brush with a French religious tribunal, the Spaniard was not attentive to this message.[43]

After his 1553 book, Miguel Servetus was arrested by a French Inquisitorial tribunal, but managed to escape from their loosely guarded jail, intending thereafter to flee to Italy. For unknown reasons, en route to Italy, Servetus stopped in Geneva and tried to meet with Calvin, perhaps to continue their interrupted correspondence with a direct confrontation. Before he could do so, however, he was recognized and arrested. Servetus was tried as a heretic and burned at the stake that October at the express orders of John Calvin. The ideas of Servetus would later become theologically significant as part of the development of Unitarianism, but for the moment, Calvin emerged trium-phant and as the key leader of a community within Protestantism not just in Geneva, but throughout Europe and beyond. Calvin's actions to end the theo-logical dissent of Servetus echoed the tactics of the Spanish Inquisition against Calvinists, but this should not have been surprising; demands for toleration by religious minorities in sixteenth-century Europe did not mean they would offer that same requested tolerance in the event their faith became dominant.[44]

Even so, Calvin's Geneva was a refuge for Spaniards and other Europeans who embraced his Protestant Reform ideas fully. Calvinism had by this point spread widely in Europe, becoming the leading Protestant denomination not just in Geneva, but in Scotland, the Low Countries, and among French Protestants (Huguenots). Although Luther's ideas were adopted more widely, there was already more than a bipolar world within European Christendom. French was to Calvinism as German was to Lutheranism, with writings spreading into other languages as the ideas became more popular across the continent and beyond. The first translation from the original French into Spanish of Calvin's catechism dates from 1550, although the translator is unknown, and apologizes for the quality of the work, given the individual's many years away from Spain. Based on a 1559 edition, which included prayers, hymns, and other elements of worship, there was a Spanish-speaking congregation in the city during these years.[45]

Other works in Spanish emerged around the same time, including *Sumario de indulgencias* (*Summary of Indulgences*) by Juan Pérez de Pineda. Pérez had fled Spain around 1550 when the Spanish Inquisition began to launch serious investigations in Seville.[46] Prior to this, Pérez had served in the Spanish Embassy in Rome during the 1520s, enduring the sack of the holy city by imperial forces in 1527. In communication with the court of Emperor Charles V, Pérez had engineered a letter by Pope Clement VII in defense of Erasmus, to be sent back to the Spanish Inquisition, and which threatened excommunication for anyone that questioned the orthodoxy of the writer. The Pope, then captive by Habsburg forces, agreed to authorize the letter at the insistence of the emperor. Returning to Spain, Pérez was appointed to head a religious *colegio* (secondary school) for boys in Seville, a teaching and administrative position he held until around 1550, when he fled in advance of inquiries by the Holy Office.[47]

As an exile, Pérez first lived in Paris, then had come to Geneva around 1556 as a refugee from the Spanish Inquisition, which had included him on their lists of accused heretics, even burning him in effigy in 1560. In his works, Pérez included dedications to Philip II, pleading with the king to break from his devotion to Rome. The king's support for the Spanish Inquisition, and that body's "destructive work" would leave his realms as nothing but "ashes and *sambenitos*" (the penitential robes worn by those convicted). Pérez quickly gained the attention and favor of Calvin and other Reform leaders. In addition to his writing, Pérez served as pastor to the small Spanish-speaking Reform congregation in the city. The Spanish congregants had formerly worshipped alongside Italian Protestants in Geneva, but their numbers had grown enough to justify their own church building. While this Spanish congregation was short-lived, this growing diversity of Protestants in Geneva was echoed elsewhere, including in London, which also welcomed Protestant exiles from Spain, France, and the Holy Roman Empire.[48]

Pérez remained concerned about events in Spain, seeing the impact of the Spanish Inquisition on friends and former colleagues. He played a role in providing books to be smuggled back to Spain, including a shipment of his Spanish-language New Testaments and Psalms from Antwerp. These books, hidden in double-barreled casks of wine with false bottoms, were brought into Spain by Julian Hernández, better known as Julianillo (little Julian) because of his diminutive stature. Hernández was a typesetter and printer, who worked with Pérez on editions of his translations. Having made his smuggling runs safely on multiple occasions, in 1557 en route to Seville, Julianillo was captured and turned over to the Spanish Inquisition for trial. He was convicted and executed at the *auto da fe* in Seville on 22 December 1560.[49]

Heartbroken and guilt-stricken by the arrest of Hernández, as well as others in Seville, in 1560 Pérez wrote the "Epístola Consolatoria" (Letter of Consolation) to comfort Spanish Protestants, including those being harassed and hounded by the Spanish Inquisition and those in exile. His assessment was that the fear and suffering being endured by his co-religionists was worse than other forms of misery, given the shared values with the perpetrators. "The persecution that we endure is cruel and very dangerous, because those that persecute us are not Turks or pagans by tradition, but rather baptized, like us, and say they have the zeal of God."[50]

Unlike many other Spanish exiles that initially fled to Geneva, Pérez remained a committed Calvinist for the rest of his life. Whatever disagreements he may have had with John Calvin personally, and which eventually led to his departure from the Swiss city, they were not based on theology and he remained a trusted collaborator with the Reform leader.[51] In the mid-1560s, Juan Pérez returned to Paris to supervise the final work on the translation and printing of the New Testament into Spanish. In France, he also served as household chaplain to Princess Renée of France, a prominent member of the French royal family. As the youngest daughter of King Louis XII, in her youth Renée was suggested as a potential wife for England's Henry VIII, eventually marrying the Italian Duke of Ferrara. Accomplished and educated, she chafed at France's Salic Law, which prohibited a woman from reigning in her own name, especially after seeing in Queens Mary and Elizabeth of England, and Mary Queen of Scots, that women were equally capably of governing.[52]

By moving to France, Juan Pérez was taking advantage of the temporary liberty granted to Huguenots in France in 1562 by a limited decree of toleration, the Edict of January, issued by regent Catherine de' Medici. Although Catholics resisted this law, which led to a state of civil war within months, it did signal the growing strength and popularity of French Protestantism, not only in the south and west, but even in the royal court and family. One of the prominent representatives of this upsurge in Protestantism in the highest circles was Renée. A prominent Huguenot noblewoman and member of the royal family, she had spent several years in Italy as the Duchess of Ferrara, before returning home to France after her Italian husband's death in 1559.[53]

Juan Pérez de Pineda, a beneficiary of the patronage of Renée, died in France in 1567.[54]

Pérez was not alone in denouncing the Spanish Inquisition among Spaniards abroad. An anonymous work in Latin, published in Heidelberg in 1567, titled *Sanctae Inquisitionis Hispanicae Artes* (*The Arts of the Spanish Inquisition*), was the first detailed criticism of the Holy Office, focused on its persecution of Spanish Protestants, especially in Seville. Recounting the process by which the Spanish Inquisition had investigated and persecuted Protestants, it named prominent victims of the Holy Office. Although the choice of a Latin text made it less accessible to educated general readers, it was a thorough and detailed critique of the methods, theology, and justifications of the Spanish Inquisition. The author's pseudonym, Reginaldus Gonsalvius Montanus, implied Spanish origins. Later editions, including in English translation, list the author as Raimundo González Montes or Reinaldo González Montes, but without asserting that this was an actual person. There is some evidence that the work was one of collaboration by several scholars familiar with events in Spain and the Spanish Inquisition, rather than the work of a single author.[55] Antonio del Corro and Casiodoro de Reina are the two authors mentioned the most; potentially, they could have collaborated on the text.[56]

Along with Servetus, Pérez, and the unknown author of *Sanctae Inquisitionis Hispanicae Artes*, another example of a Spaniard who gained a following, some notoriety, and contributed to Spanish Protestantism outside the reach of the Spanish Inquisition was Juan de Valdés. He worked at the University of Alcalá, and as with other Erasmians had originally been sponsored by Cardinal Cisneros. In 1529, Valdés published his *Diálogo de Doctrina christiana* (*Dialog on Christian Doctrine*), a book inspired by and dependent on Luther's idea of justification by faith. Although it was published anonymously, the Spanish Inquisition quickly determined authorship of the work and added it to the Index of Forbidden Works.[57] By 1530 Valdés had fled from the Spanish Inquisition to Italy, given his family experience with the Holy Office, which encouraged him to be wary. The descendant of *conversos*, four of his great-grandparents had been Jewish before converting to Catholicism; one uncle, Fernando de la Barrera, had been burned by the Inquisition after being convicted of being a relapsed Jew.[58]

As an educated Spaniard, Valdés was sought after by both Church and imperial officials to serve in administrative and executive roles, holding positions of trust on behalf of Italian nobles. He even served as Charles V's agent in Rome, keeping watch over political developments and the emperor's interests. Even more significantly, in 1536 Juan Valdés met Giulia Gonzaga, Italian Countess of Rodigo, who became his patron. Widowed and refusing to remarry, ostensibly because she feared losing her lands either to a new husband or to her estranged daughter, Isabella, Giulia was famous not only for her ruling capacity, but for her humane education and great beauty. She gathered around her a group of scholars, including Valdés, encouraging their scholarly efforts, sponsoring their publications, and reading their works.

Many were initially Italian Erasmians, but among them were some who later would be identified by the Inquisition or other Catholic tribunals as Protestants. Valdés was the most prominent among this group and continued to identify as a Catholic his entire life, even though increasingly the Church suspected him of being less than devoted to orthodox Catholicism.[59]

During his career as an administrator, advisor, and courtier, Valdés would receive accolades from many corners, including "(t)wo popes, the emperor, and the most beautiful woman in Italy." It was his literary and Reformist accomplishments, including his notable works, *Alfabeto Christiano, Diálogo de la lengua*, and *Diálogo de la doctrina Cristiana*, the latter of which continued to be of grave interest to the Spanish Inquisition, that explained why Valdés never returned to Spain.[60] As an author and spiritual leader, he played a somewhat ambiguous role in the Reformation and its impact on Europe and the Church. While Valdés endorsed the theological idea of justification by faith, he opposed the Reformation cause. Although a Reforming Catholic, he disagreed with Luther and Calvin for breaking the unity of the Church. Some of his followers were Protestant Reformers, but others remained Catholics, as did Valdés, even if his approach to orthodoxy embraced Erasmian reforms.[61] Erasmus also took an interest in Valdés, with the two exchanging letters during the late 1520s. In one, Eramus expressed his concern for the treatment Valdés received at the hands of the Spanish Inquisition, noting:

> How sensibly I feel, my dear Valdés, by your letter what great troubles and dangers have afflicted you: and yet, on the other part, how lively was my satisfaction to know that you had escaped the shipwreck safely, and already found yourself secure in port! I greatly regret to behold Spain afflicted with so many evils. Oh, that God would turn the hearts of kings to the love of peace! ... it gives me great pain that, in a country favored with so many privileges, such nests of vicious hornets multiply there, that, not to me alone, but to them also that I love, they should cause such painful disturbance.[62]

While Valdés would grow in fame (or from the Church's perspective infamy), it was his sponsoring noble who drew the greatest attention at the time. Even in the Ottoman Empire there were stories of the lovely Italian countess. The infamous North African corsair and naval commander Hayreddin Barbarossa launched an unsuccessful raid in 1534 with the aim of kidnapping Giulia, to present her to Suleiman the Magnificent as a gift for the sultan's harem in Istanbul. Barbarossa (so named because of his red beard), had the previous year been named an admiral in the Ottoman fleet, and had conquered the city-state of Tunis from a Muslim ally of Charles V. Giulia escaped just barely in advance of the Muslim pirates, slipping past their forces near her castle, riding on horseback "scantily clad in her nightclothes."[63] Perhaps seeking additional security, soon thereafter in that same year the countess moved to a convent in Naples. Countess Giulia did not take on religious orders as a nun, despite her residence among women religious. Defying cultural expectations, she also continued to refuse remarriage, despite an abundance of eligible and interested parties in Italy and beyond. She instead continued to exercise her secular authority over her domains as a widow, albeit from a more secure and protected location.[64] Giulia left the convent in 1541, returning to her palace in Naples, in spring 1541, to maintain closer control over her estates, as well as to contest claims over them by relatives of her late husband.[65]

After the death of Juan de Valdés in 1541, his followers fled from persecution, as he was denounced to the Spanish Inquisition as a heretic for his belief in justification by faith, his devotion to the scripture in contrast to loyalty to the institution of the Church, and his association with known Protestants.[66] After a brief period of promoting and funding his religious publications posthumously, even Countess Giulia began to retreat from her enthusiasm for his writings. Even so, unlike other former supporters, she never disowned him, although she did express her disagreement with some of his religious and philosophical positions. In 1541, she conveyed her lands and privileges to a male relative, her nephew Vespasiano I Gonzaga, returning to her conventical life. Vespasiano would later serve Prince Philip, soon to be King Philip II, becoming a high-ranking commander and noble in Spain. Some have called Valdés the most prominent Reforming theologian "South of the Alps."[67]

As a devout Catholic, like Erasmus seeking reform from within the Church, Valdés would not have embraced the labels of Protestant, much less Calvinist or Lutheran. Even so, the Spanish Inquisition identified him in his early writings as approaching heresy, and after his death, embraced the label of heretic, lumping him with Luther and Calvin in condemnations, book burnings, and pursuit of his followers.[68] By 1559, his works figured prominently on indexes of forbidden books, not only in Spain, but throughout Europe's remaining Catholic states.[69] The Holy Roman Empire survived Martin Luther, but not as a theologically united federation. Indeed, from the 1520s onward, even though at times it united through treaties or coalitions, principally against the external threat of the Ottoman Empire, the Holy Roman Empire because less accurately described as such with every passing year. By the late sixteenth century, the key states of the Holy Roman Empire of the Germans were effectively not only politically independent, but their princes were free to choose the religion of their state: Catholic, Lutheran, or Calvinist. Luther's ideas triumphed in the north and northeast, Calvinism in the northwest and west, and Catholicism in the south. While the Counter-Reformation initiatives of the late sixteenth and early seventeenth century reclaimed much of this terrain, especially in the center and west of the empire, the divides remained.

For all of Charles V's frustrations with Martin Luther and Spaniards who embraced ideas of the Protestant Reformation, there was an even more confounding state on the verge of causing him and his son no end of challenges: the little kingdom of England. Over the course of a few years, these islands shifted dramatically, from ally of the empire to joint domain with Spain, to bitter enemy and global adversary, not only dynastically, but in matters of religion and faith. Just as Spain exemplified the crusade within Europe to strengthen Catholicism, England would become the champion for the Protestant Reformation. Even more than the small states within the Holy Roman Empire that were the first supporters of Luther, or the doughty Dutch rebels that caused so much angst for Spain, England would be the first state to promote a worldview as adversarial to Spain, even defined by this opposition, a perspective that continues to echo.

Notes

1 Fernández Álvarez, *España del Emperador Carlos V*, Vol. XX, 719.
2 Croft, "Englishmen and the Spanish Inquisition 1558-1625," 267.
3 Francisco Ruiz de Pablos, "Carlos V y su persecución del Protestantismo," *Cuadernos de Historia Moderna*, 2018, Vol. 43, No. 2, 505–518.
4 Tracy, *Emperor Charles V, Impresario of War*, 20–23.
5 Fernández Álvarez, *España del Emperador Carlos V*, Vol. XX, xxxii.
6 Ivana Elbl, "'The Elect, the Fortunate, and the Prudent': Charles V and the Portuguese Royal House, 1500-1529," in Alain Saint-Saëns, ed., *Young Charles V (1500-1531)* (New Orleans: University Press of the South, 2000), 89–91, 104.
7 Green, *A New History of Christianity*, 128–130.
8 Green, *A New History of Christianity*, 130–131.
9 Hugh Thomas, *The Golden Age: The Spanish Empire of Charles V* (London: Penguin Books, 2010), 11–12.
10 Fernández Álvarez, *España del Emperador Carlos V*, Vol. XX, 870.
11 Rady, *The Habsburgs*, 67–68.
12 Massing, *Fatal Discord*, 464.
13 Fernández Álvarez, *España del Emperador Carlos V*, Vol. XX, xxi.
14 Alain Saint-Saëns, "Charles V's Reply to Martin Luther and the German Princes at the Diet of Worms, 19 April 1521," in Saint-Saëns, ed., *Young Charles V*, 58–63.
15 Massing, *Fatal Discord*, 463. Fernández Álvarez, *España del Emperador Carlos V*, Vol. XX, 720, 737–738, 806.
16 Fernández Álvarez, *España del Emperador Carlos V*, Vol. XX, 807.
17 Mikhail, *God's Shadow*, 373–376.
18 Mikhail, *God's Shadow*, 379–381.
19 Grantley McDonald, "'Burned to Dust': Censorship and Repression of Theological Literature in the Habsburg Netherlands during the 1520s," in Soen, Vanysacker and François, eds., *Church, Censorship and Reform in the Early Modern Netherlands*, 29.
20 Green, *A New History of Christianity*, 141–142.
21 McDonald, "Burned to Dust," 30–31. Alonso Burgos, *El luteranismo en Castilla durante el siglo XVI*, 53.
22 McDonald, "Burned to Dust," 32–35.
23 McDonald, "Burned to Dust," 39–44.
24 Els Acten, "Ottavio Mirto Frangipani, First Papal Nuncio to Flanders (1596-1606) and His Thoughts on Book Censorship," in Soen, Vanysacker and François, eds., *Church, Censorship and Reform in the Early Modern Netherlands*, 80–81, 84.
25 Arjan Van Dixhoorn, "The Claim to Expertise and Doctrinal Authority in the Struggle for Anti-Heresy Policies in the Habsburg Netherlands (1520s-1560s)," in Soen, Vanysacker and François, eds., *Church, Censorship and Reform in the Early Modern Netherlands*, 52–57, 69–71.

26 James D. Tracy, *The Low Countries in the Sixteenth Century: Erasmus, Religion and Politics, Trade and Finance* (Aldershot, Hampshire, UK: Ashgate Publishing, 2005), IX, 56–57.

27 Massing, *Fatal Discord*, 403.

28 Tracy, *The Low Countries in the Sixteenth Century*, VII, 151–152.

29 Tracy, *The Low Countries in the Sixteenth Century*, VI, 284–286, 293–294; VII, 163–164; IX, 53–54.

30 Bénéton, *The Kingdom Suffereth Violence*, 36.

31 Rady, *The Habsburgs*, 70. Norwich, *Four Princes*, 134–138.

32 Isidoro Jiménez Zamora, "La Emperatriz Isabel de Portugal ante la división religiosa," in Borreguero Beltrán and Retortillo Atienza, *La memoria de un hombre*, 326–330.

33 Norwich, *Four Princes*, 190–192.

34 Lynch, *Spain 1516-1598*, 350–352, 357.

35 Mullett, *The Catholic Reformation*, 44–46, 55–56.

36 Mullett, *The Catholic Reformation*, 62–63.

37 Mullett, *The Catholic Reformation*, 67. Green, *A New History of Christianity*, 167.

38 Mullett, *The Catholic Reformation*, 74–77.

39 Lynch, *Spain 1516-1598*, 363–369. Mullett, *The Catholic Reformation*, 98–99, 181, 194–195. Green, *A New History of Christianity*, 164.

40 Green, *A New History of Christianity*, 170.

41 Massing, *Fatal Discord*, 769. Miguel González Ancín and Otis Towns, *Miguel Servet en España (1506-1527)* (Tudela, Spain: Imprenta Castilla, 2017).

42 Monter, *Frontiers of Heresy*, 83.

43 De la Torre, *Breve Historia de la Inquisición*, 110.

44 Massing, *Fatal Discord*, 769–771.

45 Boehmer, Wiffen, and Wiffen, *Bibliotheca Wiffeniana*, Vol. II, 43.

46 Boehmer, Wiffen, and Wiffen, *Bibliotheca Wiffeniana*, Vol. II, 51–52.

47 Boehmer, Wiffen, and Wiffen, *Bibliotheca Wiffeniana*, Vol. II, 57–58, 60. Luis Usoz y Rio, Benjamín B. Wiffen, and Eduardo Boehmer, eds., *Reformistas antiguos españoles*, Vol. 2 (Barcelona: Librería de Diego Gomez Flores: 1848), iii–v, x.

48 Boehmer, Wiffen, and Wiffen, *Bibliotheca Wiffeniana*, Vol. II, 67.

49 *Reformistas antiguos españoles*, Vol. 2, xiv–xv. John E. Longhurst, "Julián Hernández: Protestant Martyr," *Bibliothèque d'Humanisme et Renaissance*, 1960, Vol. 22, No. 1, 90–118, http://www.jstor.org/stable/20674167.

50 *Reformistas antiguos españoles*, Vol. 2, xviii, 5.

51 Juan Pérez de Pineda, "Epístola consolatoria," in Emilio Monjo Bellido, ed., *Obras de los Reformadores Españoles del Siglo XVI* (Seville: Editorial MAD, 2007), 9–11.

52 Boehmer, Wiffen, and Wiffen, *Bibliotheca Wiffeniana*, Vol. III, 15.

53 Kinder, A. Gordon, "Two Previously Unknown Letters of Juan Pérez de Pineda, Protestant of Seville in the Sixteenth Century," *Bibliothèque d'Humanisme et Renaissance*, 1987, Vol. 49, No. 1, 111–20, http://www.jstor.org/stable/20677441. Kelly Digby Peebles. "Renée de France's and Clément Marot's Voyages: Political Exile to Spiritual Liberation," *Women in French Studies*, 2018, Vol. 2018, 33–60.

54 Boehmer, Wiffen, and Wiffen, *Bibliotheca Wiffeniana*, Vol. II, 69–70.

55 Boehmer, Wiffen, and Wiffen, *Bibliotheca Wiffeniana*, Vol. II, 113–117. *Reformistas antiguos españoles*, Vol. 5, "Artes de la Inquisizion Española," 1851.

56 Reinaldo González Montes (pseudonym), "Artes de la Santa Inquisición Española," in Francisco Ruiz de Pablos, ed., *Obras de los Reformadores Españoles del Siglo XVI* (Seville: Editorial MAD, 2008).

57 Luttikhuizen, *Underground Protestantism in Sixteenth Century Spain*, 71–73.

58 Peter Elvy, "A Tale of Two Sitters: Juan and Alfonso de Valdés," *Bulletin for Spanish and Portuguese Historical Studies*, 2015, Vol. 40, Issue 1, 105–106. "Juan

de Valdés," Real Academia de la Historia, accessed 20 March 2022, https://dbe. rah.es/biografias/4664/juan-de-valdes.

59 Boehmer, Wiffen, and Wiffen, *Bibliotheca Wiffeniana*, Vol. I, 69.

60 Daniel Crews, *Twilight of the Renaissance: The Life of Juan de Valdés* (Toronto: University of Toronto Press, 2008), 4–5, 31, 37–39. Juan de Valdés, "Diálogo de doctrina," in Emilio Monjo Bellido, ed., *Obras de los Reformadores Españoles del Siglo XVI* (Seville: Editorial MAD, 2008).

61 Bruce Gordon, "Italy," in Pettegree, ed., *The Reformation World*, 286–287. Luttikhuizen, *Underground Protestantism in Sixteenth Century Spain*, 75–76.

62 *Reformistas antiguos españoles*, Vol. 15, "Alfabeto Cristiano," Xxv. Letter, 21 March 1529, Erasmus to Juan de Valdés.

63 Crews, *Twilight of the Renaissance*, 80.

64 Boehmer, Wiffen, and Wiffen, *Bibliotheca Wiffeniana*, Vol. I, 69–70.

65 Crews, *Twilight of the Renaissance*, 152–153.

66 Luttikhuizen, *Underground Protestantism in Sixteenth Century Spain*, 77.

67 Elvy, *A Tale of Two Sitters*, 107. Crews, *Twilight of the Renaissance*, 155.

68 Crews, *Twilight of the Renaissance*, 151–159.

69 Olivar-Bertrand, *La revolución erasmista y los españoles*, 15.

4 Perfidious Albion[1]

England of the sixteenth century was not the same island as would rule the seas in the eighteenth and nineteenth centuries. The centuries of global British power were yet to come. Small, isolated, relatively poor compared to France, Spain, the Low Countries, and the Holy Roman Empire – England nonetheless posed an ongoing challenge to Spain and the Habsburgs. In the early sixteenth century, Tudor England and Habsburg Spain seemed natural allies, on their way to a permanent alignment of interests and dynasties: both ardently Catholic with close political and economic ties. Common interests, including "(m)utual fear of France, and the strong economic linkages forged by the Habsburg inheritance of the overlordship of the Low Countries, made Anglo-Imperial friendship almost mandatory."[2]

Among the states of Europe and its vicinity, only England and Persia seemed likely allies for the Habsburgs, with the balance of states hostile or, at best, neutral to Charles V and Philip II. Indeed, three times in the sixteenth century, with the marriage of Prince Arthur (who died soon after) then of his brother, King Henry VIII, to Catherine of Aragon and the later marital union of Philip II to Mary I, there seemed every opportunity and expectation that this nascent alliance would be consummated not only in the marriage bed, but on the battlefields of Western Europe. War between the two seemed highly unlikely for the first 60 years of the century; indeed, for most of this time, it was a question of how deeply intertwined would be the Tudors and the Habsburgs, rather than of the depths of their conflicts.[3]

These unions held the promise of strengthening the unity of Catholic Christendom, adding an invaluable partner to Spanish strategic ambitions, and thwarting France. In both cases, however, the marriage ended in disappointment, resulting in worsened conditions not only for Spain, but for Catholicism. Protestants would rejoice in these results, seeing the failure of both marriages as bringing to power champions for their theological and political cause: Henry VIII, as the initiator of what would become the Church of England, and his daughter, Elizabeth I, who would prove to be Philip II's most daunting rival, after decisively spurning his courtship, institutionalized England as the leading Protestant power in Europe.[4] Elizabeth would be portrayed in books and films as a heroic monarch, resisting alien rule by distant Spain, but it was a dramatic reversal in a relatively short period of time; the

DOI: 10.4324/9781003197676-5

history of the two nations and the dynasties that ruled them were far more intertwined, and the division that came between Elizabeth and Philip in keeping with the shifts in coalitions during the sixteenth century.

Charles V attempted to forge an alliance with Henry VIII in the 1520s, even visiting the king in England twice in the effort.[5] In many ways, England was an ideal partner for the Holy Roman Empire, as a counterbalance to France, with trade connections to the Low Countries, and with the city of Calais on the Continent, a long-term English enclave amidst the French coast. Added to Spain and the Empire, England could provide a third front against France. The partnership failed over a botched effort to coordinate an offensive against France, and later over the English king's quest for a divorce from Catherine of Aragon, the aunt of the emperor, a disunion that would eventually lead to Henry's break from the Catholic Church and creation of the Church of England.[6]

Although not immediate, the shift from ally to adversary proved enduring; by the last quarter of the sixteenth century the two states were engaged in a global war. Over time, with the establishment of the Henrician church in England, and its development into a fully Protestant institution, the English became identified in the minds of many Spaniards as their primary theological enemy; "English" became synonymous with "heretic" or even "Lutheran," generalities that may have been technically inaccurate, but in practice quite meaningful to both the subject and the monarchs of both countries. The emergence of a distinctively English form of Protestantism, which would evolve into Anglicanism, was not yet clear in the initial decades of clashes between England and Spain.[7] Even more importantly, relations between the two kingdoms began not with conflict, but with an alliance, cemented by a promising marital union.

The marriage between Henry VIII and Catherine began well. He was handsome and strong, she beautiful and graceful, and both expressed their joy at their 1509 union. They initially seemed inseparable at court, in the country, and on their travels throughout England. They danced, hunted, and took counsel together, presiding over their court and kingdom happily and well. Henry was clearly smitten by her appearance, noting to his father-in-law, King Ferdinand of Aragon, that "if I were still free, I would choose her for wife above all others."[8] Her education was superior to that of her husband's; Erasmus noted the queen's intellectual qualities, which included an impressive proficiency with Latin, an eloquent capacity for writing in multiple languages, and a depth of reading on par with the best educated Europeans of her time.[9]

This was, despite their initial physical attraction and affinities, more of an alliance between powerful kingdoms than a match between two young people. Henry hoped both Aragon and Castile would join him in alliance against France, in addition to the normal expectation of a king that his wife, in this case Catherine, would provide him with male heirs to ensure the continuity of the Tudor dynasty and the stability of the kingdom. As king of Aragon and regent of Castile, Ferdinand expected the couple would ensure England would join a three-way alliance that also included the Holy Roman Empire, guaranteed to chasten the French. After almost a decade of negotiations, hard fought between the English and Aragonese, terms were agreed just after the death of Prince Henry's father, King Henry VII, in April 1509.[10]

Initially, the two seemed well-matched monarchs, sharing a love for courtly dancing, finery in clothing and decor, court entertainments, church and secular ceremonies, and galloping at top speed on excellent horses. Catherine served ably as a good-mannered foil for his excesses, including feigning surprise when he revealed himself from under outlandish costumes, granting him favors for tournaments, being at his side in court, and offering informed and tactful feedback to him privately on matters of statecraft. Although she was Spanish by birth and upbringing, she presented herself as a loyal wife and Englishwoman well-matched to an English king. She was careful to be seen by her subjects to speak and act with an eye first and foremost to English interests, rather than those of the Spanish or other Habsburg royals on the Continent.[11]

While Henry VIII led his armies into a war against France in 1512, supported unevenly and at times duplicitously by forces from Aragon and the Holy Roman Empire, Catherine remained in England, serving able as Governor of the Realm, in charge of its defense against the Scots and other potential invaders. Not only did forces under her direction hold back the Scots, but England's armies also made appreciably more progress to the north than did Henry on the Continent against the French. By 1514, after several years of unproductive conflict, abandoned at critical times by his father-in-law, Henry made peace with France. Catherine, similarly, frustrated by her father's machinations, resolved to be loyal to England and to her husband, despite Ferdinand's efforts to manipulate her in his interests and those of the Empire.[12] Also in 1514, Catherine gave birth to her second child but, alas the boy was stillborn.

Finally, in 1516, she gave birth to a child that lived beyond the bedchamber: a daughter, Mary. Although Henry had hoped for a boy, the couple's young age – Henry, 25, and Catherine, 31 – augured time for more attempts to produce a male heir. Unlike in France, where the presumption, later codified as the Salic Law, was that a woman could not rule, there was no such code in England, much less in Spain, where Isabella of Castile had reigned so spectacularly. The absence of a previous female sovereign, however, meant that an attempt to raise one to the English throne would tempt other powers to assert rights of their male progeny with familial ties to England. Because of this danger, and out of his personal preference, England's king clearly wanted a son and male heir and began to express disappointment in his wife. Their earlier comity and collaboration also began to fade, with Henry seeking advice elsewhere, and finding comfort in the company of mistresses, as Catherine's previous attractiveness to him faded through pregnancy, childbirth, the responsibilities of the reign, and her withdrawal into piety and religious observance.[13]

Another war against France, 1522–1526, went similarly disastrously for Henry, with bad feelings multiplying between England and the Holy Roman

Empire (under Charles V).[14] Each side accused the other of failing to fulfill commitments to coordinate their war against the French and of seeking a separate peace treaty at the expense of their ostensible ally. Henry, with the fewest resources and greatest vulnerability, began to feel increasingly betrayed by Charles V, a vulnerability even greater given the relative weakness of England in comparison to France and the Holy Roman Empire. This sense of inferiority and disappointment with the pro-Habsburg alignment no doubt was a contributing factor to Henry's growing emotional and physical distance from Catherine.[15]

By early 1527, Henry resolved to seek an annulment of his marriage to Catherine, who at 40 was unlikely to produce a male heir, and to the king's eye was less attractive than the woman he had married two decades earlier. Henry was no longer faithful to his wife, behavior quite common for monarchs, but which would lead to complications in this case. Henry's claims that his marriage to Catherine had been illegitimate, based on her brief marriage to his brother Arthur before he died, thus violating the provision of Leviticus 20:21, were theologically weak, even if based on the Bible. This argument was even weaker given that Henry and his father had gone to great pains to receive papal dispensation on this concern in advance of Henry and Catherine's marriage in 1509. The king was now in the odd situation of claiming his earlier request had been made in error, and that the decades of marriage to Catherine, recognized by both Church and state and having produced a surviving child, should be annulled.[16]

The earlier theological maneuvers of Henry, by which he had gained papal approval to marry Catherine, were in 1527 and thereafter replaced by countervailing ones, arguing that the original sanctions setting aside the affinity of the bride and groom had been flawed, thus rendering the marriage invalid. Indeed, even before proving this theological case, Henry was already planning a marriage to Anne Boleyn, one of Catherine's ladies-in-waiting. While some court officials recommended a French marriage to advance claims to formerly English territories on the Continent, the king's eyes were set firmly on Anne.[17] Henry's timing was fortunate; with the rising popularity among his people of the ideas of Luther and Calvin, "it was much easier to quarrel with Rome when half of northern Europe was doing much the same thing."[18]

Had Catherine consented to be shunted away to a distant castle or country manor, Henry no doubt would have gained Church approval to end the marriage quietly, without spectacle, and proceed to marry Anne. Even better would have been the queen's agreement to join a religious order, as there was precedent for taking on the vows of a nun being sufficient to dissolve a marriage. However, Catherine was made of sterner stuff; the daughter of Isabella of Castile refused Henry's request to support an annulment, asserting with all justification that she was his legitimate queen, married with the full endorsement of the Church, and any of his misgivings would not move her from the throne. Even the direct pleadings of a papal legate, asking Catherine to consider entering a convent under special conditions, enabling the dissolution of her marriage while preserving her financial means and her daughter, Mary, in the line of succession, went for naught. Catherine refused all direct and indirect pleadings, from the king, court advisors, and clerics. The queen proudly asserted that she had been a virgin at the time of her marriage to Henry, that their bond in the eyes of God and the Church was indissoluble, and that she would not make the way easy for her husband. In this, she was also resisting the Catholic Church, which hoped for a quiet and consensual resolution.[19] Catherine was strongly supported by both Emperor Charles V and Empress Isabella, then acting regent of Spain. Isabella marshaled a legion of theologians to buttress Catherine's position, intervene with the Catholic Church and the Pope directly, and attack Henry's arguments in public and private.[20]

Henry's single-minded focus on producing a male heir, rather than preparing his daughter for the throne, also reflected his concern that a future husband of Mary, whether French, Spanish, or German, could lay claim to England in the interest of another dynasty. With no clear example in England of royal rule by a woman, he sensed the vulnerability especially from France, with the multiple succession claims that intertwined noble families on both sides of the English Channel. The king's concern would prove prescient in the choice of husbands for Mary, even though it would be a Spanish prince, rather than a French one, who would cause concern in England about the kingdom's potential subordination to the Habsburg "superpower" of the Iberian Peninsula.[21] To Henry and some of his key advisors, the survival of the Tudor dynasty might likely rest on the king's ability to sire a male heir; certainly, the kingdom's odds did not improve without one.[22]

Upon hearing from Henry directly of his intentions and his view that their marriage was theologically illegitimate, the queen broke down in tears of anger, furious at her husband for his false claims and denial of their 18 years as king and queen, husband and wife.[23] For Catherine, preserving the sanctity of marriage, the claim of her daughter to the throne, the legitimacy of her queenship, and the truth of her virginity at the time of her marriage, were worth fighting for. The eventual dissolution of England's connection to the Catholic Church was not an outcome that Catherine welcomed in any way; she remained a true daughter of the faith, preserving for her daughter the possibility of restoring Roman Catholicism to England.[24] From 1531, the last year that she saw Henry, to her death in 1536, she did not waver from her devotion to the Church, her crown, and her daughter.[25]

With this determination by Catherine, and the prospect of a long and bitter legal proceeding ahead, with complicated theological arguments likely to drag a trial on for years, Henry made a stark decision: he would break from Roman Catholicism and receive a divorce from an entirely English church. Even before his clash with Catherine, Henry had tolerated low levels of Protestant activity, including the importing of books by Luther and Calvin. One can imagine his new-found agreement with Protestant writings on the duplicitousness of the Church, and now finding little support from the Pope on the matter of his marriage.[26]

A king that had been named "Defender of the Faith" by Pope Leo X for his arguments against Luther's reform, had by the end of 1533 married Anne and had her crowned queen, divorced Catherine, declared his daughter Mary illegitimate, and set England on a path that, within five years, brought it fully within the Protestant Reformation.[27] It is far too simple to regard Henry's break from Catholicism as a mere result of his desire for a divorce; he had been devoted to the Church, had written works of theology, and had been intimately involved in Church issues.[28] Even so, he was not beyond nudging the Church in directions that favored his personal interests, as was the case with his treatment of Catherine. Soon after his marriage to Anne Boleyn, his new wife had also given birth to a daughter, Elizabeth, future queen of England. Although the term would not come into use until later, in practice Anglican would join Lutheran and Calvinist as the major Protestant groupings within Europe – each a direct challenge to the unified Roman Catholic Christendom advocated first by Charles V then Philip II, both of whom aspired to lead it. Having been denied what he wanted from the Roman Catholic Church, Henry VIII created his own church. Although the Church of England would hardly be universal, at least in the ways that mattered to Henry, it would be triumphant at least within the borders of the kingdom.[29]

The subsequent actions of Henry to create a formal Church of England, including purging those loyal to Rome, seizing the assets of the Catholic Church and religious orders for distribution to his loyalists, naming himself the head of the new church, and incorporating new religious practices and ideas from the continental Reformation into the new institution, consolidated the power of the monarch over religion in his kingdom. He also set the terms that would define religious conflict within England over the next century, building obstacles to the restoration of Catholicism that both of his daughters, Mary and Elizabeth, would face in their terms as monarch. Enabling Henry to make these changes was the slow response of Pope Clement VII; by the time the Roman Church issued its decision, decreeing in March 1534 that the marriage of Henry and Catherine was legitimate and could not be annulled, or the king granted a divorce, the king was married to Anne Boleyn, Catherine humiliatingly received the title "princess dowager" and was essentially imprisoned at various castles and manors, and the writ of the Pope no longer mattered in formerly devout England. As an added cruelty, Catherine was not allowed to see Mary, her only surviving child, and one for whose future she felt nothing but dread. Catherine died in January 1536; her pleas to Henry, to her nephew Charles V, and to the new pontiff, Pope Paul III, who had succeeded Clement VIII, to recognize her daughter Mary as heir to the throne were unavailing.[30]

Initially, there was not much of the Reformation in Henry's declaration of a new church for England, merely replacing the leadership and authority of the Pope with himself as highest church leader. This was indeed something new: a national church, severed from Rome, but in form essentially the same as before the dissolution of the link. Reactions from devout Catholics were understandable, with one Jesuit describing the new institution in stark terms, still bitter three hundred years later: "Like a monster it stood alone: all the nations of the earth refused alliance with it; it stands alone now; not Lutheran nor Calvinist even consenting to a union with it."[31] Over the years that followed, however, Henry VIII led what would become the Church of England through substantial structural and spiritual reforms. Under his theological guidance, the English church reduced the number of sacraments from seven to three, privileged scripture over tradition – without abandoning the latter in the pattern of Luther. Henry's church also encouraged the adoption of English vernacular, rather than Latin, as the language of religious practice, worship services, and for the reading of the Bible. The king also confiscated Church and monastery lands, weakening the power of both secular and regular clergy, and fought to eliminate the veneration of icons and other images. Stripping the fiscal and legal advantages away from the clergy, he made them more vulnerable to the king's justice, rather than having first recourse to episcopal courts. Determined to identify the Church of England as not only outside Catholicism, but from the faith of Luther, whom Henry loathed, the king's church could best be described as a hybrid between Catholicism and the Protestantism of Luther and Calvin.[32]

King Henry's conversion to de facto Protestantism, through the vehicle of a church created for his personal convenience, transformed the strategic position of England. Even though Henry did not want to become a Protestant, and would have balked at the title, his reforms in the end led to this result.[33] Even after establishing his de facto Protestant church he endorsed the persecution of Protestants in England and on the Continent, including William Tyndale, who through Anne Boleyn had been an influence on the king.[34] Historians still debate the role of the woman who would become Queen Anne, but it does seem clear that she had read widely from Protestant works, supported a vernacular Bible – having read it in French while on the Continent – and was in many ways sympathetic to Protestantism, even while remaining ostensibly loyal to the Catholic Church prior to Henry's moves toward institutional theological independence.[35]

Henry's institutional revolution was more strategic than theological to the end; from an ally of Spain and the Holy Roman Empire, to one of France, and then again into an alliance with Charles V, Henry hoped to reclaim lost lands in France, unite Scotland with England under his rule, and remake England as a major power in Europe, despite its demographic and economic inferiority to France, the Empire, and Spain. He was unsuccessful in all three objectives, enduring battlefield defeats, national bankruptcy, and desertion by his wartime allies. His final peace treaty with France in August 1546 resulted as much from the exhaustion of both the king and his kingdom – indeed, Henry VIII would pass away five months later. He was, however, successful in handing his kingdom to his long-sought male heir, Prince Edward.

As Henry stated in his will, passing his realm to a son was the king's "chief labour and study in this world," for which he defied the Pope, established a new church, and executed or sequestered his many wives.[36] Henry VIII would earn the distinction of having named not just his immediate successor, but the two following ones, as he restored both Mary and Elizabeth to the line of succession through his testament. By restoring the legitimacy of his two daughters, the king ensured that it would be his children who took the throne should Edward, who was always sickly, pass away before producing heirs. Consistent with this, Henry did make allowances for any sons of Mary or Elizabeth, or even of his current wife, Catherine Parr, to inherit the kingdom should his immediate heir die. The new king, Edward VI, son of Henry and his third wife, the late Jane Seymour took the throne at the age of ten in 1547.[37]

Henry's son Edward VI, on whose behalf ruled a regency council and other delegates, did not hold the crown long; he died in July 1553, leaving Mary – despite a brief and failed attempt to substitute the king's Protestant cousin Lady Jane Grey – to take the throne, which she did in October. Unlike her father, and her two cousins, Edward VII and Jane Grey, Mary was a devout Catholic, following the example of her mother, Catherine. Indeed, she had refused direct orders from her half-brother and his ministers to abandon Catholicism during his reign, continuing to hold Catholic Mass in defiance of the Church of England. She would take this personal piety, which for so many years had remained confined to her private life and restricted connections, to the throne of England.[38] In support of this agenda, her eventual marriage to Prince Philip, heir to Habsburg Spain, was a rational choice, but among England's Protestants "throughout England a marriage alliance with Spain was regarded with indignation and horror."[39]

Mary's ambition as queen was to extirpate Protestantism from England, restoring to it the faith of the Catholic Church, ties to the Vatican, and the close connection to Spain that England had enjoyed during the early years of her parents' marriage.[40] Indeed, at times her cousin Charles V, and even her future husband, Philip II, would encourage her to proceed with less fanaticism and more patience in the restoration of the True Church; she would have none of these admonishments. As queen, she was in a hurry to purge all of her lands of the Protestant heresy as quickly as possible. In this goal, she would lean heavily on the influence and resources of her future husband, Philip of Spain. Just as important were the more than 2,000 Spanish courtiers, officials, and clerics Philip would bring to his marriage to England's queen, who would offer advice from their years of extirpating Protestants from Spain.[41] For many English subjects, the arrival of a Spanish husband for Mary, as well as the tide of Spaniards that accompanied him, raised "fear of the prospect of cultural extinction that the rising wave of Habsburg power seemed to presage."[42] For Mary, the opportunity as queen to reverse her father's theological adventurism and strike against Protestantism was consistent with her view that Calvin, Luther, and other Protestant heretics were, as one Jesuit noted, "far beyond all abominable miscreants in wickedness" in their "sacrilegious impiety."[43]

Mary faced many obstacles, including her father's undermining of the economic strength of the Catholic Church through land confiscations and the dominance of Protestants among English printing houses, which hindered the queen's ability to counter Reformation propaganda and to reissue Catholic works of theology and worship.[44] Despite her public prohibitions against Protestant publications, London and other cities continued to see books and other printed materials in support of Reform, with nimble printers able to outmaneuver not only the monarchy's censors, but the far few numbers of Catholic printers. Indeed, it seems that most pro-Marian materials were printed on the Continent and imported to England, delaying even more the ability of Mary, Philip, and their court to respond to attacks or defend their own policies.[45]

Even with these challenges, had Henry been the only monarch to rebel from the Catholic Church, Mary's task would have been achievable. Many historians, reversing earlier views about the establishment of the Church of England, argue that Mary's promise of a restoration of Catholicism was popular among the English people. True believers in Protestantism were a minority until much later during the Elizabethan decades.[46] However, while Henry VIII's break from Rome had emerged for entirely personal and dynastic reasons, rather than theological ones, the church he created by fiat existed in the broader milieu of Reform Protestantism, with a significant minority of influential English clerics, theologians, and active lay leaders deeply attracted by Calvinist and Lutheran ideas from the Continent, and seeing in Henry's irruption, as well as the faith of Elizabeth, the opportunity to constitute an entirely English brand of Protestantism, despite the reactionary ambitions of the new Catholic queen.[47]

For Catholics, "heretic England" was the bane of Europe, with France, Spain, and the papacy determined to reclaim the lost kingdom. For English Protestants, the goal was the opposite: to resist the efforts of Catholic Europe to force a reversal.[48] While Elizabeth remained moderate in her views, hoping until the outbreak of war with Spain that there might yet be an accommodation, many in her court viewed a conflict with Spain as not only likely, but desirable. Her chief advisor on foreign affairs, Sir Francis Walsingham, for his part, believed that England, along with Dutch Calvinists, and others were "the upholders of Protestant truth ... locked in a cosmic struggle with the dark powers of the papal Antichrist."[49]

Walsingham was not a man to encourage accommodation with Spain. Having witnessed the St. Bartholomew's Day Massacres in Paris in 1572, he viewed Roman Catholics as "the limbs of Satan" and Rome as "the whore of Babylon." Whatever his capacity for diplomacy and flexibility, he did not waver from his belief that Catholicism "must never, ever, under any circumstances whatsoever, be allowed to re-establish itself in England."[50] As a young man, he had experienced the attempt by Queen Mary and her husband, Philip II of Spain, to launch "a full restoration of the Catholic faith" to England.[51] Throughout his time as advisor to Elizabeth, master of her espionage network, and her lead foreign policy manager, he remained committed to supporting fellow Protestants throughout Europe, chafing at the queen's hesitation, even as he remained personally loyal to her.[52]

The marriage of Philip and Mary provided an opportunity for both to show their devotion to Catholicism, by returning England to the fold of the Church. By all accounts the Spaniard was not thrilled with the idea of this particular marriage, given Mary's shortage of admirable characteristics, but he accepted it as a dutiful Habsburg son, who shared with his bride the goal "to return England to Catholicism and its allegiance to the Pope."[53] Indeed, his welcome to London was far from warm; he was not crowned king of England, did not become Mary's designated heir, and did not even receive grants of lands and titles as compensation for not wearing the crown.[54] The wedding provided an opportunity to restore Catholicism to England, which Philip embraced. There were long-term ambitions raised during the negotiations for the match about uniting England and the Netherlands in a single Catholic reign, to be entrusted to the heirs of Mary and Philip, although in the event this dynastic plan did not come to fruition.[55]

The marriage was not popular in England. Disturbances were reported across England, with four major conspiracies launched against the marriage, including an abortive anti-Spanish revolt led by Thomas Wyatt.[56] Although these rebellions were quickly suppressed, the widespread mistrust of Spain was not. Bad feelings continued from the long-fought divorce between Henry VIII and Catherine, along with concerns that England would be drawn into Spain's wars in Italy, the Low Countries, and against France. Sympathies for Elizabeth also ran high, with crowds calling for her to rule in place of Mary, even as this Protestant daughter of Henry VIII, now legitimized under the will of the deceased king, remained under house arrest and vulnerable to actions of her Catholic half-sister.[57] The measures Mary and her advisors put in place to limit Philip's power, such as Parliament's 1554 Act Concerning Regal Power, maintaining her as both queen and king, were humiliating to the Spaniard, but with an eye to the greater benefit to the Habsburg grand strategy and the return of England to the Catholic fold, he assented.[58]

Even before the wedding in 1554, Spanish officials and clergy began to arrive in England, tasked with supporting Philip in his role as consort, aligning Spanish and English foreign and trade policies, and just as importantly with extirpating Protestant heresy from the island. Among the officials was the Dominican priest Bartolomé Carranza, former confessor to Emperor Charles V, who took the lead in establishing tribunals on the island and also served as confessor to Queen Mary. By early 1555, Parliament had restored the previous heresy laws, and Carranza and his allies among the English clergy had initiated tribunals to root out Protestants.[59] Closely allied to Cardinal Pole, and with the confidence of both Philip and Mary, he promoted persecution, rather than reconciliation, with recalcitrant Anglicans who refused to embrace the return to Catholicism.[60] Carranza would later claim that 30,000 English Protestants had been returned to Catholicism, exiled, or executed, in the campaign against heresy under his direction.[61]

Beyond reversing the success of the Reformation in Britain, Mary and especially Philip and his father, Emperor Charles V, hoped to bring England into alliance with the Habsburg domains, joining it in the fight against Protestantism and Islam. Under Philip, the Inquisition came to England, charged with extirpating Reformers. After a formal ceremony in November 1554, through which England, through Mary and Philip, were absolved of breaking away from the Catholic Church, Parliament reimposed previous laws against heresy. Trials soon began, starting in in February 1555, with thousands investigated and almost 300 burned at the stake for heresy. Cardinal Reginald Pole, the Pope's legate in England, Bishop Edmund Bonner of London, and Father Bartolomé Carranza, a priest in Philip's court, were among those leading this process. Carranza was especially noted by Philip and Mary for his "sterling work for the Catholic cause" in England.[62] The story of these and other Protestants executed in England and elsewhere at the behest of Mary and Philip would be the basis for many Protestant writings, most famously Foxe's Book of Martyrs, first published in 1563.[63]

Although the pace of executions was not especially high, averaging one per week, their public nature drew attention and built the queen's reputation, and earned her the epithet "Bloody Mary" among Protestants.[64] Approximately 300 Protestants were executed by order of the queen, with another 1,000 fleeing abroad into exile in advance of potential sentencing by Catholic tribunals in England.[65] Among those executed were Thomas Cranmer, Archbishop of Canterbury and leader of the Church of England, executed in 1556 after Pope Paul IV deprived him of the protection of his bishopric. Cardinal Pole, who had led the anti-Protestant purge, was named successor as Archbishop. For Mary, Cranmer's death was especially welcome, given his role in abetting her father King Henry VIII's divorce from her mother, Catherine of Aragon – a dissolution opposed vehemently by Catherine.[66] Even more fled into exile, or hid their true beliefs, enduring revived Catholicism with resentment and "bitter discontent" that would prove the undoing of Mary's reign.[67] While Philip did not return the tremendous affection that Mary held for him, he did his best to serve as a dutiful husband, focusing especially on religious matters, and hoping she would deliver an heir who would give meaning to his sacrifices.[68]

This hope was not to be realized. Indeed, Philip and Mary failed to produce a child, despite a long period during which the queen showed every evidence of being pregnant. In September 1554, Mary began to gain weight, stopped menstruating, and endured bouts of morning sickness. Rejoicing and relief were obvious in the court; even Elizabeth was freed from house arrest in spring 1555 to join in the celebration. Philip had his doubts about the pregnancy, a skepticism that others began to share as 1555 continued with no birth. By the end of summer 1555, Mary was no longer showing signs of pregnancy, having lost the weight and returned to court. Humiliated and frustrated by his and the queen's failure to produce an heir, in early September, despite the pleadings of Mary, Philip left England for the Low Countries, to address the Calvinist rebellion among his subjects.[69]

The union of England and Spain would face another humiliation, this time at the hands of the French. Furious at France's support for Mary Queen of Scots, as well as for rebels who in 1557 had launched a brief insurgency, Mary and Philip declared war on France. A failed attempt by Philip and English forces during 1557–1558 to invade France led to the loss of Calais, the last English enclave on the Continent. Although it had been Mary that had called for war on the French, many blamed Philip, who did not return to England.[70] His challenges in the Low Countries forced him to focus there, but no doubt he was more than happy to be away from the gloom of the English court.

Mary, not fully recovered from her false pregnancy, and feeling defeated not only in war, but in her obligation to restore Catholicism and produce an heir with her husband, died on 17 November 1558.[71] She and Philip had made progress in their efforts to return England to Catholicism; only their failure to produce an heir, and the embrace of Protestantism by Elizabeth, reversed the Counter-Reformation gains the couple had made.[72] The death of the queen was met with relief and rejoicing by those that had opposed her Catholic advocacy or the alliance with Spain; England could now be England, and Protestant, rather than an appendage to the universal Habsburg monarchy.[73] Elizabeth is alleged to have responded to the death of her half-sister with this comment: "This is the Lord's doing and it is marvelous in our eyes."[74]

Another hope of Philip was that he and Mary would succeed in making England the first nation to reverse its rebellion from Catholicism, using royal decrees, expected parliamentary assent, and the support of Cardinal Pole, Archbishop of Canterbury, a strong advocate for returning the English people to the Catholic Church. During his time as a leader of exiled Catholic loyalists after Henry's break from Rome, Pole had urged Pope Paul III and Charles V to make war on England to restore Catholicism; under Mary and Philip he had that opportunity.[75] Serious challenges remained, including whether and how to restore the lands and properties of the Catholic Church that had been seized by King Henry VIII, as well as whether to maintain the Church of England's independence as a national church in the Catholic tradition, as some English argued, or to petition for reintegration under the rule of Rome.[76] Mary and Philip were able to devise several compromises along these lines, which for a time seemed to be tipping the scales toward a Catholic reconquest of England. Indeed, despite later accounts, the English queen and her Spanish husband in only five years nearly overcame the establishment of Protestantism by Henry VIII. Roman Catholicism was too deep, and the distinctively English version of Protestantism too shallow, for the former to triumph completely over the latter in just a few years.[77]

Francis Walsingham, a known Protestant, joined the exile community in Basel, Switzerland in 1553, alternating study with travel on the Continent until Mary's death, and the beginning of Queen Elizabeth's rule in 1558. Although Elizabeth hoped to avoid constant warfare with Catholicism, the 1563 Council of Trent concluded with little theological space for confessional accommodation. This Catholic body reaffirmed Protestantism as entirely heretical. Indeed, "the principal focus of Rome's ire was England," empowering Philip II, shunned as suitor by Elizabeth, to launch his resources against this sanctuary for Reformers. Elizabeth was herself declared both "heretic and abettor of heretics" and an illegitimate monarch.[78] For a queen who had assumed power over a kingdom where Roman Catholicism was the state religion, Protestants had been executed or driven into hiding, and bishoprics and key religious posts were held almost universally by devout and orthodox Catholics, treading lightly was wise.[79] In the aftermath of the passage of the Act of Supremacy in 1559, with all English clergy forced to swear allegiance to Elizabeth or resign, all but one of the 25 bishops refused and left office; by 1561, the queen had filled these vacancies with Protestants, but realized the scale of the challenge ahead.[80]

Although she shrugged off her excommunication by Pope Pius V in 1570, a gesture that did nothing to the queen, but made even more perilous the situation for English Catholics, she did remain well-attuned to religious developments on the Continent. The Pope's denunciation of Elizabeth as "the pretended queen of England and the servant of crime" did little to gain Catholics tolerance in her realm. Indeed, his admonition that the faithful should ignore her "orders, mandates and laws" upon pain of their own excommunications put lawful English Catholics in an impossible quandary.[81] Elizabeth's efforts to find a "middle way seeking to avoid the excessive ceremonialism of Catholicism and the creedal certitudes of Protestantism" may have been the best approach for her and to maintain peace in England but was destined to be unacceptable to Philip II, Pius V, and the ardent Catholic faith of these two men.[82] Philip did realize that he could not wage war on France and England at the same time as he faced rebellion in the Low Countries by Dutch Calvinists. In the short term, he kept relations with England cool, rather than allowing the most passionate adventurers on his side to clash with those on Elizabeth's and gain the war both sides craved.[83]

Spain's king was concerned not just about the resurgence of the Church of England under Elizabeth, but also with the dramatic rise of Calvinism in Scotland, spurred by John Knox, founder of Presbyterianism. Although there were significant theological and political differences between Anglicanism and Scottish Calvinism, both were ardent enemies of Spain. Fears of the Scots allying with Dutch and French Calvinists, either alone or in concert with England, were an ongoing concern for Philip II. To overcome this challenge, many Spaniards put their hopes into the idea that Mary, Queen of Scots, Catholic cousin of Elizabeth, would one day reign over both Scotland and England. This hope enabled the launching of many schemes with French and Spanish support, but to no avail, a failure compounded by Mary's arrest for treason in 1567.[84]

Philip had initially hoped in the 1560s to maintain good relations with England, and perhaps entice Elizabeth, if not into marriage, at least back into the Catholic fold. Reluctant as he was to marry Elizabeth, whom he knew from his time as husband to Mary, he considered the preservation of Catholicism in England worth the sacrifice of his own preference for a marriage to a Portuguese or French princess. As an indication of his primary focus, he insisted that, should Elizabeth agree to marriage, she would also have to personally embrace Catholicism as well as promise to cooperate with him, as had Mary, in the final and complete extirpation of Protestantism from England.[85]

Philip had previously suggested Elizabeth might marry his cousin, Emmanuel Philibert, who was Duke of Savoy, Prince of Piedmont, and the king's governor in the Netherlands. She demurred, as she would do later with other candidates, including Archduke Ferdinand, son of the Holy Roman Emperor, Charles of Austria, grandson of the emperor, and Don Carlos, the sickly and erratic son of Philip, who would die in 1568 at the age of 23. Although responding with civility and initial interest, in each case she rejected these Catholic and Habsburg loyalists, supported in this by most of her court, rejoicing as they were to be free of the "ill-fated" Spanish Catholic connection.[86] King Philip deeply regretted his failure to convince Queen Elizabeth to marry a Spanish Habsburg, either himself or one of his subjects. This was about more than keeping her connected by bonds of marriage to Philip; absent a pro-Habsburg marriage, this almost certainly meant England would be lost to him and to the Catholic Church, likely now to "fall back into its former errors."[87] In her responses, and those on her behalf, the English pointed out the impropriety of a Catholic Habsburg marrying someone considered a heretic; a clear message that Elizabeth was not of a mind to become a Catholic, even much less so after being called "the daughter of the devil" by a Spanish diplomat.[88]

Even so, with support from his ambassador, Diego Guzmán de Silva, the Spanish monarch sent marriage offers and encouragements to abandon heresy. He also tried to gain positive results for England during peace negotiations with France, ending with the Peace of Cateau-Cambrésis in April 1559, which ended the war of England and Spain against France. Unfortunately, England was forced to accept French occupation of Calais, the last English territory on the Continent, only slightly mitigated by a French promise to return the city, or compensate England, after eight years. Spanish territorial gains elsewhere, especially in Italy, made the surrender of Calais even more unpopular, and consequently increased hatred for Spain and its king.[89]

The loss of their last continental outpost was received bitterly in England, even though they gained French pledges to withdraw their previous support for the claims of Mary, Queen of Scots, to the English throne. Ending the war was also a tremendous relief to Elizabeth's treasury, which her half-sister Mary had drained in the conduct of the war. Even so, the English saw this treaty as further evidence of the negative impact of a close connection to Spain. While Philip and Elizabeth maintained civil relations in the immediate aftermath, their respective courts had by this point turned solidly against even neutrality by the early 1560s. Only the relationship between the two monarchs, and their mutual reluctance to embark on a war, held back a potential conflict, accelerated by Elizabeth's full embrace of the Protestant Reforms of her father.[90]

The queen's prudence was a source of frustration then and later among the most ardent of her Protestant supporters, who welcomed a chance to war against Spain. As Sir Walter Raleigh noted, "her majesty did all by halves" and because of this did not beat "that great empire in pieces" despite propaganda to the contrary.[91] Even so, England held off Spain, which unlike England was a great empire in the 16th century. The surprise was not that Elizabeth did not conquer Spain, but that she avoided being conquered by Spain. England, despite the bluster of men such as Raleigh and Drake, remained "critically weak" at the strategic level, when compared to Habsburg resources. The course of England's gradual change from ally to enemy of Spain has been the subject of discussion by many historians, but over the course of the decade 1568–1579, disputes rose dramatically, as did the mutual recognition by both Spain and England that their interests had become irreconcilable.[92]

Another point of contention was Elizabeth's offering refuge and protection to Spanish Protestants, who by 1560 had a small congregation in London "under the Queen's favour and protection, for the sake of true religion." Their pastor, Cassiodoro de Reina, had originally been a Spanish friar, most likely attached to the monastery of San Isidoro del Campo, a center for Lutheran sentiments among the Hieronymite monks.[93] The Spanish ambassador, Bishop Alvaro del la Quadra, wrote to Philip II in 1562 about the group of "Spanish heretics," complaining bitterly about their protection by the English, who not only granted them a building, the former Church of St. Mary of Axe, but allowed their flagrant public worship three times per week. Philip responded that the ambassador should work to have the Spanish pastor expelled, on whatever pretext might be available, presumably in order that Spanish authorities might lay hands on these heretics. Cassidoro did leave England in 1563, with the Spanish church closing shortly thereafter due to declining numbers.[94]

Reina moved first to Frankfurt and then to Basel, Switzerland, where he continued the major translation he had begun elsewhere: a complete Bible in Spanish. Finally completing this in 1568, by 1572 he had succeeded in printing the first copies of this tremendous achievement. Although corrected and updated by later scholars, including Cipriano de Valera around 1600, the text of Reina remains the basis for the contemporary Spanish-language Protestant Bible. He dedicated the first edition to Queen Elizabeth, under whose patronage and protection in London much of the initial work was possible, and in whose realms he initially expected to publish his edition.[95] Reina would later serve during the early 1590s as a Lutheran pastor, preaching to French-speaking congregations in Antwerp, before passing away in 1594.[96]

Even with these events and gestures toward supporting Protestantism, Philip still hoped to retain at least a neutral position regarding England; he did not need another enemy in Europe and at sea. These notions ended after England seized five ships in November 1568, full of Spanish treasure and other cargo, headed to the Low Countries to support Spain's war against Dutch Calvinist rebels. The Spanish retaliated with trade sanctions, which the English reciprocated, confirming the new state of affairs: persistent hostility in Hispano-British relations. Although Elizabeth did not have the means to lead European-wide Protestant resistance to Spanish Catholicism, she did become a symbol both in her realm and in the Habsburg Empire of practical resistance to Philip II's vision for a united Christendom. Concerned about coming into conflict with both Spain and France, Western Europe's two leading Catholic powers, she had to be cautious in both warfare and theology, while championing the unity of her realm under the Church of England.[97]

Throughout the late 1560s, 1570s, and early 1580s, Philip II and his diplomats supported – or, more often, were accused of supporting – various schemes and conspiracies to overthrow Elizabeth. In 1569, for example, the Revolt of the Northern Earls attempted to march south and replace the queen with the imprisoned Mary, former Queen of Scots.[98] The expectation of Spanish gold, papal approval, and military support from Habsburg armies encouraged whispered discussions and plots of varying significance, often hatched with assistance from Spain's ambassadors. With rumors of assassination, plots to release Mary from imprisonment, and Spanish armies always seeming to be on the verge of landing, and the real threat of prominent English Catholics joining in rebellion, it took very little to keep tensions high in the 1570s. Philip encouraged every possibility for a change of regimes and religions in England, even promoting the most dubious schemes, the failure of which legitimately exacerbated English fears of a Spanish invasion.[99]

On the Spanish side, the presence of John Man as Elizabeth's ambassador to Philip II from 1567 made things progressively worse. As a former Oxford warden, he was an "ardent Calvinist" who had driven away some long-time faculty members through his abrasive personality and dour devotion. In Spain, he attempted to argue theology with Catholic leaders, denounced the Pope, and attempted to encourage Calvinist conversions through disseminating pamphlets. Philip II loathed the envoy, refusing to meet him and informing Elizabeth in a letter that the ambassador was worthy of being burned at the stake.[100] At the same time, English merchants trading goods in Spain and Spanish colonies were highly sensitive to the real danger of being brought before the Inquisition upon charges. If they swore loyalty to Queen Elizabeth as monarch and head of the Church of England, they were admitting heresy, since the Catholic Pope was the only legitimate leader of Christians. In addition to the risks to individual English traders, sailors, and other travelers, this issue greatly complicated treaty and commercial relations between England and Spain, and the rise of these incidents caused outrage in both countries.[101]

The collapse of Anglo-Spanish negotiations after 1570 was in large part due to this issue; Philip II refused to allow English diplomats, merchants, or other residents or visitors to enjoy religious liberty on Spanish soil, and was willing to endure another war, at a time when his hands were already full of it, to insist on this point of universal Catholic supremacy within his domains. At the same time, England refused to reign in piracy or even de facto privateering among its subjects.[102] The most diplomatically embarrassing incident occurred in January 1562, when officers of the Spanish Inquisition seized the servants and baggage of Sir Thomas Chaloner, the new English ambassador to Habsburg Spain. Particularly egregious was the tribunal's impounding of the envoy's personal and diplomatic papers, a violation of standard ambassadorial privileges. Chaloner had the double misfortune of being both Protestant and Erasmian, having translated "In Praise of Folly" from Latin into English. While his papers, effects, and servants were returned, it was a challenging moment for both governments.[103]

An ongoing source of tension between Elizabeth and Philip was the treatment of English merchants and sailors in Spain. Although, as noted earlier, there were few cases of English Protestants being brought before the tribunal, the ongoing treatment English visitors to Spain was a point of contention. Spanish *comisarios* (commissioners) of the Spanish Inquisition would routinely ask English sailors in port whether there were Anglican services being held on board. These events were routine and required on all English-chartered ships, but both sides tried to maintain the fiction that there were no services of this kind happening. On occasion, a poorly prepared or undisciplined sailor would blurt out to the commissioner that there were services happening, or confess to being a practicing Protestant, which could lead to trouble for the captain and the entire crew. British merchants and sailors constituted the largest numbers of foreigners in some ports, including Las Palmas, Canary Islands, where they traded English textiles for Spanish wheat, wine, and sugar. By 1576, as the Protestant threat was subsiding in Spain, Spanish commissioners agreed that Protestant services on board merchant ships at sea were no longer punishable by the Inquisition; the prohibition remained in place for merchant vessels in port, regardless of the country of origin. However, even this limited protection ended with the Anglo-Spanish War that began in 1585; merchants continuing to visit Spanish ports after this date, and until peace in 1604, could be arrested as pirates.[104] Even thereafter, the issue of foreign commerce in Spanish ports was not fully resolved, so smuggling remained a recourse for English merchants, even if privateering was no longer authorized by the crown.[105]

Investigations by officials of the Spanish Inquisitions continued in ports and harbors, however, looking for illegal Lutheran and Calvinist books being smuggled into Spain on foreign vessels. All ships entering Spanish waters were supposed to be searched by *comisarios*, with harsh penalties for attempting importation of works on the Index of Forbidden Works or obviously Protestant in their subject matter, even if previously unknown to the Inquisition. While *comisarios* varied in the thoroughness of their searches, and presumably a financial consideration might divert their attention, once these allegations reached the local tribunal there could be serious consequences for those responsible, including a sentence of galley service. While only six Englishmen were known to have been burned at the stake in sixteenth-century Seville, other forms of physical punishment, imprisonment, or hefty fines were also among the potential penalties for smuggling. Merely being written in a foreign language could draw the unwanted attention of the Spanish Inquisition, at least until a reliable translator could be found, to assure everyone that the book was innocuous.[106]

Some Englishmen were able to avoid execution, such as Thomas Pillyn, arrested in March 1580 and accused of Protestantism. His testimony to his Catholic faith was so convincing, as was his promise to reveal the names of actual Protestants among the English in Toledo and elsewhere, that he was absolved of any wrongdoing. His statement of loyalty to "the Holy See and Roman Church" and "the true Catholic and Apostolic faith," along with his denunciations of all "heresies and apostasies (that deny) the Catholic faith and evangelical rule of our Redeemer and Savior Jesus Christ" convinced the tribunal to impose no punishment on him, other than a solemn oath to say multiple rosaries, attend additional Masses, and inform for the Inquisition.[107]

Overseas, English adventurers such as Francis Drake took advantage of weak garrisons to raid Spanish colonies in the Caribbean, Atlantic coasts, and even in the Pacific. While few of these attacks were made explicitly in the name of Queen Elizabeth, much less the Church of England, Spanish officials did see them as a manifestation of conflict with Protestants, with heresy conflated with piracy. Indeed, both Drake and the English government preferred to maintain some ambiguity about the relationship of these expeditions to the state; plausible deniability meant more diplomatic room to maneuver for the queen, as well as potentially greater financial returns for Drake and his fellow sailors.[108]

Drake's raids were not devoid of religious significance, however; typically included in his modus operandi was the looting and desecration of any Catholic churches his men encountered, such as when they attacked the small Mexican port city of Huatulco on 13 April 1575. At Huatulco, Drake forced his Spanish prisoners, including the town's Catholic priest, to attend an Anglican Protestant service.[109] The religious implications for these raids did matter, although of more proximate benefit to Elizabeth was the financial shares she received from these voyages. Drake's return in 1580, for example, brought the crown £140,000 in plundered wealth from Spanish ships and colonies. By comparison, the total annual expense for the queen's household during these years was £40,000–£50,000, and her total debt on assuming the throne in 1558 had been £300,000.[110]

Later attacks, such as those led by Thomas Cavendish, also targeted Catholic churches and symbols. Among these were a 1587 attack on Huatulco, Mexico, which saw the English attempt to burn a large wooden cross erected by the Spaniards, but to no avail. When the Spaniards reoccupied the town, the survival of the scorched *Santa Cruz* (Holy Cross) took on great religious significance as a symbol of resistance to English heretics. This was a consolation given the successes of Cavendish and Drake, who between them took nine Spanish ships as prizes, including cargos from Manila and Peru. They had also raided multiple Spanish coastal settlements in the Americas.[111]

In England, although initially Queen Elizabeth's monarchy tolerated Catholics who confined their activities to private homes or quiet, out-of-the-way parishes, after 1571, with an exclusively Protestant parliament, the situation began to become more challenging. English Catholics were forced to choose between Pope and Queen, the conversion of Protestants to Catholicism became equated with treason, and English priests who had been trained in Spain, France, or elsewhere in foreign Catholic seminaries, were immediately suspect as alien subversives.[112] On this latter point, there was some merit to English Protestant concerns; Philip II did fund seminaries in Paris and elsewhere, hoping to prepare English and especially Irish natives to return home with pro-Spanish and anti-Elizabethan attitudes. The oldest, the Irish College in Paris, opened in 1578. During the 1570s and 1580s, these small colleges, subsidized by Spanish treasure, supported Catholic seminarians, priests, and bishops, turning "militant Irish migrants into potentially useful agents of Spanish influence." While Philip did not have an established goal in mind, he viewed anything that strengthened the Catholic Church within Protestant-controlled lands, especially Elizabeth's England, as worthy of investment and effort.[113]

Despite later events, war between Spain and England was far from certain. Indeed, the two nations enjoyed much longer periods of formal peace between them than declared conflict, albeit with covert operations against each other during many of these interbellum times. While Elizabeth surely coveted Spanish wealth and placed few objections to the extractions of her privateers from the Spanish, provided the crown received its portion, she preferred not to risk open warfare and its associated risks and costs, no matter how much Spanish silver she might gain.[114] Elizabeth's stated intent was to maintain England's "splendid isolation ... to keep out of continental squabbles," not only out of a preference for peace, but necessary as a "cost-saving policy."[115] She had also seen the costs of entanglements during her father's and sister's reigns, with little gained and much lost from their alliances and interventions. Piracy tends to emerge in areas with weak governments, near territories with insufficient naval protection, or where maritime powers seek irregular allied forces to supplement their own navies. Arguably, all three factors applied in the pending contest between Tudors and Habsburgs, with English "individual adventurers and small syndicates" probing into Spain's colonies from the 1540s onward, including its Portuguese possessions after 1580, in search of ports into which to smuggle and prizes to seize at sea. That this occurred even when the two states were ostensible allies showed the limits of Habsburg naval power and the modest capacity of England to limit the behavior of its subjects.[116]

Philip, for his part, had sufficient enemies in France, the Ottoman Empire, and among his own rebellious Protestant regions that he was in no mood to seek additional foes at sea, on land, or in a position to ally with his existing foes. He and his Spanish courtiers had, nonetheless, created enemies in England, not only among Protestants outraged by his and Queen Mary's attempts to reinstate Catholicism, but by English losses as an ally of Spain, such as Calais. As one historian noted, Philip's presence and attempts to link Habsburg and Tudor policies into a more formal alliance had not only caused anti-Spanish sentiment, but an accelerated "enduring hatred of foreigners rather than any degree of constructive engagement."[117]

By the early 1580s, however, both England and Spain had had enough of each other. Philip II was increasingly frustrated by Elizabeth's support for Dutch insurgents, her protection of privateers that plagued Spanish shipping and colonial lines of communication, and especially her increasing devotion to the cause of the Reformation. The Treaty of Nonsuch, signed in 1585 between England and the Dutch rebels, pledging English financial and military aid against Spain, was the final offense from the Spanish perspective.[118] Support for war increased especially among Spanish commercial interests, who saw competition and piracy from England as continual threats to their survival, control over Spain's overseas empire, and trade throughout Europe and in Spain's colonies.[119]

For Queen Elizabeth, Spain continued to pose a threat, supporting Catholic spies and coup plotters in England, denying England free access to ports and markets in the Americas, and persecuting English Protestant subjects who fell into the hands of the Spanish Inquisition. The public images of the two monarchs, Philip as favored son of the Catholic Church, and Elizabeth as "Protestant saviour ... the godly champion against the Romish Antichrist" also contributed to the inflammation of hostilities between their two realms.[120] Neither monarch especially wanted the Anglo-Spanish War, despite the coolness of their personal relations: "had they believed themselves to possess the choice, would have avoided it as happily as they would each other's company."[121]

Philip, for his part, embraced paeans to his role as "a great monarch with grave global responsibilities," leading the Catholic nations in the struggle not only against Islam in the Mediterranean, but even more critically against the heresy of Protestantism within Christendom. This was more than just an image; his banner had led the Holy League, a union of Catholic states, in the victory against the Ottoman Empire at the apocalyptic naval battle of Lepanto.[122] While he was not the only Catholic monarch in Europe, he was the most powerful, most ardent in his faith, and most committed to unremitting warfare against the Protestant Reformation. Wherever heresy was, Philip and his allies were likely to be nearby, planning to fight any rebellion against the Catholic Church.

Philip II imagined that his great Armada, which he began planning in 1583 and assembling in 1587 for a campaign against England, could achieve at least the same kind of victory.[123] Supported, albeit reluctantly, by Pope Sixtus V with Church tithes and loans, this naval force had the blessing of the Catholic Church as an expedition against heretical Elizabeth and her Church of England. In addition to a financial pledge, the Pope also named a new Cardinal, William Allen, to be "future interim governor of England following its conquest" by Spain.[124] While Philip's ultimate strategic goal was unclear, since forces by themselves seemed insufficient to conquer England, at a minimum he seems to have intended a punishing assault against Elizabeth. Among the opportunities discussed by the king and his commanders were to destroy the English navy, clearing lines of communication between Spain and the Low Countries, ending the alliance between England and Calvinist rebels, and being prepared to lend support should there be a Catholic uprising against Tudor rule in Ireland, or even in England itself.[125] His delays and strategic uncertainty enabled the English to be warned well in advance of this maritime threat, and even for Francis Drake to launch pre-emptive raids in Cadiz and elsewhere, in 1587 destroying some of the fleet preparing for the campaign against England.[126]

Assembled near Lisbon, once ready in 1588 the Armada contained 130 sea-worthy ships, over 2,400 artillery pieces, and 22,000 sailors and soldiers, to be joined in case of an invasion of England by Spanish and allied reinforcements from the Low Countries.[127] There has been some debate about the strategic goals of this massive maritime expeditionary force. Was it meant to conquer England? Clear the naval channel for reinforcements to the Low Countries? Or encourage a rebellion by Irish Catholics against London? In the event, it accomplished none of these goals, foundering against the adversaries of weather in the English Channel and North Sea, as well as England's small but effective navy and allied privateers. There was nothing inevitable about the failure; with more cooperative weather, including clear sailing when Spain was en route and rain when England attempted to launch its fire ships, the outcome could easily have been otherwise, with a successful Spanish landing on English soil.[128]

The ultimate disaster of the Spanish Armada, and the failure to control either the English Channel or the North Sea, would be ongoing obstacles to Spain's ability to defeat England or repress the Dutch Revolt, two ongoing Protestant threats to the Spanish Empire. The resources spent on the Armada were also sunken costs in both the financial and maritime senses, no longer available for the wars against the Ottomans, counterinsurgency against the Dutch, or maritime engagement elsewhere with the English or French to secure communication lines to the far-flung Spanish Empire.[129] Even after the defeat of the Spanish Armada, Philip and his advisors continued to plot for the destruction of Elizabeth's monarchy and the restoration of Catholicism to England. In 1596, for example, the English Jesuit priest Robert Persons, who had supported the Armada from a distance, wrote a detailed proposal outlining how to govern England to bring it back into the Catholic fold. Among his recommendations were creating a Council of Reformation to extirpate heresy, since the name Inquisition "may be somewhat odious and offensive" to the English. Magnanimously, he offered a transition period of 4–6 years for Protestants to recant their heresies and return to Catholicism. He volunteered himself to serve as Archbishop of England.[130]

Religious warfare was no less earnest at sea during the war against England, which lasted from 1585 to 1604. Although Mass could be not held, given the potential for the host to fall in unsteady seas, there was ample accommodation for other forms of Catholic religiosity in the Habsburg fleet. Prayers, hymns, invocations of the Virgin Mary, the wearing of crucifixes, saints' medallions, and the presence of other religious items, all attested to the devotion of sailors and others aboard Philip's maritime crusading vessels. While priests were present only on the larger vessels, ship's masters and other crew stepped in, to the best of their competences and devotion, to ensure an appropriately Catholic atmosphere as Spain's ships entered battle against the hated English heretics.[131]

Indeed, as historian Philip Fernández-Armesto has noted, both the English and Spanish would have agreed with a characterization of the spiritual intent of the Spanish Armada "as an engine of Catholic vengeance, launched to subvert the English Reformation."[132] Spain would lament the failure of this seaborne enterprise, while England would celebrate the catastrophic failure of the Armada. In their foreign policies, their national narratives, and subsequent actions, both Spain and England magnified the legend of this naval confrontation as it shaped their respective self-image, as well as their perspective on their chief maritime foe. Spain mourned and England celebrated, but both kept the battle in recent memory.

In the end, the ostensible defeat of the Spanish Armada in August and September 1588 by English ships and unfavorable weather can only be partially described as a loss for Spain. The overall strategic balance remained essentially unchanged at sea and on land. Spain remained a global superpower, while England, although reinforced in its Protestantism, remained a peripheral state. While as the actions of Drake and other privateers showed, the English would continue to nip at the heels of the Spanish, they would not, except as one component of the global Protestant threat, truly threaten Habsburg dominance in Europe and the world.[133] As historian James McDermott noted, "If Goliath could not slay David, David had neither the reach nor resources to bring the giant to his knees."[134]

It was not the English alone who posed an existential threat to Spain; it was English efforts, in concert with those of Dutch rebels, French Huguenots, and Protestants within Spanish territories that together endangered Philip II's monarchy. There was never a formal coalition or coordinated efforts against Spanish Catholicism by these forces, but that does not mean that it was far from the minds not only of the King of Spain, but from that of the Queen of England. A limited intervention in France in support of the Huguenots in 1562–1563 had ended badly for the English, with defeat at the hands of French Catholics, failure to recapture Calais, the loss of Le Havre after briefly holding it, and the humiliation of the Treaty of Troyes, which forced England to pay a substantial fine to France to end the war.[135]

Elizabeth, despite the encouragement of many of her advisors, especially Walsingham, resisted the idea of creating a Protestant mirror image of Philip II's Holy League. There did exist the commonality of interests and, most importantly, a common enemy among the Protestant states and movements in Europe. There were the northern Lutheran states of Denmark, Sweden, and German principalities, Dutch and French Calvinists, and her own Church of England, all of which could have been forged into a coalition against Habsburg-led Catholics. Before his conversion to Catholicism in 1593, King Henry IV (also King of Navarre) figured prominently in these schemes.[136] Even though Elizabeth was distraught at Henry's conversion to Catholicism, the two maintained positive relations. Elizabeth was encouraged by his hostility to Spain and his expulsion of the Jesuits in December 1594, after a Jesuit student attempted to assassinate him.[137]

After Henry's conversion, however, Queen Elizabeth was even less enthusiastic about the idea of forging a global Protestant alliance, recognizing England's limited resources. There were no ships full of American silver to fuel these ambitions, apart from those rare ones captured from the Spanish. While the queen was willing to provide limited support to the enemies of the Habsburgs, and to fight when directly threatened, she recognized that England would be most prosperous and safest when it was at peace with the superpower of her day, not at the vanguard of Protestant armies in Europe.[138] The failure of a retaliatory effort in 1589, the so-called "English Armada," a joint attack on Spain and Portugal by English, Dutch, and Huguenot ships, was an additional warning to Elizabeth of the risks of expeditionary warfare on the Continent and at sea.[139]

For Phillip II and his monarchy, England's identity became inseparable from the Protestant threat. The mutual enmity between England and Spain was based primarily on this theological divide; even under later truces or peace treaties, there remained a significant barrier to more advanced partnership. Despite periods of peace, between decades of warfare, Catholic Spain could never truly embrace England as a partner and ally, at least not after the Elizabethan era confirmed it in its Protestantism. In less than 50 years, England had shifted from natural ally of Spain to persistent adversary at sea, on land, and in the faith.[140] Elizabeth continued to keep a watchful eye on potential enemies of Britain, for example warning James VI of Scotland against "the wicked conspirators of the Spanish faction" that were ever plotting to encourage Spanish invasion and restoration of Catholicism in Scotland.[141]

Spanish armies, as well, embraced this aura of crusading fervor and "Catholic triumphalism."[142] Even more than their maritime compatriots, Spain's soldiers were far more likely to be accompanied by priests to celebrate daily Mass, receive confessions, and offer last rites. These chaplains accompanied Spanish soldiers on the march and at times even into battle, where they came into direct contact with Protestant enemies through direct fire weaponry, small-arms fire, and even bloody hand-to-hand combat. Whether in the forces preparing to land on English soil or in the armies fighting in the Low Countries to preserve the Kingdom of the Netherlands as a Catholic realm, their obvious and outward devotion to the Church was a phenomenon for all of Spain's forces during the sixteenth century.[143]

The Anglo-Spanish War continued until 1604, although less apocalyptically after the failure of Philip's Armada. The king continued to explore ways to undercut Protestantism in Britain. For example, his patronage of Irish colleges enabled their founding in Spain and France to train seminarians in exile from Ireland. The Royal College of Irish Nobles, Salamanca, received a royal charter in July 1592, to provide a "focal point" among the Irish diaspora and prepare to send priests back to Ireland to counter the Protestant heresy. This Irish College, which would operate continuously until 1951, trained many generations of parish priests for Ireland, centuries after open warfare between Catholics and Protestants no longer plagued the European continent. While educating Irish students may seem a distant question from the affairs of the heart and state that characterized the relationship between England and Spain during the sixteenth century, the Irish College and its equivalents elsewhere on the continent remained as an echo of the messy religious and institutional entanglements between Habsburgs and Tudors. For Philip II, who fought other campaigns during this period, there could hardly be a better legacy than the establishment of Catholic seminaries to undermine Protestantism in the British Isles.[144]

The end of the Anglo-Spanish Wars also enabled greater tolerance for Catholics in England. Absent the fear that they represented a potential source for foreign support or internal rebellion, Elizabeth and her successors reduced somewhat the persecution of Catholics, allowing the 20% of the population that remained Catholic to retain this faith quietly, away from court and public life, and without the ability to proselytize. Even though the restrictions remained harsh, they were far more accommodating to this religious minority than the comparable situation in Spain, where Protestantism remained officially illegal until the late nineteenth century (1868), three decades after the final closure of the Spanish Inquisition. England expected that Catholics would remain "the most modest, quiet, and faithful Subjects" of the monarchy, according to Father Matthew Kellison, president of the English College at Douai, France, "notwithstanding their confiscations, confinings, Seizings, imprisonments, (and) deathe" imposed by the Tudors.[145] According to Kellison, even though Calvin and Luther urged rebellion against Catholic monarchs, "which doctrine they in Holland have practiced in rebelling and deposing their King of Spaine; yet our conscience and Religion telleth us that we must obey our kings though they differ from us in Religion."[146] Anti-Spanish attitudes among the English remained strong, even if official tolerance resumed. There continued to be a powerful bias against the Habsburgs, Catholicism, and all things Spanish, such that even the Anglo-Spanish peace treaty of 1604 was met with grumbling by those who wanted to continue the conflict. English literature, as well, maintained a bias against Spain and all things Spanish.[147]

Although English Catholics attempted, with mixed success, to assert their loyalty to Elizabeth and her successors, the same opportunities were by no means open for Spanish Protestants. Especially in regard to Spain, Philip II was absolutely intransigent about Lutheranism, Calvinism, and other forms of Protestant practice. He endorsed, without hesitation, the ardent persecutorial approach of the Spanish Inquisition toward Protestants, their writings, and their efforts in Spain, leading in the 1550s and 1560s to a concentrated and successful effort to extirpate them from the heart of Philip's empire, to pursue them throughout Europe, and to bring Habsburg influence to bear, in collaboration with the papacy and other Catholic states, to fight against Protestant Reform everywhere and always.

Notes

1 The phrase originated in the late Middle Ages among French audiences but later referred to England's switching sides during the religious conflicts of the sixteenth century. H.D. Schmidt, "The Idea and Slogan of 'Perfidious Albion'," *Journal of the History of Ideas*, October 1953, Vol. 14, No. 4, 604–616.
2 James McDermott, *England and the Spanish Armada: The Necessary Quarrel* (New Haven: Yale University Press, 2005), xii.
3 Lynch, *Spain 1516-1598*, 105. McDermott, *England and the Spanish Armada*, 51.
4 Newcombe, *Henry VIII and the English Reformation*, 23.
5 Norwich, *Four Princes*, 52–53, 59–60.
6 Rady, *The Habsburgs*, 65.
7 Marshall, *Religious Identities in Henry VIII's England*, 120–122.
8 Mattingly, *Catherine of Aragon*, 126.
9 Norwich, *Four Princes*, 38–39.
10 Mattingly, *Catherine of Aragon*, 121–122.
11 Mattingly, *Catherine of Aragon*, 133–137.
12 Mattingly, *Catherine of Aragon*, 155–157, 160–163.
13 Mattingly, *Catherine of Aragon*, 174–177.
14 Mattingly, *Catherine of Aragon*, 218–229.
15 Retha Warnicke, *The Rise and Fall of Anne Boleyn* (Cambridge: Cambridge University Press, 1989), 39–40, 52–54.
16 Newcombe, *Henry VIII and the English Reformation*, 23–25.
17 Mattingly, *Catherine of Aragon*, 246–247.
18 Norwich, *Four Princes*, 19.
19 Mattingly, *Catherine of Aragon*, 250–253, 268–270; Newcombe, *Henry VIII and the English Reformation*, 28–30.
20 Isidoro Jiménez Zamora, "La Emperatriz Isabel de Portugal ante la división religiosa," in Borreguero Beltrán and Retortillo Atienza, *La memoria de un hombre*, 331–334.
21 Wilson, *Sir Francis Walsingham*, 21.
22 Warnicke, *The Rise and Fall of Anne Boleyn*, 48–49.
23 Norwich, *Four Princes*, 96–97.
24 Mattingly, *Catherine of Aragon*, 433–435.
25 Warnicke, *The Rise and Fall of Anne Boleyn*, 100, 103.
26 Mattingly, *Catherine of Aragon*, 278–280.
27 Norwich, *Four Princes*, 71. Warnicke, *The Rise and Fall of Anne Boleyn*, 131.
28 Lipscomb, *The King is Dead*, 57–59.
29 Mattingly, *Catherine of Aragon*, 303, 363–364, 370–372, 385.
30 Mattingly, *Catherine of Aragon*, 388–390, 413–415, 420–422, 425–430.
31 Rev. W. Waterforth, S.J., *England and Rome: or, The History of the Religious Connection between England and the Holy See, from the Year 179, to the Commencement of the Anglican Reformation in 1534* (London: Burns & Lambert, 1854), 370.
32 Suzannah Lipscomb, *The King Is Dead: The Last Will and Testament of Henry VIII* (New York: Pegasus Books, 2016), 14–15; D.G. Newcombe, *Henry VIII and the English Reformation* (London: Routledge, 1995), xi.
33 Newcombe, *Henry VIII and the English Reformation*, 1–3.
34 Newcombe, *Henry VIII and the English Reformation*, 12–13.
35 Warnicke, *The Rise and Fall of Anne Boleyn*, 110–113.
36 Lipscomb, *The King Is Dead*, 118–119.
37 Lipscomb, *The King Is Dead*, 9–12, 34–35, 56, 66, 68–69.
38 Duncan, *Mary I*, 8–9.
39 Wilson, *Sir Francis Walsingham*, 22–23.

40 Lipscomb, *The King is Dead*, 100–103.
41 Norwich, *Four Princes*, 215–216. McDermott, *England and the Spanish Armada*, 42–43.
42 McDermott, *England and the Spanish Armada*, xvi.
43 Henry Fitzsimon, S.J., *A Catholike Confvtation of M. John Riders Claymé of Antiqvities, and a Calming Comfort Against His Caveat* (Rouen, France: 1608), 16, 98.
44 Andrew Pettegree, "Printing and the Reformation," in Marshall and Ryrie, eds., *The Beginnings of English Protestantism*, 176–177.
45 John N. King, "John Day: Master Printer of the English Reformation," in Marshall and Ryrie, eds., *The Beginnings of English Protestantism*, 197–200.
46 Marshall and Ryrie, *The Beginnings of English Protestantism*, 3.
47 Newcombe, *Henry VIII and the English Reformation*, 3–6.
48 Derek Wilson, *Sir Francis Walsingham: A Courtier in an Age of Terror* (New York: Carroll & Graf Publishers, 2007), ix.
49 Wilson, *Sir Francis Walsingham*, xi.
50 Wilson, *Sir Francis Walsingham*, 2.
51 Wilson, *Sir Francis Walsingham*, 20.
52 Hammer, *Elizabeth's Wars*, 87.
53 Sarah Duncan, *Mary I: Gender, Power, and Ceremony in the Reign of England's First Queen* (New York: Palgrave Macmillan, 2012), 1.
54 MacCulloch, *The Reformation*, 272–273. Rodríguez-Salgado, *The Changing Face of Empire*, 82–84.
55 Rodríguez-Salgado, *The Changing Face of Empire*, 81.
56 Duncan, *Mary I*, 44–45. Hammer, *Elizabeth's Wars*, 46. Patterson, *With the Heart of a King*, 48–49.
57 Norwich, *Four Princes*, 216–219. Duncan, *Mary I*, 46.
58 Duncan, *Mary I*, 58–59, 61.
59 John Edwards, "The Spanish Inquisition Refashioned: The Experience of Mary I's England and the Valladolid Tribunal, 1559," *Hispanic Research Journal*, 2012, Vol. 13, No. 1, 45.
60 Rodríguez-Salgado, *The Changing Face of Empire*, 198–199.
61 Luttikhuizen, *Underground Protestantism in Sixteenth Century Spain*, 129–136.
62 Edwards, *The Spanish Inquisition Refashioned*, 45, 47. Patterson, *With the Heart of a King*, 56–58.
63 Maltby, *The Black Legend in England*, 33–35.
64 Norwich, *Four Princes*, 222.
65 Wilson, *Sir Francis Walsingham*, 23, 103.
66 Edwards, "The Spanish Inquisition Refashioned," 45.
67 Wilson, *Sir Francis Walsingham*, 23.
68 Rodríguez-Salgado, *The Changing Face of Empire*, 90–91. Patterson, *With the Heart of a King*, 55.
69 Norwich, *Four Princes*, 219–220.
70 Hammer, *Elizabeth's Wars*, 49–50. Norwich, *Four Princes*, 220–221.
71 Norwich, *Four Princes*, 221–222.
72 Duncan, *Mary I*, 2.
73 McDermott, *England and the Spanish Armada*, 44–45. Wilson, *Sir Francis Walsingham*, 33.
74 Patterson, *With the Heart of a King*, 102.
75 Marshall, *Religious Identities in Henry VIII's England*, 249–251.
76 Rodríguez-Salgado, *The Changing Face of Empire*, 95–97.
77 Rodríguez-Salgado, *The Changing Face of Empire*, 198–199. Massing, *Fatal Discord*, 687.
78 Wilson, *Sir Francis Walsingham*, 44–45.
79 Bayne, *Anglo-Roman Relations*, 17.

80 Patterson, *With the Heart of a King*, 118–119.
81 Mullett, *The Catholic Reformation*, 119. McDermott, *England and the Spanish Armada*, 96. Pope Pius V, "Regnans in Excelsis: Excommunicating Elizabeth I of England," 1570, accessed 24 March 2022, https://www.papalencyclicals.net/pius05/p5regnans.htm.
82 Massing, *Fatal Discord*, 687.
83 C.G. Bayne, *Anglo-Roman Relations, 1558-1565* (Oxford: The Clarendon Press, 1913), 31.
84 Wilson, *Sir Francis Walsingham*, 50–51, 54.
85 Rodríguez-Salgado, *The Changing Face of Empire*, 321–323.
86 Chris Skidmore, *Death and the Virgin Queen* (New York: St. Martin's Press, 2010), 49, 115–117, 137–140.
87 Skidmore, *Death and the Virgin Queen*, 117.
88 Patterson, *With the Heart of a King*, 124–125.
89 Norwich, *Four Princes*, 234–235. Paul E.J. Hammer, *Elizabeth's Wars: War, Government and Society in Tudor England, 1544-1604* (Palgrave Macmillan, 2003), 55.
90 Skidmore, *Death and the Virgin Queen*, 120–122.
91 Hammer, *Elizabeth's Wars*, 1–2.
92 For a documentary account of this change in international relations, see Martin A.S. Hume, ed., *Calendar of Letters and State Papers Relating to English Affairs, Archives of Simancas*, Vol. II. Elizabeth, 1568-1579 (London: Her Majesty's Stationery Office, 1894).
93 Boehmer, Wiffen, and Wiffen, *Bibliotheca Wiffeniana*, Vol. II, 165–167.
94 Boehmer, Wiffen, and Wiffen, *Bibliotheca Wiffeniana*, Vol. II, 169–171.
95 Boehmer, Wiffen, and Wiffen, *Bibliotheca Wiffeniana*, Vol. II, 173–176.
96 Boehmer, Wiffen, and Wiffen, *Bibliotheca Wiffeniana*, Vol. II, 184–185.
97 Wilson, *Sir Francis Walsingham*, 56–57, 82.
98 Mullett, *The Catholic Reformation*, 175–176.
99 Wilson, *Sir Francis Walsingham*, 70–72, 176–177, 181–183. Hammer, *Elizabeth's Wars*, 82–84.
100 Wilson, *Sir Francis Walsingham*, 73–74. Colin Martin and Geoffrey Parker, *The Spanish Armada* (Manchester: Manchester University Press, 1999), 61.
101 Hoffman, *The Spanish Crown and the Defense of the Caribbean*, 111. McDermott, *England and the Spanish Armada*, 63.
102 Hoffman, *The Spanish Crown and the Defense of the Caribbean*, 111–112.
103 McDermott, *England and the Spanish Armada*, 58. "Sir Thomas Chaloner," UK National Portrait Gallery, accessed 23 March 2022, https://www.npg.org.uk/collections/search/person/mp00823/sir-thomas-chaloner.
104 Croft, "Englishmen and the Spanish Inquisition 1558-1625," 259. Leonora de Alberti and Annie Beatrice Wallis Chapman, *Los mercaderes ingleses y la Inquisición Española en las Islas Canarias*. Translated from the English by José Delgado Luis. Original edition London: Royal Historical Society, 1912 (Tenerife, Canarias: Publidisa, 2010), 10–11, 25.
105 Hammer, *Elizabeth's Wars*, 234.
106 Croft, "Englishmen and the Spanish Inquisition 1558-1625," 259–261.
107 AHN, Inquisición, Legajo 112, Exp. 3. Inquisición, Toledo, 1580, Pillin, Tomás (Thomas Pillyn). March 1580.
108 Gerhard, *Pirates on the West Coast of New Spain*, 61–70.
109 Gerhard, *Pirates on the West Coast of New Spain*, 71–72, 88.
110 Allegra Woodworth, "Purveyance for the Royal Household in the Reign of Queen Elizabeth," *Transactions of the American Philosophical Society*, 1945, Vol. 35, No. 1, 12. https://doi.org/10.2307/1005579. McDermott, *England and the Spanish Armada*, 131, 146, 154.
111 Gerhard, *Pirates on the West Coast of New Spain*, 85, 240.

112 McDermott, *England and the Spanish Armada*, 92, 97. Bayne, *Anglo-Roman Relations*, 33.

113 Liam Chambers and Thomas O'Connor, eds. *College Communities Abroad: Education, Migration and Catholicism in Early Modern Europe* (Manchester: Manchester University Press, 2018), 9–10, 96, 97, 105. *Centre Culturel Irlandais*, "History and Building," accessed 24 March 2022, https://www.centreculture lirlandais.com/en/discover/history-building.

114 Philip Fernández-Armesto, *The Spanish Armada: The Experience of War in 1588* (Oxford: Oxford University Press, 1988), 72–74.

115 Wilson, *Sir Francis Walsingham*, 43.

116 McDermott, *England and the Spanish Armada*, 10, 17–18, 27.

117 McDermott, *England and the Spanish Armada*, xv.

118 McDermott, *England and the Spanish Armada*, 157. Hammer, *Elizabeth's Wars*, 81, 86.

119 Lynch, *Spain 1516-1598*, 197–198.

120 Fernández-Armesto, *The Spanish Armada*, 34–35.

121 McDermott, *England and the Spanish Armada*, xvi.

122 Fernández-Armesto, *The Spanish Armada*, 36.

123 Lynch, *Spain 1516-1598*, 440–444.

124 McDermott, *England and the Spanish Armada*, 166.

125 Lynch, *Spain 1516-1598*, 379–382. McDermott, *England and the Spanish Armada*, 82, 162, 182.

126 Patterson, *With the Heart of a King*, 231–235.

127 Lynch, *Spain 1516-1598*, 453–454.

128 Parker, *Success is Never Final*, 61–62.

129 Geoffrey Parker, *The Army of Flanders and the Spanish Road, 1567-1659. The Logistics of Spanish Victory and Defeat in the Low Countries' Wars* (Cambridge: Cambridge University Press, 1972), 4–5.

130 Robert Persons, *The Jesuit's Memorial for the Intended Reformation of England under their Firft Popish Prince*. Originally published in 1596, Seville. With Intro by Edward Gee (London: Rose and Crown, 1690), 33–34, 70.

131 Fernández-Armesto, *The Spanish Armada*, 56–59.

132 Fernández-Armesto, *The Spanish Armada*, 60.

133 Fernández-Armesto, *The Spanish Armada*, 273–276. Lynch, *Spain 1516-1598*, 456–458.

134 McDermott, *England and the Spanish Armada*, 314.

135 Hammer, *Elizabeth's Wars*, 62–67.

136 R.B. Wernham, *After the Armada: Elizabethan England and the Struggle for Western Europe, 1588-1595* (Oxford: Oxford University Press, 1984), 143.

137 Letter, Elizabeth of England, "To Henry the Fourth, King of France," December 1594. G.B. Harrison, ed., *The Letters of Queen Elizabeth I* (Westport, Connecticut: Greenwood Press, 1981), 232.

138 Wilson, *Sir Francis Walsingham*, 57.

139 Luis Gorrochategui Santos, *The English Armada: The Greatest Naval Disaster in English History* (London, Bloomsbury Academic, 2018).

140 Marshall, *Religious Identities in Henry VIII's England*, 122–123.

141 Letter, Elizabeth of England, "To James the Sixth, King of Scotland," January 1593. Harrison, ed., *The Letters of Queen Elizabeth I*, 223.

142 Fernández-Armesto, *The Spanish Armada*, 36.

143 Fernández-Armesto, *The Spanish Armada*, 60–62.

144 Regina Whelan Richardson, ed., *The Salamanca Letters: A Catalogue of Correspondence (1619-1871) from the Archives of the Irish Colleges in Spain in the Library of St. Patrick's College, Maynooth, Ireland* (Maynooth, Ireland: St. Patrick's College, 1995), v–vii.

145 Matthew Kellison, Doctour of Divinitie, *A Treatise of the Hierarchie and Divers Orders of the Church Against the Anarchie of Calvin* (Doway, France: Gerard Pinchon, 1629), v, 400.

146 Kellison, *A Treatise of the Hierarchie and Divers Orders of the Church Against the Anarchie of Calvin*, 407.

147 Mark G. Sanchez, *Anti-Spanish Sentiment in English Literary and Political Writing 1553-1603* (Leeds, UK: University of Leeds, Ph.D. dissertation, 2004). Maltby, *The Black Legend in England*, 100.

5 Philip II and the Spanish Inquisition

Philip II inherited the western Habsburg domains in 1555 and 1556, upon the abdication of his father, Emperor Charles V. Charles surrendered his power voluntarily, burdened by the weight of his responsibilities. He welcomed a retreat from the heights of power, preferring the solace of the monastery of Yuste, in the southwestern Spanish region of Extremadura. The former emperor's comment on his time as Europe's most powerful monarch expressed his frustrations and what prevented him from reaching his dream, which was:

> bringing peace among the Christian peoples and uniting their fighting forces for the defense of the Catholic faith against the Ottomans. It was partly the German heresy and partly the envy of rival powers that prevented me from fully achieving the goal of my efforts.[1]

At times, the emperor could seem indecisive about how to react to Luther, Calvin, and their followers. By the end of his life, however, the "ambiguity, vacillations, and doubts" of his earlier years was gone, although perhaps also the hope he had to unite Christendom under a single banner.[2] Among the other regrets of Charles was not having executed Luther after the Diet of Worms, despite the promised safe conduct. It would not have been the first or last time that the interests of state prevailed against a solemn oath.[3]

With the abdication of his father, which took effect in January 1556, Philip II was monarch over vast lands, from Spain to the Low Countries, Italy to Burgundy, in a region that is in modern-day eastern France. At the time, Philip was also married to Queen Mary of England, sharing her throne, although he did not receive the title of king of England nor exercise direct monarchical authority in Britain. While Central and Eastern Europe – the Holy Roman Empire, Hungary, and some assorted territories – remained in the hands of the new emperor, Ferdinand I, brother to Charles, Philip was nonetheless master of a world domain, including much of the Americas, the Philippines, and outposts throughout north Africa and the Mediterranean. Some historians have expressed the idea that Philip's empire "was never viable," with too few resources and too many enemies, and a failure to achieve the greatest goals of the king, including the destruction of Protestantism in his domains and the reclamation of England for Catholicism. Even so,

DOI: 10.4324/9781003197676-6

Habsburg Spain endured, remained Catholic, and continued to be a great power with the world's largest empire well into the seventeenth century.[4]

Through his various titles, kingdoms, and ranks, his empire was a large and powerful institution, or rather interconnected set of institutions, to the strengthening of which he dedicated the remainder of his days. United only "by the King and by the Faith," in Philip's domains, except for the Jewish quarter of Oran, Catholicism was not only the official religion, but it was also the only legal one allowed for his subjects. This religious unity was even more important given the diversity of Philip's Habsburg lands: "the Spanish Monarchy, in addition to being geographically multi-territorial, was multi-jurisdictional, which is to say, its component parts were substantially differ-ent in their laws, institutions, tribunals, languages, coinage or, in general terms, culture."[5]

Would the king be able to unite this disparate collection of inherited realms? There was great skepticism about Philip's capacities, which likely played a role in the handing of the Holy Roman Empire not to him, but to his uncle Ferdinand. Even so, by 1558 his father, Emperor Charles V, was dead and the western Habsburg kingdoms remained entirely under the authority of Philip.[6] Unlike his father, however, Philip ruled almost exclusively from Spain, which more than ever was the center of the empire. While Charles had relied on a multinational group of advisors, ministers, and ecclesiastics, Philip increasingly heard, and spoke through, Spanish voices.[7] Born and raised in Spain, and serving as his father's regent since 1543, when he reached the age of 16, he was truly a Spaniard. In this regard, he began his leadership of Spain potentially more connected than his Flemish father, whose extensive travels kept him less apprised of the mood in Spain.[8] However, this connec-tion to Spain caused Philip problems in relating to his other realms. For example, he never returned to the Netherlands after 1559, leaving this critical territory in the hands of regents, military, and religious officials. The king also did not keep his initial promise to send his son, Don Carlos, to rule as regent, given the increasing incapacity of the prince.[9]

Many of his advisors viewed the king as especially blessed by God as a chosen vessel and expected glorious achievements to be always on the cusp of completion. He could defeat England, keep France subdued, drive back the Ottomans, suppress the Protestant revolt across Europe, seize all the Americas, and even extend Christianity to China, if he would only stretch out his hand and believe that God would provide a means for these victories. At times, Philip took these admonitions seriously; at other times, he acted more prudently to understand and fulfill God's destiny for Spain.[10] As king, Philip did tend to become increasingly messianic in his approach. Historian Geoffrey Parker outlined the three key elements to this worldview:

> First, Philip believed that God had chosen him to rule expressly to achieve His purpose for the world. Second, he was equally convinced that God held him under special protection, to enable him to achieve these goals (although the process might prove neither obvious nor easy).

Third, he felt certain that, if necessary, God would intervene directly in order to help him succeed.[11]

One manifestation of this perspective was that Philip II was devoted to the Catholic Church, viewing himself as a loyal son of Rome and its arm, albeit on his own terms, for unrelenting struggle against heresy within Christendom and Islam beyond its frontier. This does not mean he did not clash repeatedly with various popes, at times treading close to open confrontation, a risky maneuver for a monarch whose image depended so much on his Catholicism. Pope Sixtus V, a pontiff with whom Philip had many conflicts, believed that the Spanish king had difficulty separating the interests of Spain from the interests of the Church. Nonetheless unquestionably pious, Philip II looked to his faith for motivation, explanations for both his victories and defeats, and impetus for his greatest efforts.[12]

For Philip, Spain had an obligation to serve in the vanguard of Europe in the defense of Catholicism against the Protestant Reformation, "as a quid pro quo for the near-miraculous acquisition of a vast and profitable empire. To challenge one was to deny the other, as Spain's future enemies well understood."[13] Even if he disagreed with a specific Pope, Philip would seek guidance from other clergy, especially Spanish ones, even forming specially constituted Committees of Theologians (*Juntas de Teólogos*) for their learned input on whether specific policies were consistent with orthodox Catholic doctrine.[14] In his personal life, Philip was consistently pious, hearing Mass daily, a sermon every week, and confessing at least four times yearly. Philip was also obsessed with relics of saints, amassing a substantial collection at great expense. His belief that his providential mission was to destroy Protestantism and return all heretical lands to true Catholic Christianity derived from this devotion, as well as his education as the heir to the legacies of his parents and grandparents.[15] Although arguably by the 1550s, Lutheranism and Calvinism were too strongly entrenched in the Holy Roman Empire and elsewhere in northern Europe to be defeated by military means alone, Philip II was not willing to accept this if it meant accommodating to religious diversity within Habsburg lands.[16]

In all these struggles, he was an ardent ally of the Spanish Inquisition and aligned tribunals elsewhere, providing resources, supporting their decisions, and exhorting them to even stronger campaigns against individual heretics, as well as what he perceived as the broader threats of false Jewish and Muslim converts to the faith. This was the legacy of the Inquisition under his great-grandparents, Isabella of Castile and Ferdinand II of Aragon, who had created it in 1478 on the cusp of their victorious final stage of the *Reconquista*, expected to bring thousands of potential new converts into the Christian fold from the Muslims, Jews, and lapsed Christians in conquered Granada and the rest of southern Spain.[17]

Philip II embraced the earlier mission of the Inquisition, hunting for false or incomplete converts, to educate or punish, depending on the severity of their straying from Catholic faith, but added to its tasks. Soon after taking on his royal mantles, however, he began to encourage the Holy Office to focus its efforts on what he saw as the greatest theological threat to his worldview: the religious movements of the Protestant Reformation, initially devotees of Luther, but later also of Calvin and of other emerging denominations. Philip II's oft-repeated statement that he "did not intend to rule over heretics," initially referring to his Calvinist subjects in the Low Countries, succinctly summarized the essential driving force behind many of his actions.[18] Even expressing political ideas, if these involved positive comments about Protestant leaders such as Queen Elizabeth, could be cause for accusations of heresy. Praising the exploits of Francis Drake, victories by the Huguenots, or joking about Philip II were all grounds, even if truly non-theological, for attracting the attention of the Holy Office.[19] The king kept himself well-informed about the campaign against Protestants, sending notes to relatives in other Habsburg states admonishing them to watch for Spanish Protestants, exhorting Inquisitors to be more ardent in their efforts, and asking his ambassadors in other countries to keep watchful eyes on known Spanish heretics in exile.[20]

In England, in Spain, and in the Americas – indeed, wherever he held sway – he was unrelenting in exhorting his soldiers, sailors, and clergy to bring war, persecution, and destruction to the enemies of the Roman Catholic Church, at times even denouncing popes, bishops, and fellow Catholic monarchs of insufficient orthodox Catholic faith and religious devotion. Philip continued to support the Inquisition's suspicion of *conversos*, even as their numbers continued to decline. In 1555, he banned *conversos* and their known descendants from being ordained as secular clergy. Previous decrees had also banned them from religious orders (such as the Dominicans and Jesuits), military orders, colleges, guilds, and cathedral chapters. These decrees were challenging to enforce, with a major effort across Philip's domains to create false genealogies to extirpate any evidence of *converso* ancestors, but the point was made: *conversos* were lesser Christians.[21]

The Protestant Reformation had a dramatic impact on the Spanish Inquisition; this new threat revived and strengthened the Holy Office at a moment when its significance and even existence were at risk. As historian Benzion Netanyahu has noted, "the Church's foundations were shaken by the earthquakes that signaled the coming of the Reformation."[22] The Inquisition remained an effective tool for Philip II, with its reputation for torture, intense questioning, and resources to pursue extensive investigations. The coming of the Protestant Reformation led the king to increase the authority of the Inquisition, while encouraging a strategic shift in Spanish foreign policy away from wars on Islam toward wars against Protestants. Prior to the 1520s, the Spanish Inquisition targeted primarily unfaithful *conversos*, Jews that had officially converted to Christianity but were suspected of continuing as adherents of Judaism. Indeed, it was fear of the heresy of "Judaizing" – combining Jewish and Christian practices – that motivated the creation of the Spanish Inquisition in 1478, an effort enabled by Pope Sixtus IV.[23]

Empowered to investigate, try, and punish, with penalties up to the death penalty – a sentence that had to be carried out by secular authorities, given the prohibition against the Church taking human life – the Spanish Inquisition built up an extensive legal system of tribunals and logistical support across the Iberian Peninsula. Death sentences had to be confirmed unanimously by the presiding judges and confirmed by the *Suprema*.[24] By 1510, however, trials and investigations, and of course executions, had declined so dramatically that there were discussions about ending the mandate of the Inquisition. The Jewish "threat" appeared to have abated.[25] Enter one Martin Luther, a German monk, providing a new reason for the survival of the Holy Office. While even during the previous period of focus on converted Jews and Muslims there had been investigations of other heresies and individual lapses of faith unconnected to Judaism or Islam, the Protestant Reformation would pose distinct challenges to Inquisitors. Rather than trying to investigate who held to another faith aside from Christianity, they faced accused who believed themselves faithful Christians, but no longer with loyalty to the Catholic Church. Especially in the first few decades after Luther's first emergence, it was often not even clear to believers where their own spiritual loyalties were most accommodated.

Not only suspected Protestants came under suspicion by the revived Inquisition, however. Spanish Inquisitors began to drag into their system those accused of a wide range of religious offenses that had not been under their purview when alleged Jews were the chief targets. Blasphemers, adulterers, and even the merely profane found themselves interrogated, tried and punished, along with accused Protestants.[26] *Moriscos*, former Muslims converted to Catholicism, also remained suspect and the subjects of many investigations and trials. The Reformation in Spain had a direct impact on the Holy Office itself, exerting an "enduring influence on the fortunes of the Inquisition," providing a much-needed spark to reignite the Inquisition and attracting the resources to maintain two more centuries of existence.[27] The Reformation revived the Spanish Inquisition at a critical time, saving it from potential inactivation at a time when its previous mandate, to extirpate Spain of false converts from among former Jews, seemed to have been achieved.

Fernando de Valdés, Inquisitor General from 1547 to 1566, refocused his investigations on Protestants, and away from the diminishing number of *conversos*, at the same time improving the administration and efficiency of the Holy Office, with an emphasis on standardizing processes, minimizing opportunities for corruption, and dismissing officials who became known for corruption or inattention to guidance from the Suprema.[28] In 1561, Valdés issued new guidelines for Inquisitors; these "Instrucciones," first published in Toledo, then reprinted many times over the years, served as a handy guide across Spain for new and ongoing officers of the Inquisition's tribunals. With 81 directives, suggestions, and guidelines for policies and procedures, these rules brought tribunals into common practice and methods, replacing the less detailed rules of Grand Inquisitor Torquemada from 1536. Included were procedures to admit evidence, methods to employ torture, conditions owed to prisoners, how to proceed if the prisoner died in the custody of the Inquisition, and how to handle appeals.[29]

For prisoners, whether still under investigation or completing sentences, there were protections under the law and these regulations. Inquisitors were supposed to visit their prisons at least every 15 days to listen to the needs of the prisoners and note down reasonable requests to order the jailers to fulfill them. Prisoners could complain of watered-down wine, inadequate food, or poor conditions, and by rule could have family members bring them food, drink, and other items. Inquisitors were also tasked with making sure prisoners were not ill-treated, charged for things (such as wine) they did not use, or spoken to harshly by jailers. Over time, the Inquisition tried to reduce prison sentences, given the costs associated and the rights of prisoners, especially prominent ones. Actual time served could also vary, with a life sentence meaning six months, a year, five years, or full term, depending on local conditions, prison capacity, and decisions by new Inquisitors. In the case of Protestants, it is not clear that the expense of incarceration encouraged harsher penalties, but long-term prison sentences were imposed far less frequently than other options, from the death penalty to galley service, to confiscation of all assets.[30]

Protestants became the primary focus, and fear, of the Spanish Inquisition, remaining so from the mid-1550s until at least the early 1570s, when the imminent threat of Spanish Protestantism seemed to subside – just as foreign Protestants in England, France, and the Low Countries, seemed an increasingly existential threat to Spanish Catholic power.[31] With this redefined mission, however, the Spanish Inquisition remained centered not on punishing all those who came under its auspices, but on determining the truth of accusations. For its historical period, the Inquisition was dedicated to following the evidence against those brought before it to punish the guilty, release the innocent, and act as a deterrent to all others, to encourage a more enthusiastic embrace of orthodox Roman Catholicism. Even though the Spanish Inquisition began its processes presuming that those who came before it were guilty, with prompt confessions, genuine repentance, and humble acceptance of punishments, many of those prosecuted were able to return to the Catholic Church with fairly light sentences. Private admonishment, orders to attend additional Masses, or to offer specific prayers – these steps were often sufficient for the most modest of offenses.[32]

Those who denied all charges, despite multiple witnesses or even material evidence, or admitted guilt but refused to accept the Church's ministrations, faced the strongest punishments, up to and including death at the hands of the secular authorities. Similarly, those who confessed to heresy, but then recanted either the confession or their desire to be welcomed back into the Catholic Church after initially expressing this desire, were the most likely to face the most extreme punishment of death. Being disputatious with the tribunal was a path toward even great punishment than the theological crimes deserved, as they could demonstrate to the judges an unrepentant heart. The safest approach was complete honesty, especially if one was not truly converted to Protestant beliefs but had expressed errors or inadvertently heretical views.[33] Estimates of final punishments vary, given the lack of complete documentation from all tribunals, but of the approximately 45,000 trials held from 1540 to 1700 in peninsular Spain, perhaps 2% resulted in immediate death sentences, with a similar percentage burned in effigy, because the convict was out of the hands of the Spanish Inquisition. Although there were few complete exonerations, since the accused were presumed guilty of some sin against the Church, most sentences were light, consisting of additional prayers, confessions, or at most short terms of service as galley oarsmen. More rarely, those convicted were sentenced to monastic enclosure or Inquisitorial detention.[34]

The greatest danger for the accused, however, was that at least initially, they were not told what specifically had brought them to the attention of the Holy Office but were instead invited to search their conscience and confess their sins, as well as all recognized sins and crimes of family, friends, and acquaintances. Through a long interview, the detainee would be asked about their upbringing, family, beliefs, education, work, and foreign travel – with the latter being of particular interest after Luther began his work, since living abroad increased the likelihood of corruption with Protestant ideas.[35] The Inquisitors also read a declaration known as the edict of faith, which listed possible heresies and moral failings to which an accused could confess. Those brought before the tribunal were asked to denounce themselves, usually with 30–40 days to reflect on their sins and produce a full confession.[36] The first question asked of most those brought before the Spanish Inquisition was often the most effective: *"¿Si sabe o sospecha por qué motivo ha sido hecho preso del Santo Oficio?"* (Do you know or suspect for what motive you have been made a prisoner of the Holy Office?) In many cases, this led to an immediate confession, either of the primary crime, or perhaps of a lesser one, in the hopes of forestalling a greater punishment. This opened the door to more extensive questioning, through which the Inquisitors were seeking not only the full confession and penitence of the initial accused, but ideally to reveal the names of others who had committed the same crimes and heresies. Even final punishments could be delayed by weeks or months in the hopes of extracting more names, holding out the promise of absolution for those who collaborated most enthusiastically.[37]

Depending on the severity of the crime, this waiting period could be completed at liberty, under supervised house arrest, or under detention at the hands of the Spanish Inquisition. If there was a high convergence between the confession and the accusations, the suspects might have a relatively smooth process. If they confessed to sins beyond those known to the Inquisitors, they might put themselves in additional jeopardy, including being under threat of torture until they remembered and repented of the additional sins, often through guided promptings by the prosecutors.[38] Compared to other courts and tribunals of the sixteenth century, the Spanish Inquisition, despite its reputation, used torture sparingly: more than 90% of those accused never experienced it. Inquisitors were aware that it could lead to false confessions. There were also limitations on the process, with the intentional spilling of blood or mutilation of detainees prohibited. Torture at the hand of the Spanish Inquisition, as one historian has noted, was "more psychological than gory."[39]

There were excesses, to be sure, but in general the physical and psychological means employed by the Holy Office were far more humane than those
likely to be encountered elsewhere at the time, with historians concluding that
those detained by the Spanish Inquisition were far less likely to be subject to
torture than those brought before secular authorities amid the "brutal spirit
of the sixteenth century."[40] Even if the image of the Spanish Inquisition came
to be associated with torture, it had other methods, including its reputation
for safeguarding denunciations as secret, as protected as confessions to a
priest. The accused might never know who had turned them into the tribunal,
or who might be prepared to do so. Fear motivated many spontaneous confessions, as those who knew they were committing heresy might prefer to
self-reveal rather than be informed on by a neighbor.[41]

There were three primary methods of torture used – water torture, the
rack, and the pulley – but even after a torture-induced confession, most
Inquisitors insisted on additional corroboration, either from other witnesses
or from the accused under conditions of less immediate duress. Many tribunals were understandably skeptical of convicting solely on confession induced
through pain, or through fear of what tortures might be coming next.[42]
A notary would be present at all torture sessions, dutifully writing down
everything said by both interrogator and interrogated, including screams of
pain and cries for mercy.[43] The goal of these proceedings, which typically
lasted an hour or two at most, was to coax the accused into reconciliation
with the Church through a full confession and subsequent penance. A reluctance to answer questions, to identify others that had contributed to the heresy or other sins in question, or to embrace the opportunity to learn how not
to repeat one's mistakes: these were all warning signs of an irreconcilable
heretic, the ones most likely to be released into the hands of the secular
authorities for subsequent public execution following an *auto da fe*.[44]

The most probable to face only modest punishment were those who self-
reported their sins pre-emptively, with expressions of full contrition; convicts
such as these would often face orders to fast, recite the rosary, or add to their
prayers. Since it was beliefs that most concerned the Spanish Inquisition,
rather than behaviors, self-denunciation seemed a clear victory. In most cases,
short of extreme cases of heresy, such as open declaration of Protestant convictions and attempt to proselytize others, this could be the end of the process without requiring additional measures. This was often the case so long as
the penitent was consistent in their story. None of this applied if the accused
had come to the attention of the tribunal through other means prior to their
confession; pre-emptive confession just prior to arrest was seen as an attempt
to game the system, unlike spontaneous self-denunciations by those not in
the sights of the local tribunal.[45]

Once there were formal charges, either before or after torture, the accused
received the benefit of being assigned an official advocate, the *letrado*, an
attorney whose task was to help organize a defense. With the likelihood of
some kind of confession already having come through questioning, the
efforts of the *letrado* were often focused on presenting mitigating evidence in

an effort to reduce the severity of punishment, to discredit witnesses through the presentation of alibis and counter-evidence from friendly witnesses, or to argue that the sin was committed out of ignorance, lack of full faculties (such as through drunkenness, status as a minor, or lack of education), or under negative influences from other individuals, against whom the accused would be delighted to testify.[46] Since no single witness was ever sufficient to lead to a conviction, the *letrado* might work to discredit one or more corroborating ones, to explain away a confession as insufficient or false, or otherwise to weaken either the charges or the penalties assigned, if conviction was the final result despite his best efforts.[47]

There were incentives for the priests and other Church and lay officials attached to the tribunals of the Holy Office to be effective in their roles; successful campaigns against heresy, executed fairly and thoroughly, could lead to advancement within the Church hierarchy, even to the rank of bishop. At the same time, efforts that were seen as too vigorous in actions against clearly innocent individuals, and stepped beyond the norms in terms of cruelty, pursuit of the obviously innocent, or venal actions that led to the enrichment of Inquisitorial officials, could lead to ecclesiastical or secular punishments, a reality that could mitigate against excesses. Clerics and others in the employ of regional tribunals had to be careful not to exceed the mandate of the Suprema or the directives of the Inquisitor General, who outlined the policies and procedures for all tribunals, and had the capacity to remonstrate against, or even remove, local officials.[48]

Philip II was a most ardent supporter of the Inquisition, making a point to attend *autos da fe* whenever possible, and never, at least as far as the evidence shows, opposing a ruling of the Holy Office. Indeed, he embraced the hard line of Grand Inquisitor Fernando de Valdés, as well as supporting an expansion of public observance of and participation in the public component of the ceremonial and juridical elements of the *auto da fe*, including parades, celebratory elements, and elaborate Masses.[49] Philip encouraged the Inquisition's persecution of Protestants especially; in 1558, he enthusiastically embraced the Inquisition's campaigns against "two Lutheran cells" in Seville and Valladolid, despite the prominent families represented among the accused. Although noted military historian Geoffrey Parker described the harshness of the Inquisition's actions against these small Protestant groups as "an overreaction," it did not seem so to Philip II, but instead a necessary, legitimate, and holy effort against a deadly heresy.[50] Before presiding over the *auto da fe* in Valladolid on 8 October 1559, the king swore to carry out his duties faithfully:

> as a true and Catholic king placed by the hand of God he would defend with all his power the Catholic faith that the holy mother apostolic Church of Rome has and believes; (that he would work toward) the preservation and increase of it and that he would persecute the heretics and apostates that oppose it, and that he would give all the necessary favor and help to the Holy Office of the Inquisition and to the ministers of it

so that the disturbing heretics of our religion would be caught and punished in accordance with the rights and sacred canon law without hesitation or exceptions for any person.[51]

For Philip, acting as a magistrate and executive of the secular state at that moment, this oath was a clear statement of his approach to governing as a devout Catholic. At the same event, when the convicted heretic Carlos de Seso spoke to the king, Philip is reported to have said "I would myself bring wood to burn my own son if he was as evil as you." Given that the prince was on the dais with the king, this was a moment that showed how ardently pious Philip was; it was also unlikely to improve the already tense and distant relations between father and son.[52]

The king exchanged letters with Fernando de Valdés, Inquisitor General, commending him for having "implemented a good system in all parts of those Spanish kingdoms" for rooting out Lutheran beliefs and writings. Valdés, for his part, petitioned Philip II for more resources and authority to extirpate the "heresies and errors of Luther and his followers," so that "by the grace of God the heart of Spain remained untouched by this stain." Although king and Inquisitor occasionally differed on minor points, overall, Philip II was the most enthusiastic monarchical supporter during the history of the Spanish Inquisition. He was also the king whose reign endured the most external pressure from Protestant enemies.[53] In a major concession to the Grand Inquisitor, in 1559 the king granted the Holy Office financial autonomy, by allowing it to retain assets seized from those convicted, whether paid in fines or through the confiscation of assets. Before this order, the crown, local bishop, or other ecclesiastical or secular domains would receive these funds, and in turn would provide operating budgets to the Inquisition. The change created an incentive for tribunals to assess greater penalties.[54]

At the same time, Valdés prevailed upon Philip II and Pope Paul IV to dedicate revenues equivalent to the upkeep of one canon priest toward the Inquisition. This was a real loss for the bishops, as well as for the general cause of spiritual formation in their dioceses, since this meant one fewer teacher; for poorer bishoprics, this could mean no cleric assigned to this task. Rooting out heresy was in this decision measured as more important to the Church than building orthodox beliefs among the Catholic faithful.[55] The king was frustrated with Valdés on other points, as well, including for resisting providing funds for Spain's wars against France, in Italy, and against rebellion in the Low Countries, costly affairs that were draining the monarchy's resources. While both king and Inquisitor/Primate agreed that the Protestant heresy was an enemy to be fought, they disagreed on the location of the greatest danger and on the immediate allocation of resources.[56] The king also refused a proposal to create a military order affiliated with the Spanish Inquisition, to be named the "Caballeros de Santa María de la Espada Blanca" (Knights of Saint Mary of the White Sword), fearing possible infringement of his royal authority.[57] In addition to his communication with the king, Grand Inquisitor Valdés also kept the Pope informed of the campaign against Protestants in Spain, noting in September 1558 the great progress happening so that "heresies are extirpated and the Catholic faith and Christian religion are increased" through the work of the Spanish Inquisition.[58]

Philip II's fear of the Reformation extended into his own family. Taking his dynastic responsibilities seriously, one of the king's primary duties was to ensure an heir for his far-flung domains, who would not only rule effectively, but carry forward Philip's Catholic imperatives. His first marriage, to Maria of Portugal, yielded a male heir in 1545. Prince Carlos, referred to as Don Carlos, would cause personal and theological heartache for the king. The result of inbreeding between double first cousins, Carlos was a sickly and unattractive child from an early age; one of his great-grandmothers, Juana I of Castile, suffered from mental illness. His grandfather Charles V was so repelled by his character that he refused to allow him in his presence. The tutors of Don Carlos found him lacking in intellectual capacity and work ethic, with some expressing doubts as to his mental stability. Frail, with a disproportionally large head, and plagued by a speech impediment and long periods of sickness, he seemed an unlikely heir to the most powerful position in the world.[59]

After initial joy at the birth, Philip II was plunged into deep distress over his wife Maria's death from complications four days after giving birth to Carlos, as well as the early and ongoing health problems of his son. The king was only 18 at the time and already regent of Spain on his father's behalf.[60] Carlos did not develop well or steadily, a source of worry, sadness, and intense prayer for Philip. By one account, at the first meeting of Don Carlos with his grandfather and namesake, Charles V, the eleven-year-old prince chastised his grandfather – the most powerful man in the world – for not crushing the Lutherans of the Schmalkaldic League decisively in Germany, a reaction the emperor found impertinent and capricious, and not befitting a potential Habsburg heir.[61] Following another account, Don Carlos insisted he would have never retreated in the face of the enemy, even after the emperor explained that sometimes this was necessary when one had too little treasure or too few soldiers to continue. Regardless of whether Charles and Carlos parted ways with affection or misunderstanding, the young heir left an impression of stubbornness, resistance to reason, and a lack of respect for his elders, aspects that would also be seen in his later life.[62]

As he continued into adolescence, Prince Carlos began to exhibit increasingly erratic behavior in private and public. Beyond proving resistant to the teachings of tutors and Spain's most accomplished educators, he also exhibited cruelty toward animals and girls, some of whom he ordered beaten, and openly criticized his father, high-ranking nobles, and ecclesiastical figures.[63] The king's concerns accelerated after Don Carlos fell and suffered a head injury in April 1562, at the age of 17. Although the prince recovered after two months of fevers and uncertainty, the damage seemed to have made his mental and physical condition even more precarious and unpredictable.[64] Formally named as heir in 1563, Carlos' health continued to be uncertain, with episodic fevers and spasms putting his fitness for the throne in doubt. Both Spanish and foreign observers noted his poor health, sickly complexion, and bizarre eating habits, which included alternatively gorging himself, drinking enormous amounts of iced water, odd temporary obsessions with specific foods, and periods of self-imposed fasting. His lack of interest in exercise contributed to concerns about his longevity and preparation to inherit the Habsburg mantle.[65]

In 1568, soon after the death of Queen Isabel, Philip's wife and step-mother to Carlos, the prince's behavior began to worsen. Not only did his unhealthy eating habits begin to resemble a mania, but his actions also began to show potential disloyalty to his father. This occurred at a time when the king was actively seeking a bride for his son, as the next step in his heir's development into a future monarch; Europe's most powerful dynasties were highly interested in connecting themselves through marriage with the Spanish Habsburgs, even as misgivings about the prince's health and mental state spread to other courts. Among those discussed most as potential matches were Mary, Queen of Scots, Elizabeth of England (who was vehemently opposed), and Anna of Austria. The latter was the strongest candidate, until the increasing infirmities of Carlos became impossible to ignore. The king reversed his initial plan, for Carlos to marry Anna and the two to rule the Netherlands, choosing instead to marry Anna himself. Carlos became enraged at both these decisions, causing a complete collapse in the relationship with his father.[66]

The prince also began to correspond with enemies of his father, behavior that was not only disloyal to Philip II, but in the context of the religious conflict plaguing the king's realms, a treason that could not be tolerated, especially from the potential heir. Carlos proposed to several Dutch nobles that, if they would assist him in traveling to the Netherlands, then in open revolt against Habsburg rule, he would declare himself monarch and grant religious liberty to his Calvinist subjects, in defiance of his father and of the Catholic Church. When Philip II heard of these conspiratorial steps by his son, he not only ended any discussions on a potential wife, but also had his son arrested and stripped Don Carlos of his potential to inherit Habsburg realms and continue covert communications.[67] He also ordered the Dutch nobles that had communicated secretly with Don Carlos arrested.[68]

There remains some debate over whether the king's 1568 imprisonment of his heir, Don Carlos, was more over concern for his son's mental state or because of his scandalous letters to Dutch Protestants, which included furtive – if farcical – plans to escape there and join the rebellion against Spain. Even the papal ambassador to Spain expressed his concern that Don Carlos could be a secret Protestant.[69] While it seems unlikely that Don Carlos was possessed of sufficient capacity in his later years to convert fully and completely to Calvinism, his secret – and not-so-secret – attempts to conspire with Dutch leaders have led to much speculation over his beliefs. What is most relevant is that the king and key advisors feared the implications were Don Carlos to become either a Protestant or their champion, neither of which would be acceptable for the heir to a kingdom in a global war against the new faiths.[70]

Both causes seemed to have contributed to the king's decisions about his son. There was no denying the accelerating mental instability of Don Carlos, among which fantasies of religious defection were but one symptom. That there could even be rumors alleging Protestant sympathies by the erstwhile heir reveals the extent to which the Protestant Reformation was a consistent and omnipresent fear among Spain's political and ecclesiastical elites.[71] While the king assured the Pope and other ecclesiastical figures that Don Carlos was not a heretic, and that his detention had been to help restore his son's health, that he addressed this issue of Protestantism in his own family forthrightly and frequently shows how significant it was in the king's mind and to those concerned about the fate of his kingdoms. In his correspondence, Philip indicated that his son was not capable of mature judgment, and that his confinement was a necessary step, taken reluctantly for his heir's safety. The death of Carlos in summer 1568 spared him from the possibility of a hearing before the Inquisition; other prominent Spaniards did not escape trial, however.[72]

Among the priests, nobles, and merchants that came under investigation by the Spanish Inquisition accused of Protestant heresies none was more prominent than Bartolomé de Carranza y Miranda, Archbishop of Toledo. His case would become emblematic not only for the potential threat of Protestantism within the Church, but the international context for these questions. A Dominican priest who earned the title of The Black Friar for the ferocity of his efforts against heresy in England, he had been a tutor of Philip II and had been the confessor of the emperor. As confessor, Friar Carranza had been summoned to the deathbed of Emperor Charles V in September 1558, to whom he gave the last rites, and whose final words he heard.[73]

An ally of the Spanish Inquisition, who had aided in the persecution of British Protestants during Philip II's time in England, he was an unlikely target for the Holy Office. He had also been with Philip in the Netherlands, where Carranza had preached and campaigned against Lutheran and Calvinist ideas and texts that were increasing in popularity in the provinces. Philip immediately selected Carranza for this position, out of the "positive esteem and personal affection" the king had for him, likely based on their relationship in England. During that challenging time, Philip had relied heavily on Carranza to help restore Catholicism to England. Given this confidence, he rejected the priest's attempts to demur from the primacy. It was in Brussels on 27 February 1558 that Carranza was consecrated as bishop and prelate of Spain, with the titles "The Most Reverend Don Friar Bartolomé Carranza, Archbishop of Toledo, Primate of the Spains, Chancellor Mayor of Castile." Carranza's elevation was resented by clerics of high noble families, who had expected the position to accrue to one of their number, rather than someone undistinguished by his ancestry.[74] It was in the Netherlands where he seems to have finished writing a catechism for priests, a work that would cause him serious troubles later.[75] In the end, it was his foreign connections that proved his undoing, even though this had been in direct assistance to king. Indeed, one of the suspicions that prompted his arrest was that his work in England on behalf of the Catholic Church involved reading of a great deal of Protestant literature, which his accusers believed had begun to influence him toward heresy.[76]

Of humble origins, Archbishop Carranza earned the enmity of more accomplished bishops of noble birth whom the king bypassed in naming Carranza chief cleric. Carranza had harshly criticized bishops and priests who did not show loving and pastoral care for their parishioners. He complained about the common practice among avaricious priests of taking on multiple religious postings to accumulate income, while neglecting the duties that came with these assignments. His denunciation of this practice, and his blame of these office holders for the rise of heresies such as Protestantism, likely enraged those that had grown comfortable through these funds:

> Observe the difference that exists between the good shepherd and the one who is merely salaried. This one, when he sees the wolf, flees, because he does not care for the sheep; that one gives his life for them! How many examples of this truth do our sad centuries provide! Wanting to be secular princes, they stopped being shepherds. The wolves came into the fold, they did not find a shepherd, and so they mistreated and dispersed the sheep, as now we see the sad errors of diverse heresies and sects.[77]

Accused by the Inquisition of Lutheran heresies, he was arrested in 1559 and held under house arrest in Spain. His arrest came as a result of three errors: first not reporting to the Spanish Inquisition his knowledge of Spaniards who had struggled with Catholic doctrine and had confessed to him their sympathies for Lutheranism. While normally a confessor could keep this knowledge private, heresy in Spain "was not only a sin, but a crime," and therefore had to be reported. Second, in 1558, Carranza had preached against considering all questioning of the Church as heresy. Finally, he had circulated a draft copy of a new work, *Commentary on the Christian Catechism*, which contained multiple errors from the perspective of the Inquisition, including passages that seemed like Luther's evangelical views on good works, prayer, and other subjects.[78] Contributing to Carranza's challenges were rumors that he had tried to pass along heretical thoughts to Charles V as the emperor lay dying, that he had refused to hear his confession, and that Carranza had diverted Charles from questions about the campaign against Protestants in Spain.[79]

The testimony of witnesses against Carranza was inconclusive. No one testified that the archbishop had declared himself a Lutheran, but several claimed that he had shared Lutheran books, discussed the ideas of Luther and other Protestant theologians, preached ideas in sermons that were consistent with Protestantism, raised doubts privately about the Catholic doctrine of purgatory without making any open declarations, and was friendly with several who would later confess to being Lutherans. Several declared Protestants also recommended his views to others. Most importantly, Carranza never confessed to heretical crimes. As an archbishop, he was not tortured, which perhaps explains why he did not confess, but his incarceration was highly unpleasant, kept in a dark, windowless cell, isolated from contacts with the Church and his supporters, and deprived of many comforts, including those normally granted to those detained by the Inquisition. The enmity of the Grand Inquisitor and other enemies within the Church did not help the primate's situation.[80]

After several years in the custody of the Spanish Inquisition, Pope Pius IV insisted that Carranza be transferred to Rome. Facing continued resistance from Philip II, the Pope threatened widescale excommunication of those who defied this order. The king relented and allowed Carranza to travel to Rome, while the stalemate over jurisdiction continued to simmer between the Spanish Inquisition and the Vatican.[81] Carranza and his advocates reminded courts in Spain and Rome that, because he was an archbishop, he could only be tried under the authority of the Pope. Inquisitors and Philip II argued that their mandate allowed for no exceptions in the persecution of heresy, and that Spaniards should be tried by Spaniards. The king himself noted that the Spanish Inquisition should be the body to try all of his subjects, rather than having these trials conducted "by foreigners unacquainted with national and local particularities."[82]

Inconclusive and episodic legal proceedings continued, with theologians arguing for and against Archbishop Carranza's alleged heresies, an highly unusual and perplexing case, given his imperial patronage, his key role in drafting the catechism approved by the Council of Trent, his Inquisitorial bona fides, and his humble character.[83] If even Primate Carranza, who had enforced Catholic orthodoxy in England and Spain and had heard the confessions of both Charles V and Philip II, could be accused of heresy, then no one, no matter how powerful or connected, was guaranteed to be loyal to the Catholic Church or, from an individual perspective, safe against the serious inquiries of the Holy Office.[84]

One Inquisitor stated, referring to Carranza, that "if Spain was going to have its Luther, he would come in the form of a renegade prelate or revered religious." While Carranza did not have the force of personality or the determination to stand up to the hierarchy of which he was the leader, or theological mind of Luther, his arrest reflected a genuine concern that the Protestant heresy could arise anywhere and would be especially dangerous if embraced by those in the Catholic hierarchy. The archbishop was able to mount a vigorous defense, forcing multiple judges of the Inquisition to recuse themselves, given their obvious conflicts. These and other initiatives delayed even the start of the proceedings until May 1561 but was not the end of the challenges. Carranza's case became a point of direct confrontation with the papacy, with Pope Pius V demanding the cardinal's release, eventually gaining his transfer in 1566 to the Vatican under a form of parole and for a final decision by a Roman tribunal. Carranza had escaped the Spanish Inquisition, but not his troubles as an accused heretic. Even so, the venue had changed to far more comfortable circumstances, before a more lenient court.[85]

Formal legal and religious proceedings continued in Rome, operating sporadically for another decade. On 14 April 1576, Carranza yielded to the pressure of the long process and admitted "sixteen heretical mistakes," expressed through errors in his writing. That same year, Carranza retired to a Roman monastery, after 17 years in various forms of detention in Spain and Rome. Although mostly exonerated, since he had merely claimed errors, rather than confessing to heresy, he was a broken man and would never resume his post as primate of Spain. In an unusual convergence, some Protestant historians agree with the Spanish Inquisition that the archbishop had converted to Lutheranism through excessive time spent reading Protestant works to refute them. Regardless of his inner beliefs, the career of Carranza would be defined by his association with the Protestant Reformation. While released, he would have little time to alter this; Carranza died shortly thereafter, on 2 May. [86]

As in the case of Don Carlos, a fortuitous death spared Spain any additional embarrassment from having a suspected Protestant in its Catholic hierarchy. The broader point – that no one, from the lowliest peasant to the highest-ranking prelate, was beyond the reach of the Spanish Inquisition – was clear.[87] In the end, Grand Inquisitor Fernando de Valdés succeeded in permanently sidelining Carranza, removing an opponent from the top of the Spanish ecclesiastical hierarchy; however, the Inquisitor did not long enjoy this triumph, being nudged out of his own position in 1566, and passing away in 1568.[88] Even though Carranza was eventually absolved by the Pope, what mattered most was that his trial proved that referencing Erasmus for theological orthodoxy was no defense, so long as the fear of Luther pervaded Spain and the efforts of the Spanish Inquisition.[89]

Foreigners in the Iberian Peninsula, especially French and Flemish artisans, were also highly vulnerable to the Inquisition, being doubly suspicious not only for their origin, but because of the strong Protestant movements in their home regions. English merchants and sailors could also face troubles from the Inquisition, especially after Henry VIII's establishment of the Church of England in the 1530s. While at times Charles V would intervene to protect prominent Englishmen caught up in these travails, this potential salvation would depend on the state of diplomatic and commercial affairs between England and the Empire. Typically, however, it was unwise choices by Englishmen – arguing in public over theology or directly confronting Catholic practices – that most often caused the Inquisition to take notice. Sailors who kept to their ships and immediate harbors, and merchants who discussed prices and markets exclusively, seldom drew the interest of the Holy Office. This also meant ignoring provocative comments from Spaniards; rushing to defend the honor of Henry VIII, the Christian piety of England, and the morals of the country against insults, in the midst of ample alcoholic spirits, was a course later regretted by many English visitors to Spain.[90] Spanish Catholics with close ties to outsiders could come under suspicion as possible vectors for the alien ideas of John Calvin, Martin Luther, or other pernicious influences.[91]

It was not just in Spain where the Inquisition drew new life from the Protestant threat, using this mandate to expand its investigatory powers. In other Habsburg lands – Sicily, Naples, the Canary Islands, and even in the Spanish American colonies – fear of Lutherans, Calvinists, Anglicans and other Reformers justified a revived Holy Office.[92] Indeed, by the 1540s, "Lutheranism was much more dreaded than Judaism," not surprising given the alignment of powerful European states with these new faiths, a dramatic contrast with the stateless Jews so long persecuted by the Habsburgs and other dynasties.[93] One major concern, especially in Sicily, was of an alliance between the Ottoman Empire and Lutherans; indeed, Luther had spoken favorably of Istanbul and the Ottoman sultan on occasion. Protestant pirates, mostly Dutch or English, did occasionally make common cause with Muslim corsairs in the Mediterranean, and Inquisitors in Sicily often interrogated captured Protestants about potential pacts with the Ottomans.[94] At a minimum, the Ottomans provided an ongoing balance to the power of Philip II "and allowed Protestants to breathe easier" given the pressure Istanbul could bring against Habsburg interests.[95]

The fear of the Reformation at sea by Spanish sailors even spread to the western hemisphere, where Spanish ship captains often referred to pirates as *corsarios luteranos*, whether these ocean-borne brigands were French Catholics, Anglicans or Dutch Calvinists or, as was often the case, mixed crews of no particular faith or loyalty beyond the decks of their ship. There were at times even Jewish and Muslim pirates among those captured by Spain, ostensibly ineligible for prosecution by ecclesiastical authorities because only declared Christians could face the Inquisition, but nonetheless facing the death penalty from Spanish secular officials for the crime of piracy.[96]

Inquisitors in the Americas shared the same sense as those in Spain's European possessions, taking "the stance that the Spanish Inquisition's trials were part of a conflict against Protestants of global dimensions."[97] Indeed, the reviving of Inquisitorial activity in the 1550s and 1560s especially came at a time when a religious civil war in France, conflict in Germany, and the final defection of England from Catholicism to Anglicanism, or at least non-Catholicism, was consecrated under Queen Elizabeth I. "Between 1557 and 1559, the Inquisitor General (Fernando de Valdés y Salas) and the Suprema repeatedly declared their pursuit of Protestant heresies, depicting Lutheran doctrine as on the advance and inflicting ever-greater harm with each passing day."[98]

Over 2,500 foreigners, along with perhaps 500 Spaniards, were accused by the Inquisition of Reformation beliefs during the sixteenth century. The largest numbers of foreigners were French, Flemish, and Dutch, with smaller numbers of English and Germans. Some historians have argued that, with perhaps ten times as many Protestants in Spain at the time, but more effective at keeping their faith hidden, there was a substantial community, thus making the campaign of the Inquisition a reasonable practice by a Catholic Church under theological threat.[99]

Philip II's efforts to crush Protestantism and other heresies involved not only investigations of individuals suspected of these beliefs, but broad policies intending to protect Spaniards from encountering the ideas of Luther and Calvin. The king banned study abroad by his subjects outside of his

Iberian domains, fearing that the renowned universities of France, the German states, and even ostensibly Spanish territories in the Low Countries would lead to Protestant intellectual corruption; Spanish teachers and students were ordered to return home, either to cease their courses or to seek affiliation with universities in Spain.[100] This was a serious blow to the intellectual development of the scions of Spanish families with means, whether noble or otherwise. Even if it did not lead to a university degree, "study abroad was considered the culmination of the humanist education of young members of the elite," providing opportunities not only for scholarly learning, but to network with other well-connected families, opportunities that could yield familial, commercial, or other benefits.[101]

The Spanish Inquisition also introduced its own index of forbidden books in 1559, following the example of the Vatican, including not only outwardly Reformist authors, but all works in the Spanish language printed outside of the peninsula. This followed a royal decree the previous year that asserted royal privilege over printing, granting to Inquisitors the right to prior censorship over all books and other printed materials throughout Spain.[102] The commissioners of the Inquisition, who guarded every port and border crossing, were generally successful at reducing the availability of Protestant literature in Spain, but like shutting off air to kill weeds, the effort starved what had been blossoming in a vibrant intellectual atmosphere in Spain, discouraging creativity, scholarship, and originality in universities and among the small reading population.[103]

Among the many foreigners that traversed through or worked in Spain and other Habsburg territories, perhaps none attracted so much suspicion as printers. These skilled workers were suspected, with good reason, of harboring heretical Protestant thoughts, of being at the heart not only of smuggling Protestant publications into Spain, but of operating Spanish printing presses surreptitiously to publish books by Luther, Calvin, and other Protestants. Given the dearth of Spaniards with these skills, the printers were most often French or Dutch, and so were suspicious on at least three levels: they were foreigners, from territories where Calvinism and other Reformist denominations were strong and worked in a profession that Luther had recognized as one of his "strongest weapons" in the promotion of his faith: the printed word.[104]

The geography of their itinerant work could also increase their jeopardy; previous experience in hotbeds of Protestantism such as Geneva, Lyon, Antwerp, or London, could increase the likelihood of Reformist influence on these skilled artisans, as well as causing a redoubling of efforts by tribunals to root out heresy among those with whom these primarily French and Dutch workers came into contact. The ongoing campaigns against foreign printers seem to have had a negative impact on the availability and quality of books and other printed materials in Spain, as these itinerant craftsmen understandably were ready to flee when word began to spread about an investigation of a friend or acquaintance; the tactic of the Spanish Inquisition to promise leniency in exchange for denunciations of other heretical accomplices was well known.[105]

Although given the relative isolation of foreign printers and other non-Spaniards there was little threat that they would disseminate Reformist ideas among the general population, especially outside the tiny population of educated readers in Spanish cities, the fear, as much as the reality, made foreigners of all nationalities suspect and vulnerable to the Spanish Inquisition's investigations, subsequent tribunals, and range of punishments from the light to the ultimate.[106] Separated from the Castilian-speaking population by language, ethnicity, profession, and often as subjects of other monarchs, these same barriers made their appearances before the Inquisition a serious and life-threatening challenge for these foreigners. Translators were not provided, except at the personal expense of the accused.[107]

At the same time, both Philip II and leading Catholic prelates recognized that the religious ignorance of Spanish subjects stemmed in large part from an ill-prepared clergy, unable to provide basic teachings, much less refute Protestant ideas. The exhortations of the Council of Trent recognized these failings and encouraged Catholic states to do better to prepare their believers to understand Christianity and engage in deeper spiritual lives. Required seminary education for clergy, new enhanced catechisms, literacy and other requirements for parish priests, and redoubled efforts to improve religious teaching at all levels: these efforts, coupled with the prosecutorial efforts and public spectacles of the Spanish Inquisition, were the primary tools to expunge heresy from Spain.[108]

While the original focus on *conversos* and the new-found pursuit of Lutherans and other Protestants drew the most high-level attention from both the Inquisitorial bodies themselves and from Philip II, the actual daily work of the Spanish Inquisition focused more on the ongoing lack of orthodoxy among the Spanish people, a characteristic that flowed more from ignorance, illiteracy, and disinterest than from outspoken opposition to Catholic teachings. It was Catholics, who thought of themselves as such, and had no interest in the doctrines of Luther, Calvin, or those within the Torah, that drew the greatest attention, in terms of the number of investigations and prosecutions in Spain by the Inquisition during the late sixteenth century. This of course reflects the population of Spain, by all accounts the most overwhelmingly united through a single religious denomination of all the countries of Europe.[109]

The Spanish Inquisition was not an institution confined to the Spanish-speaking lands of the Iberian Peninsula. There were instances of clerics acting in lieu of Inquisitorial authority in the Americas as early as 1520, with both regular and secular clergy taking on this role.[110] However, it was not until Bishop Juan de Zumárraga y Arrazola was named Bishop of Mexico in 1535 that the New World saw its first formal Inquisitorial investigations, albeit through the bishop's spiritual and legal authority, rather than through an institutionally separate Inquisitorial tribunal. Initially dedicated to rooting out hidden Jews and Muslims among the Spanish-speaking population of Catholics, its mandate would expand to other forms of policing heresy, including watching for Protestant theological incursions among both

Europeans and the indigenous population. While the mandate of Inquisitions only extended to those within Christendom, it could apply to local converts to Catholicism, who upon accepting Christianity were immediately responsible for maintaining absolute orthodoxy in thought, word, and deed, even if their religious education in their new faith was inadequate or even entirely absent.[111] In 1571, Philip II had to reinforce to Inquisitorial and other tribunals in the Americas that indigenous populations who had not yet accepted Christianity were not subject to the Spanish Inquisition.[112]

The Mexican episcopal Inquisition was successful at prosecuting Protestants during Bishop Zumárraga's time leading the diocese, 1536–1543, even if the number of heretics facing this accusation was small compared to those facing other charges; five of the 152 actions were trials of accused Lutherans. While this represented only 3% of the trials, overshadowed by 56 cases of heresy (37%), 23 of sorcery (25%), and 19 of *conversos* – converted Jews denounced as maintaining Judaism (12.5%), it was still an indication that Protestants were considered a global threat everywhere, whether in the Iberian Peninsula or in distant colonies, only a few decades removed from first contact between Spanish *conquistadores* and the native populations of the Americas, Africa, and the Far East.[113]

The pursuit of Protestants continued under later episcopal leaders, including the Dominican friar Alonso de Montúfar, who served as Archbishop of Mexico from 1551 to 1572. His time in office coincided with the height of Philip II's campaigns against Protestant Reformers in Spain, an approach that the archbishop echoed in his efforts against heresy. While English and French merchants, sailors, and even captured pirates were among those who came to trial under the auspices of the Spanish Inquisition in Mexico, there were also Genoese, Spaniards, Greeks, Dutch, Germans and others from Habsburg and other Catholic and non-Catholic lands accused of Lutheran beliefs. Although usually tried in Mexico City, in the episcopal see, most accused were first taken into custody in the Caribbean coastal area. In littoral cities such as Veracruz and Acapulco, possibilities for trade and smuggling attracted a diverse cast of non-Spaniards for merchant activity, both licit and illicit.[114] There were few foreigners, and even fewer Habsburg subjects, such that the archbishop could assure Philip II in 1561 that heresy was well under control in Mexico.[115]

Indeed, as one historian has noted, "the word foreigner (*extranjero*) became a synonym for Protestant, and Catholic foreigners in Mexico were usually suspect."[116] Throughout the period of the Spanish Inquisition, whether considering tribunals in Spain or in its colonies, foreigners were disproportionally reported by informers, investigated, and convicted by the religious body. The year 1571 saw the formal institution of the Holy Office in Mexico replacing the episcopal Inquisitorial processes of the previous decades. The arrival of Inquisitors from Spain was not especially welcome to the colonial and episcopal authorities in Mexico, but they complied with the establishment of the Holy Office, given the king's mandate to it.[117] This date also coincided with the end of large-scale campaigns in Spain against Spanish Protestants, with subsequent efforts by Philip II focused on Anglicans, Lutherans, and Calvinists outside Spain proper, along with military campaigns on land and at sea against Dutch and English Protestants. Most of those convicted of Protestantism thereafter were foreigners, rather than Spanish subjects. With the religious home front secured, and the internal threat crushed through aggressive persecution over the previous decades, the battles between Philip II's Spain and Protestants everywhere continued unabated in Europe and the Americas.[118]

The defeat of English pirates at the naval battle of San Juan de Ulúa in 1568, near the Mexican port of Veracruz, launched trials against foreign Protestants. These English sailors, a surviving group of just under 100 left behind by their captain, John Hawkins, faced investigation and trial by the Spanish Inquisition. They were accused – with powerful evidence including their own confessions and religious items – of being heretical Anglicans, landed on Habsburg soil. While some faced only modest punishments and were allowed to convert to Catholicism, those unwilling to abandon Protestant Christianity eventually faced a public *auto da fe* and execution: 13 out of the original group of abandoned English sailors endured this fate.[119]

An example of an accused Protestant from the Hawkins company was the English sailor, Michael Morgan, who had come to the Caribbean in 1568 and was captured during the campaign in 1572. He initially denied Lutheranism through extensive questioning. The Inquisition in Mexico reverted to torture, including subjecting him to the rack in January 1574, during which he confessed to his Lutheran views. The conviction for heresy, along with the questioning, featured insistence by the Inquisitors that Morgan confess to Lutheran beliefs. This highlights the conflation of all Protestant theology, whether Calvinist, Anglican, or truly based on the ideas of Luther, into the same heresy.[120] Morgan was executed with others from the same group. Admittedly, with the death penalty for piracy applied nearly universally, whether in Spanish, British, or French territories, these sentences were not inconsistent with prevailing notions of secular and maritime justice in the sixteenth-century Caribbean. Later Inquisitorial efforts in Mexico would follow the same guidelines against accused Protestants and other heresies.[121]

In Spanish colonies with less exposure to foreign merchants and sailors, far fewer were charged with this heresy. In Peru, for example, the Spanish Inquisition was far more concerned with policing popular medicine, paganism, and astrology than Protestantism, which was essentially nonexistent. Indigenous "superstition and magic," rather than imported ideas of Calvin and Luther, were a more serious threat to the Holy Office and colonial authorities during the Habsburg era. In Peru, as well, the Inquisition struggled to contain its activities to converts among the indigenous population, since there could be great uncertainty in defining what it meant to be Catholic in colonies that remained overwhelmingly non-European, non-Spanish-speaking, and lacking Christian education even to the most basic level of Catholic doctrine and practice.[122] In the Philippines, the Spanish Inquisition focused on accusations of witchcraft and moral crimes, such as bigamy, rather than investigating potential Protestants. The late date of the Holy Office's introduction to this Pacific colony, as well as the minimal interactions with non-Spanish Europeans, played a role in this reduced campaign against the Protestant heresy. The first documented cases of Protestants convicted in the Philippines came after 1600, consisting primarily of Dutch and English sailors.[123]

Philip's empire spanned the globe, and so did the Spanish Inquisition, although it did not have the same pervasiveness or consistency of methods in other parts of Spain's imperial lands. Although its tribunals were limited to Spain and territories controlled directly by it – which excluded realms such as the Low Countries and Habsburg lands in the Italian peninsula – the impact of it was much broader. Spaniards noting the practices of the Inquisition often fled abroad, or if living elsewhere feared being captured and sent home. While other Inquisitions existed, including one in Rome, none equaled that of Spain for endurance, intensity, and effectiveness. In close alliance with Philip II during the last half of the sixteenth century, the Spanish Inquisition shepherded Iberia through the height of theological tumult in Europe, successfully preventing widespread Protestant conversion in Spain and consolidating religious activity around the Catholic Church, and helped encourage broader and deeper theological education among the priesthood and believers, implementing the decisions reached at the Council of Trent with thoroughgoing and fierce dedication.

Unlike other institutions, the Spanish Inquisition could reach all subjects of the monarchy resident in Spain, as well any foreigners passing through temporarily or living in Spain. There were no exempted classes based on birth, title of nobility, wealth, profession, or religious bona fides. Only bishops of the Catholic Church, at least in theory, could not be judged by the Spanish Inquisition; as Archbishop Carranza discovered, however, even bishops were not immune from the interest of the Holy Office. Whether peasants or nobles, university professors or printers, the Spanish Inquisition applied its search for heretics with enthusiasm across all social classes, regions, professions, and nationalities present in Spain. In large measure, the Spanish Inquisition helped define and defend what it meant to be Spanish, Habsburg, and Catholic in the sixteenth century and the years beyond.[124]

Allied with Philip II, the Holy Office would shape religious practice, define the outlines of heresy, and determine the development of the Catholic Church in Spain over the course of the monarch's rule. While its reach did not extend outside of Spain's territories, its impact did echo throughout Europe, and support Spanish military and diplomatic campaigns against the Protestant Reformation and other enemies of Philip II in Europe and beyond. The Spanish Inquisition played an indispensable role within Spain, especially in the midst of Catholicism's reactions to Protestantism. While by 1560, only 60% of Europe remained loyal to Catholicism, by 1650, the Counter-Reformation, led by Spain, had reclaimed much lost territory. By some estimates, as much as 80% of Western and Central Europe was once again back under the influence of Rome.[125] The actions of the Spanish Inquisition, strongly endorsed by Philip II, were the highest priority of the king, who noted "rather than suffer the least damage to the Catholic Church and God's service I will lose all my states, and a hundred lives if I had them."[126] The Spanish Inquisition did not serve Spain, so much as Spain was dedicated, through its monarch, to serving the same goal as the Holy Office: the absolute extirpation of Protestantism and all other heresies from Spain. In this regard, at least within Spain, the king and the Inquisitors could proclaim victory. In the broader struggle for Europe, against a wider range of enemies, the final tally was much more complicated.

Notes

1 Luttikhuizen, *Underground Protestantism in Sixteenth Century Spain*, 89–90.
2 Garcia Cárcel, "Lutero y Carlos V," in Borreguero Beltrán and Retortillo Atienza, *La memoria de un hombre*, 59.
3 Luttikhuizen, *Underground Protestantism in Sixteenth Century Spain*, 91.
4 Geoffrey Parker, *Success Is Never Final: Empire, War, and Faith in Early Modern Europe* (New York: Basic Books, 2002), 3.
5 "La configuración de la Monarquía Hispánica," by Fernando Bouza. David García Hernán, ed., *La historia sin complejos: La nueva visión del Imperio Español* (estudios en honor de John H. Elliott) (Madrid: Actas, 2010), 74.
6 Norwich, *Four Princes*, 226–232.
7 Lynch, *Spain 1516-1598*, 267.
8 Patterson, *With the Heart of a King*, 9.
9 Bruquetas and Lobo, *Don Carlos*, 253.
10 Wilson, *Sir Francis Walsingham*, 54. Cristina Borreguerro Beltrán, "Logros del Imperio Español: el poder militar y diplomático," in García Hernán, David, ed., *La historia sin complejos*, 100–101.
11 Geoffrey Parker, *Success is Never Final*, 30.
12 Lynch, *Spain 1516-1598*, 259, 372–373, 384–385.
13 McDermott, *England and the Spanish Armada*, xii.
14 Parker, *Success Is Never Final*, 31–33.
15 Mario Escobar Golderos, *La historia de una obsesión: Felipe II y su época* (Madrid: Consejo Evangélico de Madrid, 2001), 46–47.
16 Luttikhuizen, *Underground Protestantism in Sixteenth Century Spain*, 88.
17 Downey, *Isabella*, 212–217, 227–232.
18 Rady, *The Habsburgs*, 86.
19 Schäfer, *Protestantismo Español e Inquisición en el Siglo XVI*, Vol. 1, 299–300.
20 López Muñoz, *La Reforma en la Sevilla del XVI*, Vol. II. Letters, Philip II, 1557-1563, 135, 165, 307.
21 Luttikhuizen, *Underground Protestantism in Sixteenth Century Spain*, 89.
22 Benzion Netanyahu, *The Origins of the Inquisition in Fifteenth Century Spain* (New York: Random House, 1995), 426.
23 Lu Ann Homza, *The Spanish Inquisition: 1478-1614: An Anthology of Sources* (Indianapolis: Hackett, 2006), xv–xvi. Netanyahu, *The Origins of the Inquisition in Fifteenth Century Spain*, 920, 1006–1009, 1011.
24 Pérez, *The Spanish Inquisition*, 152–153.
25 Edward Peters, *Inquisition* (New York: Free Press, 1988), 89–90.
26 Homza, *The Spanish Inquisition*, xxviii, xxx–xxxi.
27 Lea, *A History of the Inquisition of Spain and the Inquisition in the Spanish Dependencies*, Vol. 3, 411.
28 Richard Kagan and Abigail Dyer, eds., *Inquisitorial Inquiries: Brief Lives of Secret Jews and Other Heretics* (Baltimore: Johns Hopkins University Press, 2011), 53.

29 Juan Carlos Domínguez Nafría, ed., *100 impresos españoles sobre la Inquisición: Instrucciones, edictos, cedulas, relaciones de autos de fe y otros* (Madrid: Bibliotheca Sefarad, 2018), 27. Fernando de Valdés, *Compilación de las Instrucciones del Oficio de la Santa Inquisición*, 1561, https://www.bibliothecasefarad.com/en/ digitalizados.

30 Leonora de Alberti and Annie Beatrice Wallis Chapman, *Los mercaderes ingleses y la Inquisición Española en las Islas Canarias*, 16–18.

31 Lynn, *Between Court and Confessional*, 64.

32 Kagan and Dyer, eds., *Inquisitorial Inquiries*, 17.

33 Schäfer, *Protestantismo Español e Inquisición en el Siglo XVI*, AHN, Inquisición, leg. 2105 and 99–17, 125. Griffin, *Journeymen-Printers*, 253.

34 Lynn, *Between Court and Confessional*, 21.

35 Pérez, *The Spanish Inquisition*, 145.

36 Pérez, *The Spanish Inquisition*, 135–136.

37 Schäfer, *Protestantismo Español e Inquisición en el Siglo XVI*, Vol. 1, 289, 291–292, 311.

38 Griffin, *Journeymen-Printers*, 49–51.

39 Domínguez Nafría, *100 impresos españoles sobre la Inquisición*, 13.

40 Schäfer, *Protestantismo Español e Inquisición en el Siglo XVI*, Vol. 1, 366.

41 Pérez, *The Spanish Inquisition*, 146–148. Monter, *Frontiers of Heresy*, 74–75. Domínguez Nafría, ed., *100 impresos españoles sobre la Inquisición*, 13.

42 Lynn, *Between Court and Confessional*, 20.

43 Schäfer, *Protestantismo Español e Inquisición en el Siglo XVI*, Vol. 1, 331.

44 Homza, *Religious Authority in the Spanish Renaissance*, 14. Pérez, *The Spanish Inquisition*, 145.

45 Schäfer, *Protestantismo Español e Inquisición en el Siglo XVI*, AHN, Inquisición, leg. 1953, 81. Pérez, *The Spanish Inquisition*, 86–87.

46 Griffin, *Journeymen-Printers*, 58–67.

47 Homza, *Religious Authority in the Spanish Renaissance*, 22.

48 Griffin, *Journeymen-Printers*, 38–41.

49 Bruquetas, Fernando and Manuel Lobo, Don Carlos, *Príncipe de las Españas*. Madrid: Cátedra, 2016, 73; Alonso Burgos, Jesús. *El luteranismo en Castilla durante el siglo XVI: autos de fe de Valladolid de 21 de mayo y de 8 de octubre de 1559*. San Lorenzo de El Escorial, Spain: Editorial Swan, 1983, 70, 119.

50 Geoffrey Parker, *Philip II*, 4th edition (Chicago: Open Court, 2002), 100–101. Peters, *Inquisition*, 131.

51 "Juramento del rey don Felipe II en el auto de 8 de octubre de 1559," AHN, Inquisición, leg. 3189/2, in Schäfer, *Ernst Hermann Johann. Protestantismo Español e Inquisición en el Siglo XVI*, Vol. 3A. "Documentos para la historia de la comunidad protestante de Valladolid" (Seville: MAD, 2014), 91–92.

52 Fernando Bruquetas and Manuel Lobo, *Don Carlos: Príncipe de las Españas* (Madrid: Cátedra, 2016). 73.

53 Letter, King Philip II to Fernando de Valdés, Brussels, 4 March 1558; Account of the V, 9 September 1558, in Homza, *The Spanish Inquisition*, 181, 187.

54 Pérez, *The Spanish Inquisition*, 127–128.

55 Pérez, *The Spanish Inquisition*, 131–132.

56 John Edwards, "The Spanish Inquisition Refashioned: The Experience of Mary I's England and the Valladolid Tribunal, 1559," *Hispanic Research Journal*, 2012, Vol. 13, No. 1, 42–43.

57 Del Valle, *Anales de la Inquisición*, 257–258.

58 "Carta e informe del inquisidor general arzobispo de Sevilla al papa Pablo IV sobre los luteranos españoles," Valladolid, 9 September 1558, in Schäfer, *Protestantismo Español e Inquisición en el Siglo XVI*, Vol. 3ª, 140–141, AHN, Inquisición, lib. 245, fol. 230–232.

59 Lynch, *Spain 1516-1598*, 262–263.

60 Patterson, *With the Heart of a King*, 30. Luis Próspero Gachard, *Don Carlos y Felipe II* (Barcelona: Editorial Lorenzana, 1963), 50.
61 Bruquetas and Lobo, *Don Carlos*, 68.
62 Gachard, *Don Carlos y Felipe II*, 64–65.
63 Lynch, *Spain 1516-1598*, 263.
64 Andrew Villalon, "The 1562 Head Injury of Don Carlos: A Conflict of Medicine and Religion in Sixteenth-Century Spain," *Mediterranean Studies*, 2014, Vol. 22, No. 2, 95–134. Bruquetas and Lobo, *Don Carlos*, 80–91.
65 Gachard, *Don Carlos y Felipe II*, 108–117, 132–134, 175–182. Bruquetas and Lobo, *Don Carlos*, 76, 108.
66 Gachard, *Don Carlos y Felipe II*, 201–227. Watson, *The History of the Reign of Philip the Second*, 138, 193.
67 Gachard, *Don Carlos y Felipe II*, 338, 369–372, 414–416, 450. Bruquetas and Lobo, *Don Carlos*, 341–344.
68 Bruquetas and Lobo, *Don Carlos*, 256–258.
69 De Castro, *The Spanish Protestants and their Persecution by Philip II*, 326–327. Bruquetas and Lobo, *Don Carlos*, 337–347.
70 De Castro, *The Spanish Protestants and their Persecution by Philip*, 278–282, 298–299, 316, 325–327. Bruquetas and Lobo, *Don Carlos*, 16.
71 Parker, *Philip II*, 90–93.
72 Lynch, *Spain 1516-1598*, 265–266. Gachard, *Don Carlos y Felipe II*, 474–486.
73 Fernández Álvarez, *España del Emperador Carlos V*, Vol. XX, 952.
74 José Ignacio Tellechea Idígoras, *Fray Bartolomé Carranza de Miranda* (Investigaciones históricas) (Pamplona, Navarre: Gobierno de Navarra, 2002), 21, 49, 55.
75 Edwards, *The Spanish Inquisition Refashioned*, 43–44.
76 MacCulloch, *The Reformation*, 291–292.
77 Bartolomé Carranza, "Controversia de necessaria residentia personali episcoporum aliorumque inferiorum pastorum," 1547, in Tellechea Idígoras, *Fray Bartolomé Carranza de Miranda*, 33.
78 Pérez, The *Spanish Inquisition*, 73. Escobar Golderos, *La historia de una obsesión*, 179. Luttikhuizen, *Underground Protestantism in Sixteenth Century Spain*, 135.
79 Tellechea Idígoras, *Fray Bartolomé Carranza de Miranda*, 65, 339–352.
80 AHN, "Testimonios de los protestantes vallisoletanos en las actas del proceso de Carranza 1558-1559." Madrid, Biblioteca de la Real Academia de la Historia, "Proceso del arzobispo de Toledo fray Bartolomé de Carranza, Testificaciones de cargo." In Schäfer, *Ernst Hermann Johann. Protestantismo Español e Inquisición en el Siglo XVI.* Vol. 3B. "Documentos para la historia de la comunidad protestante de Valladolid." Translated and edited by Francisco Ruiz de Pablos (Seville: MAD, 2014), 979–1078.
81 Henry Kamen, *The Spanish Inquisition: A Historical Revision* (New Haven, CT: Yale University Press, 1997), 160–163. Lynn, *Between Court and Confessional*, 47. Pérez, *The Spanish Inquisition*, 73–74, 168.
82 Pérez, *The Spanish Inquisition*, 154.
83 MacCulloch, *The Reformation*, 291–292.
84 Griffin, *Journeymen-Printers*, 6–7.
85 Lynch, *Spain 1516-1598*, 373–374. Mullett, *The Catholic Reformation*, 120. Lynn, *Between Court and Confessional*, 64–74.
86 Lynn, *Between Court and Confessional*, 75–76, 89. De Castro, *The Spanish Protestants and their Persecution by Philip*, 189.
87 Lynn, *Between Court and Confessional*, 69. Pérez, *The Spanish Inquisition*, 74.
88 Monter, *Frontiers of Heresy*, 41.
89 Alonso Burgos, *El luteranismo en Castilla durante el siglo XVI*, 50.
90 Marshall, *Religious Identities in Henry VIII's England*, 109–110, 112–114, 117.
91 Kagan and Dyer, eds., *Inquisitorial Inquiries*, 53–54.
92 Peters, *Inquisition*, 99–100.

93 Henry Charles Lea, *The Inquisition in the Spanish Dependencies* (New York: Macmillan, 1922), 24–25, 67–70, 153, 199.

94 Lynn, *Between Court and Confessional*, 149–150, 153.

95 Rafael Vargas-Hidalgo, ed., *Guerra y diplomacia en el Mediterráneo: Correspondencia inédita de Felipe II con Andrea Doria y Juan Andrea Doria* (Madrid: Ediciones Polifemo, 2002), xv.

96 Clarence Haring, *Trade and Navigation between Spain and the Indies in the Time of the Hapsburgs* (Gloucester, MA: Harvard University Press, 1918), 235.

97 Lynn, *Between Court and Confessional*, 42.

98 Lynn, *Between Court and Confessional*, 64.

99 Werner Thomas, *Los protestantes y la Inquisición en España en tiempos de Reforma y Contrarreforma* (Leuven, Belgium: Leuven University Press, 2001), 632–633.

100 Luttikhuizen, *Underground Protestantism in Sixteenth Century Spain*, 93.

101 Els Agten, "Traveling Scholars and Circulating Ideas in Early Modern Europe. The Case of Francisco Enzinas," in Borreguero Beltrán and Retortillo Atienza, *La memoria de un hombre*, 244.

102 Griffin, *Journeymen-Printer*, 5; MacCulloch, *The Reformation*, 290-291. Lynch, *Spain 1516-1598*, 344–345.

103 Rady, *The Habsburgs*, 91. Griffin, *Journeymen-Printers*, 3.

104 Griffin, *Journeymen-Printers*, 2.

105 Griffin, *Journeymen-Printers*, 27–30, 32–35, 56-57.

106 Griffin, *Journeymen-Printers*, 10–11.

107 Griffin, *Journeymen-Printers*, 70–73.

108 MacCulloch, *The Reformation*, 406–408. Mullett, *The Catholic Reformation*, 63–66.

109 Griffin, *Journeymen-Printers*, 14–15.

110 Richard Greenleaf, *The Mexican Inquisition of the Sixteenth Century* (Albequerque: University of New Mexico Press, 1969), 7–11.

111 Woodbury Lowery, *The Spanish Settlements within the Present Limits of the United States* (New York: Russell & Russell, 1959), 386, 456–457.

112 Patricia Lopes Don, *Bonfires of Culture: Franciscans, Indigenous Leaders, and the Inquisition in Early Mexico, 1524-1540* (Norman: University of Oklahoma Press, 2010), 9.

113 John F. Chuchiak, IV, ed. and trans. *The Inquisition in New Spain, 1536-1820: A Documentary History* (Baltimore: Johns Hopkins University Press, 2012), 10. Richard Greenleaf, *Zumárraga and the Mexican Inquisition, 1536-1543* (Washington, DC: Academy of American Franciscan History, 1961), 32, https://hdl.handle.net/2027/txu.059173023908390.

114 Greenleaf, Zumárraga and the Mexican Inquisition, 15-16. Daphne Alvarez-Villa, Jenny Guardado, "The long-run influence of institutions governing trade: Evidence from smuggling ports in colonial Mexico," *Journal of Development Economics*, 2020, Vol. 144, 102453, https://www.sciencedirect.com/science/article/pii/S0304387820300286.

115 Fernández Campos, *Reforma y contrarreforma en Andalucía*, 115.

116 Greenleaf, *The Mexican Inquisition of the Sixteenth Century*, 82.

117 Yolanda Mariel de Ibáñez, *El Tribunal d la Inquisición en México (siglo xvi)* (Mexico City: Universidad Nacional Autónoma de México, 1979), 62–63.

118 Greenleaf, *Zumárraga and the Mexican Inquisition*, 98. Pérez, *The Spanish Inquisition*, 111, 112.

119 Greenleaf, *The Mexican Inquisition of the Sixteenth Century*, 162–167.

120 Chuchiak, *The Inquisition in New Spain*, 1536–1820, 138–144. Ibáñez, *El Tribunal d la Inquisición en México*, 80, 90.

121 Jessica J. Fowler, "Process and Punishment: Alleged Alumbrados before the Mexican Holy Office, 1593–1603," *Colonial Latin American Review*, 2020, Vol. 29, No. 3, 357–375.

122   Adam Warren, *Medicine and Politics in Colonial Peru: Population Growth and the Bourbon Reforms* (Pittsburgh: University of Pittsburg Press, 2010), 34–35.
123   José Toribio Medina, *El Tribunal del Santo Oficio del la Inquisición en las Islas Filipinas* (Santiago, Chile: Imprenta Elzeviriana, 1899). F. Delor Angeles,"Bibliographical Data on the Philippine Inquisition," *Silliman Journal*, Third Quarter 1976, Vol. 23, 239–260.
124   Pérez, *The Spanish Inquisition*, 169–170.
125   Parker, *Success is Never Final*, 7.
126   Parker, *Success is Never Final*, 33.

6   French, Ottomans, and Protestants

Spain under Philip II was beset by enemies all around. While England and the Dutch rebels would prove the most persistent military threats, France and the Ottoman Empire were the most powerful ones. The French on land and the Ottomans at sea both presented dire challenges to Spain, and arguably neither could be permanently defeated by the forces at the disposal of the Habsburgs. Even clear tactical victories, such as the Ottoman naval defeat at Lepanto, did not change the structural difficulties for Spain, beset by both states. Indeed, when France and the Ottoman Empire temporarily allied, there was little that Spain could do to directly threaten such a powerful coalition. The added threat of the Protestant movement, especially if allied to France or even the Ottoman Empire, was even more terrifying to Philip II and his Catholic supporters through the Habsburg realms.

The kingdom of France posed a constant challenge to Charles V and later to Philip II. As one historian noted, given its location, leadership, and resources, it was "the natural enemy of Habsburg power." Powerful, large, and blocking easy territorial connections between Habsburg territories in Spain, the Low Countries, and the empire, France would also serve as a warning sign for kingdoms that did not take seriously the danger of the Protestant insurgency.[1] Although the sum of Habsburg lands were potentially more than a match for those of the Valois, the French had the additional advantage of interior lines of communication, a large population able to mobilize into a substantial army, and fewer of the financing challenges faced by the Habsburgs. Even more challenging in facing the French was the persistence of other enemies, chiefly the Ottomans and Protestants in both the empire and the Low Countries With as many as three main simultaneous foes, in multiple directions, Charles V was never able to devote all his resources against a single adversary. Even so, over the course of the sixteenth century, it was Protestantism that was the most daunting enemy, threatening not only external warfare, but the possibility of theologically based insurrection.

Spain had only to look to the north to see what potential dangers awaited, should Protestantism flourish or be tolerated. In France, where Calvinism had found a ready audience among some members of the nobility and urban classes, perhaps 10% of the population had converted by the early 1560s, and the rest of the century featured what became known as the French Wars of

DOI: 10.4324/9781003197676-7

Religion between Catholics and Calvinists. While there were never enough Protestants in France to aim for majority status, there were too many for their easy extirpation.[2] The strong Protestant presence just across the border – "Calvinist, organized, and armed" – set Philip on edge not only as an augur of what could come to Spain should the Reformation take hold in his lands, but as a direct threat should the Huguenots succeed in overtaking French Catholicism, and begin to look south for opportunities to spread the faith by force.[3] In France itself, some Catholics even pined for the efficiency of the Spanish Inquisition; just before his death in 1559, French King Henry II asked for detailed information on the operations and procedures of the Holy Office, perhaps considering imitating the institution in his campaign against the Huguenots. His reliance on bishops for this effort suffered, given the known sympathies of some ecclesiastical leaders for Protestant ideas, as well as the unwillingness of other leaders to persecute Huguenots in regions where they were influential or predominated.[4]

Mere association with France or French subjects could raise suspicions in Spain; long-standing ties to French cities where Calvinism had taken hold was something that those under investigation would often go to great pains to hide from Inquisitors during the recounting of biographical information, a consistent part of the process for all those who came before the Holy Office.[5] Despite Philip's efforts to fortify and patrol his northern border with France, the Pyrenees remained a highly permeable region, with its mountains filled with passes and pathways used not only by contraband smugglers and those seeking work in Spain, but by others hoping to bring Protestant ideas across the frontier. In some cases, in the 1560s small Huguenot groups attempted forays across the border to spread Calvinist ideas, leading Philip to fear Catalonia might welcome these interlopers. Although his fears were unrealized, and the region remained loyal and Catholic, the concern remained for decades, at least until France finally crushed its homegrown Protestant movement.[6]

Skilled French craftsmen, including printers, stone workers, and other artisans, were among those susceptible to be brought under the eye of the Spanish Inquisition. Even those that assimilated into society, through marrying Spanish wives, attending Mass, and espousing devotion to the Church, could because of their alien origins be at risk. Such was the case of Esteban Jamate, a stone cutter, originally from Orleans, France, brought before the local tribunal in Cuenca in April 1557. Accused of being a Lutheran, he admitted to having read several Protestant works, and to having consorted with Protestants. Although he was convicted of heresy, thanks to his prestige as the most talented stoneworker in Cuenca, famous for his work in the cathedral and other area churches, his death sentence was reduced to the confiscation of his assets, the humiliation of a public confession, the wearing of the *sanbenito* for three years, and the loss of his commissions from his work. The tribunal concluded that, although he had dabbled in Reformation thinking, he remained a Catholic, if a faulty one, and could be redeemed through true penitence and appropriate punishments.[7]

Concerns about the French were not only that their religious conflict could spread to Spain, but even more so that Protestantism would be exported elsewhere, including to Spanish territories and claims in the Americas. While French-speaking Calvinists north of the Pyrenees or in Calvin's Geneva were the most immediate concern to Philip II, this danger was not limited to the European continent nor to the barely controllable border between Catalonia and southern France.[8] One especially violent example of this global warfare took place in what would become the state of Florida. Claimed by Spain since 1513, when Ponce de León landed on the east coast of Florida, some French leaders and explorers saw this territory as a potential area for colonization and exploitation.

A first attempt in 1562, by a contingent of over 150 French Huguenot sailors, soldiers, and adventurers, landed initially on the east coast of North America, establishing Charlesfort, a settlement on what is now Parris Island, South Carolina. Hunger, mutinies, and a lack of agricultural interest or capacity among the colonists led to the abandoning of the site, with the survivors sailing for France in 1563.[9] A more determined effort began shortly thereafter, leading to the most dramatic struggle between Catholics and Protestants in the New World of the sixteenth century, with the French determined to establish an enclave in the Caribbean and Spaniards just as determined "to expel the Lutherans."[10] This was to Philip an extension of the problems Huguenots caused him in Europe, where they had disrupted his maritime trade and communications with the Low Countries, through piracy and privateering out of western and northern French ports, the Isle of Wight, and other Atlantic and North Sea ports.[11]

Florida in the 1560s was vital to Spain's Caribbean empire. After decades of neglect, the arrival of French soldiers and colonists dramatically increased Spanish attention to this region; the threat of Calvinists among the French served as an accelerant, expanding what was a conflict between Habsburg and Valois into a religious war. Indeed, Spanish defense spending on their Florida territories grew significantly, becoming the single largest element of their Caribbean military budget during the 1560s and early 1570s, and second only to the Spanish Main (the coastline of North and South America) in the 1580s.[12] The arrival of French Calvinists, in uneasy truce with French Catholics, had transformed an ignored area into "the (Spanish) crown's greatest military liability," as a successful French presence could sever the sea lanes back to Spain, passing as they did along the east coast of Florida.[13] Unfortunately, the recently concluded Treaty of Cateau-Cambrésis (1559) between Spain and France, while ending war between the two kingdoms in Europe, left ambiguous the status of claims in the New World. While the French regarded this as an opening for potential settlement, the Spanish resolved to defend what they saw as their rights – a difference of opinion that would soon go from diplomatic to deadly, accelerated by theological differences.[14]

Between 1562 and 1565, rival Spanish and French (mostly Huguenot) expeditions arrived on the northeast coast of what is now Florida, establishing fortified positions within 50 miles of each other. The French site, Fort Caroline, and the Spanish, Saint Augustine, were both intended to reinforce claims to the region by both controlling access to the sea, trading with the indigenous population, and serving as bases for additional colonization. Because Protestants predominated in the French colony, the conflict with the Spanish settlement soon took on an apocalyptic aura, with no mercy, no prisoners, and no capacity for coexistence, given the already difficult relations between outposts of Europe's two most powerful kingdoms. Europe's wars within Christianity were spreading to the New World.

Huguenot leaders, including Admiral Gaspard de Coligny, the Protestant leader of the French navy, hoped to gain much from encouraging settlements in Florida. The French government was truly interested in gaining a stronger foothold in the Americas; men such as Coligny also hoped to promote an improved status for Calvinists in France, by showing their worth to the state through expanding the French empire. Ideally, they could do so without direct confrontation with Spain, hoping to achieve de facto recognition of French territorial claims, a small piece of the vast American landscape. The Spanish possessed tremendous resources but as always, were pressed on many sides by rivals throughout Europe, the Mediterranean, and the broader world. Indeed, even as Philip II authorized a Spanish expedition to launch a counter-offensive against the French in Florida, the Habsburgs faced an Ottoman attack on Malta, reducing resources available to reinforce the Caribbean.[15] Given these additional stresses on Habsburg resources, the French understandably were willing to risk challenging the Spanish; perhaps a small and non-confrontational settlement could escape their notice long enough to become enduring.[16] As with English Protestants who would seek refuge in more northern areas, also hoping to escape both "papal tiara" and "the scourge of the Muslim Ottomans," the Huguenots saw this backwater of the Caribbean, not yet firmly settled by Spain, as an opportunity to create a foothold in the New World as an enclave for Protestants within French lands.[17]

The key asset of Florida was not in the sandy and unproductive soil of the peninsula, but offshore: the Gulf Stream current that enabled a return to Europe from the Caribbean; control over this route was indispensable for Spain to ensure the safe return of cargoes from the Americas, especially the silver upon which its imperial finances depended. There was, therefore, little chance of Spain tolerating an armed French community able to threaten this passage; the Protestant nature of the French outpost ensured Spain would see its existence as a mortal threat, despite attempts by the French expeditions to find alternative routes across the Atlantic Ocean to avoid Spanish shipping and naval vessels. Being French and within his claimed territorial sphere was sufficient reason to raise Philip's ire; being French and Protestant guaranteed the Spanish monarch would not rest until he had expunged this settlement from what he saw as his patrimony.[18]

Attempts by French Huguenots to challenge Spain in Brazil and Florida, however, did not end in success. Despite encouragement from the French monarchy, which hoped to export its own troubles into Spanish terrain, the limited resources of these expeditions, as well as tactical mistakes by their leaders, prevented the establishment of enduring Protestant enclaves.[19] Catherine de' Medici, widow of King Henry II, and queen regent of France, hoped to pursue a policy of de facto toleration of Calvinism in France, despite the protests of Catholics, and supported the scheme of Admiral Coligny. She similarly embraced the idea of French colonies as a source for raw materials, markets, and military strength against France's rivals.[20] Because of French failures to keep their expeditions secret, as early as 1563, Philip II was aware of their plans to dispatch ships from Normandy to the region. Although his orders to Havana to scout possible sites accomplished little in 1563 and 1564, Spanish forces were now alert to an incursion by French Protestants, an intolerable affront to Philip II's empire and faith.[21]

The French landings in Florida went badly almost from the start. Their expeditions were prepared for the voyage and landing, but not to be self-sustaining. Indeed, although the initial contacts with indigenous tribes were positive, the French reliance on native populations for food soon became a serious handicap. Unwilling or unable to grow their own crops, harvest the abundant fish offshore, or otherwise provide their own sustenance, the French relied on charity from the Indians and limited trade. As one historian noted, "too many Frenchmen played while supplies of food brought from France dwindled away."[22] With decreasing Indian interest in the limited trade goods the French brought, the colony began to face hunger and disease. By summer 1565, the French at Fort Caroline were in a desperate situation, with only temporary relief by the handful of resupply or trade ships that arrived.[23]

The conflict between Spanish Catholics and French Protestants in Florida culminated in September and October 1565. An attack on Saint Augustine was frustrated by the inability of the French to land safely, as well as the arrival of an unexpected hurricane, which forced the small French fleet to sea. During a brief confrontation at sea, as the small rival navies maneuvered and skirmished, the Spanish promised the French "to hang and behead all the Lutherans ... on this land and sea" highlighting the stakes involved.[24] As the French sailed away to avoid an incoming hurricane, St. Augustine was saved. Taking advantage of tactical surprise, the Spanish immediately set out overland, during tropical storm winds, to attack Fort Caroline. In his comments before leading his forces north, Pedro Menéndez exhorted the Spaniards in terms that reflected Philip II's apocalyptic dialectic.

> For this reason our war with them – and theirs with us – has to be one of blood and fire, since they as Lutherans seek us Catholics to prevent us from spreading the Holy Gospel in these provinces, and we seek them for being Lutherans, to prevent them from spreading their harmful and hateful sect in this land and teaching it to the Indians.[25]

With only limited defenses, and the bulk of their force still at sea, the French were defeated, with Fort Caroline overrun on 20 September.[26] The Spanish commander, Pedro Menéndez de Avilés, followed up this victory by rounding up the remaining French, most shipwrecked by the hurricane, and executing all who were not loyal Catholics. In various operations after the fall of Fort Caroline, Menéndez ordered the deaths of more than 300 French Protestants, an act in what was seen by both sides as a war for survival.[27] Pleadings by the French that their two nations were at peace and that they were fellow Christians did nothing to appeal to Menéndez.[28] At the request of Father Francisco López, the Spanish chaplain, Menéndez did allow the priest to question the French to determine if any were Catholic. Of the approximately 125 prisoners, about a dozen were able to prove themselves sufficiently Catholic, through recitations of prayers, descriptions of religious practices in their parishes, and the attestations of others in their company accepted by the Spanish as sufficiently devout: the remaining French captives "died for being Lutherans and against our Holy Catholic Faith."[29]

The Spanish leader justified these killings as justice for declared heretics, imposing on them the same punishment they would have earned had they been shipwrecked in Spain and come before a tribunal of the Inquisition. Given his modest forces, he would have been unable to secure and sustain large numbers of prisoners, but in any event Menéndez reported on his actions to Philip II with no remorse or regret; the mere presence of Protestants in the New World posed the same existential threat to Spanish Catholicism as those in Europe.[30] Among the Spanish were fears that the French would, if allowed to live, attempt to foment slave rebellions in Cuba and other Spanish colonies among the increasing numbers of Africans imported as manual labor.[31]

Wherever the king encountered them, Protestants were to receive no mercy, no pardon, and no quarter from secular or religious authorities. As Philip II noted in a letter to Menéndez, "we believe that you have done this (the summary executions) with full justification and prudence and hold ourselves well-served thereby."[32] There were also practical considerations; considering the precarious food situation endured by both French and Spaniards, adding dozens of additional mouths to feed would have spread the threat of starvation even wider among the colony had these French prisoners lived. There would also have been the challenge of guarding these prisoners, or implementing some form of work parole, either of which approaches would have posed risks to the Spanish colony.[33] Menéndez himself noted that the St. Augustine colony was "suffering much hunger," pleading for the dispatch of additional supplies in order to be prepared to face additional threats from "the odious Lutheran doctrine."[34] Indeed, given what Menéndez had seen of the king's actions elsewhere, any tolerance for a continued presence of French Protestants in the Americas, whether captive or free, would have been disobedient to Philip II's vision and mandate.[35]

Back in France, the failures in Florida did little to help promote positive relations between Catholics and Huguenots. The French government did not send additional forces to continue the struggle in Florida, not wanting to endorse what had been a primarily Huguenot enterprise.[36] Coligny himself became a key leader in the next round of religious civil war, erupting in 1567. His own assassination in 1572 was the spark that launched the St. Bartholomew's Day Massacre, a pre-emptive attack that killed thousands of Huguenots on the night of August 23–24 of that year. There are some suspicions that the murder of Admiral Coligny came at the initiative of Philip II; certainly this would be consistent with his enmity toward French Protestantism, and fitting retaliation for the man who nearly caused the loss of Florida to the Spanish Empire.[37] Regardless of Philip's involvement, or those of other Spanish representatives, the French Civil War between Catholics and Huguenots threatened Philip's rule. Not only were French Protestant exiles fleeing to the Low Countries and southern France going over to Calvinism, there was fear that Huguenots would come across the Catalan border, into Spain's colonies, or into other Habsburg territories, magnifying the task of the Spanish Inquisition. Protestants worried that Spain and the papacy would ally with French Catholics for a final assault on Protestantism, with the St. Bartholomew's Day Massacre in France in 1572 leading to rumors of this becoming widespread.[38]

The most proximate threat to Spain was just to its north, in the kingdom of Navarre. Upper Navarre had come under Spanish control in 1494, with the formal acquisition by Castile of this region in 1515. Lower Navarre, centered around Saint-Jean-Pied-de-Port, and including the adjacent principality of Béarn, retained its independence until its monarch, Henry IV, became king of France in 1589. Henry IV, who converted from Calvinism to Catholicism to bring peace to France, would grant limited religious liberty to Huguenots, through the Edict of Nantes in 1598.[39] During the mid-sixteenth century, many Navarrese converted to Calvinism; none more prominent than Jeanne d'Albret, Queen of Navarre, who on Christmas Day 1560 embraced the new faith.[40] This declaration, although likely confirmation of a decision she took years previously, was a direct challenge to both the French and Spanish monarchies, given the small kingdom's long-standing territorial claims against both Habsburg and Valois dynasties.[41] Couching her conversion in terms of a mother's duty to her children, to France, and to God, her published letters and memoirs were a challenge to Catholic monarchy in France, and indeed throughout Europe.[42]

Jeanne's mother, Queen Marguerite of Navarre, sister to French king Francis I, had never declared herself to be Protestant, but during her time as a leading member of the royal court, she had protected Reformers, attempted to mediate between Catholic and Huguenot factions within the kingdom, and wrote Reform-influenced letters, prose and poetry.[43] Marguerite's writing supported humanism, criticized corruption within the Catholic Church, and called out abuse of women by priests, often through a mystical or allegorical method. Even though much of her writing was not published until after her death, her intervention saved the lives of humanists and Reformers, such as Jacques Lefevre, translator of the New Testament into French. Erasmus, noting her writing and her support for humanism, wrote to her twice, in 1525 and 1527, although apparently without a response.[44]

Her moderation drew criticism from Catholic and Protestant leaders alike, including from John Calvin, who preferred that she choose a theological side. However, Navarre's queen hoped to support a united French kingdom, rather than endorse one faction in what seemed an increasingly contentious milieu.[45] Her daughter maintained no such intention, openly affiliating with the Protestant cause. As niece of Francis I, and sole heir to Navarre, Jeanne would become the most powerful and important Protestant woman in France.[46] Indeed, it would be Queen Jeanne d'Albret's dynasty, the Bourbon, that would reign over France after 1589, although perhaps not in the way she would have preferred.[47] As queen, she offered refuge to Protestants, ordered the New Testament translated into Basque, launched a campaign to expunge Catholicism from her kingdom, and gave aid to Huguenot conspiracies in France.[48]

As a young girl, Jeanne had already showed the determination that she would demonstrate on behalf of the Reformation, refusing in 1540 to consent to a marriage to Duke Wilhelm of Cleves, a Protestant who was twice her age (24 versus 12). Realizing that the marriage would infuriate Philip II, who would not abide a German Lutheran reigning in Navarre, and supporting her daughter's loathing of her proposed groom, Marguerite attempted to persuade her brother to cancel the proposed union. King Francis I rejected this plea, ignoring two written protests from Jeanne herself, who in 1541 had to be physically dragged down the aisle at her own wedding. Her refusal continued after the ceremony, with her and her mother's insistence that she had not yet menstruated buying time against consummation of the marriage; by 1545, with Francis I now focused on war in Italy, and Wilhelm having declared a renewed Catholic faith and obedience to Charles V, Pope Paul III granted the annulment for which Jeanne had been pleading since the ceremony, citing the lack of marital consummation as well as the violence used to force the bride to wed as justifications.[49]

After Jeanne rejected a particularly audacious proposal by Philip II that she should marry one of his sons or other male relatives, Spain's king took every opportunity to wage war against Navarre's territories and the queen's allies. It is not clear whether the Spanish had any expectation of this idea being taken seriously, since acceptance would mean Jeanne adopting both the Catholic faith and rule from Madrid, but it certainly was consistent with common monarchical practice to use marriage to mitigate strategic threats, as well as the rejection of these offers as a justification for military campaigns to redress the affront.[50] In this, Philip was also carrying forward the policies of his grandfather, Ferdinand of Aragon, who had seized a large portion of Navarre as part of a dynastic dispute in 1512, an argument that preceded the Reformation.[51]

Philip II was "a particularly dangerous enemy" to Jeanne, and presumably the Spanish king felt similarly toward her, given their shared border, her moral support for her coreligionists rebelling against Spain in the Netherlands, and the grievance she held at the lands taken from her family by Spain earlier in the century. The mutual enmity could have been as great as it was out of a sense of mutual betrayal; Jeanne's husband King Antoine had in the 1550s offered secretly to support Charles V and Philip II in their wars against France, in exchange for the restoration of Spanish Navarre to him, or even for the throne of France. Philip II offered to Antoine the restoration of all Navarre to his throne, divorce from Jeanne (with dispensation from the Pope), and marriage to Mary Stuart of Scotland, if he would renounce Reform and purge it from his kingdom. He accepted the offer but died in 1562 before he could act on it. Philip II then asked for authorization from the Pope to dethrone Jeanne as a heretic and seize her lands. Although by the end of the decade Jeanne was estranged from her husband, and in 1559 Spain and France had made peace, Jeanne's embrace of Protestantism seemed even more of an affront to the Habsburgs, coming as it did from an erstwhile ally.[52]

Navarre had in the 1550s become known as a safe place for Calvinist ideas; King Antoine and Queen Jeanne, although they had not openly embraced the Reformation, and continued to attend Mass, ended prosecutions based on heresy, and welcomed Calvinist pastors sent from Geneva to teach and preach. As early as 1557, disappointed by his failed conspiracies with Spain, Antoine declared his affiliation with Reform. Jeanne followed him reluctantly, joining him publicly in the faith in 1560.[53] This was unwelcome news south of the Pyrenees; King Philip II, for his part, urged Pope Pius IV to excommunicate the royals, and plotted for her overthrow or assassination.[54] By 1561, however, Antoine had begun to vacillate, with his ambitions to rule all of France at odds with his conversion to Calvinism. In 1562, he returned to Catholicism, attempting unsuccessfully to bring along his wife, and to leverage his restored fidelity to the papacy to gain support in the French court, as well as from Spain, for him to assume the throne.[55] At the death of Antoine in November 1562, Jeanne became sole monarch of Navarre, accelerating her identification with Calvinism. Praised for her faith by both John Calvin and Queen Elizabeth of England, the Navarrese queen was nonetheless vulnerable, given her kingdom's location between the two most powerful European states, both led by ardent Catholic monarchs, and open attempts by Spain to hoist a pro-Spanish candidate, such as Antoine, onto the throne.[56]

For the next six years, she remained focused on her small kingdom, remaining neutral during the religious civil war between Huguenots and Catholics that ravaged France. Vulnerable to both Spain and Catholic France in her lands, she attempted a middle course – embracing Calvinism and supporting its spread among her people, while remaining carefully apart from committing her modest resources to war. From 1562 to 1568, Protestantism grew among her people, not only due to conversion, but through the arrival of refugees from France, fleeing from Huguenot defeats to one of the few places where there was protection.[57] Jeanne continued her husband's policy of negotiating with Philip II, hoping to avoid Habsburg entanglements, rather than embrace them. In 1563, soon after the death of Antoine, Spain's king proposed that Jeanne should marry a Habsburg, perhaps even his son, Don Carlos. This would have been a disastrous marriage for Jeanne. Not only would she have been forced to abandon her faith, but she would also have lost her authority as a sovereign queen, and likely Navarre would have been absorbed in the Habsburg empire, surrendering its independence. She could not directly reject Philip's suggestion that she marry a Habsburg, since to defy him could mean invasion, but her attempts to defer the discussion could only delay the reckoning.[58] Philip's ambassador to Jeanne, Don Juan Martinez Descurra, grew increasingly frustrated with her delays and demurs. In July 1563, he threatened that if she continued to promote Protestantism within her domain and to refuse Spanish marriage entreaties, "within a month you will lose all your possessions ... the house of Navarre and Foix will disappear."[59]

Similar threats came from Pope Pius IV, who was alarmed by the rise of Huguenots to such influence in France and Navarre. Through French Cardinal d'Armagnac, the papacy sent a stern admonishment to the queen, hinting at great unpleasantness for her and her kingdom should she continue to embrace Calvinism. Predicting a rebellion among her subjects, the cardinal reminded Queen Jeanne that "the King of Spain will not tolerate [heretics] as neighbors," and that her kingdom did not possess the defense of the English Channel that allowed Queen Elizabeth to defy Philip II and the Roman Catholic Church. Infuriated by these messages, she responded immediately, expressing her defiance over her faith, expressing full confidence in the love of her people, and refusing to yield to the explicit and implicit threats on behalf of the Pope and Philip II.[60] She also ordered the intensification of military preparations against a possible Spanish invasion. Fortunately, Philip's concern for military commitments elsewhere prevented his mounting of a war in the Pyrenees.[61]

In September 1563, Pope Pius IV condemned Jeanne as a heretic, excommunicated her, and demanded she appear before the Roman Inquisition. This decree gained Jeanne sympathy even among Catholics in France, who rejected the idea of the Vatican attempting to judge a French sovereign, even one mistaken in her beliefs. France at that time was also in a brief interlude of peace between Catholics and Huguenots, following the policies of queen regent Catherine de' Medici. At this affront, France expelled the papal envoy, and by the end of 1563 had made clear that Jeanne would not be sent to Rome.[62] Jeanne took advantage of her relative security to intensify the conversion of her kingdom to Calvinism, prohibiting Catholic practices, including processions and displays of statues, icons, and other religious art. She carried austere Calvinism into civil life, also banning card games, dancing, and prostitution. She expelled Catholic religious orders and ordered the destruction of altars, images and statues, and other objects of veneration, enraging the Catholic population. An uprising, encouraged by the Jesuits, began in 1567. The rebels hoped to ask for help from Philip II, but he was fully committed to counterinsurgency in the Netherlands. Requests for help from King Charles IX of France arrived too late; Jeanne repressed the uprising.[63] With the Pope's excommunication and proposed trial of Jeanne a failure, Philip initiated a plan to kidnap her and expatriate her across the border for trial by the Spanish Inquisition. While this initiative also failed, due to

Jeanne's temporary move to the French court in 1564, and reliance on a loyal bodyguard of more than 300 cavalry, she remained on the alert for threats to her personal security.[64] Despite her location along Spain's northern border, and her active measures in support of Protestantism, surprisingly there seemed little direct impact in Philip II's domains; few Protestants brought before the tribunals of the Spanish Inquisition of Aragon, whether of French origin or Spanish converts to these beliefs, could be traced back to the queen's realm. Whether this came from a deliberate policy to avoid provoking Philip II, or because if anything Protestants would be migrating to Navarre, rather than away from it, is unclear.[65] While there were occasional rumors of an alliance between Huguenots and *Moriscos*, potentially also incorporating landings of Ottomans forces, a direct threat to Aragon, this proved to be an unfounded concern.[66]

Another round of France's religious civil wars broke out in 1568. Although Jeanne hoped to remain neutral, realizing that her realm was vulnerable and her subjects divided between Calvinism and Catholicism, this proved the most serious challenge to her rule. With Philip II and Pope Pius V, who had taken office in 1566, encouraging a hard line by French Catholics, even offering funds toward this end, the campaign against Huguenots became especially hard fought.[67] Pius V refused to embrace the indifferent approach toward French Calvinism of some in the Catholic Church, showing his seriousness of purpose by excommunicating eight French bishops who had become too close to heretics. With this new support from the papacy, Philip began to hint at intervention against the Protestants along his border.[68]

Indeed, threats from Spain convinced Jeanne to flee Navarre in 1568 and seek refuge in the coastal Huguenot stronghold of La Rochelle. Her forces in the Pyrenees continued to fight, however, receiving support from Huguenots elsewhere, as well as from Queen Elizabeth. With Jeanne's move to La Rochelle, however, she effectively surrendered direct control over her domains along the Spanish frontier, and became far less of a concern to Philip II, despite her efforts to elicit more active support from Elizabeth of England. From the fortress city of La Rochelle, Jeanne served as one of the key supporters of Reformism in France through its religious civil wars, raising funds, writing exhortations to her fellow Huguenots, and attempting to correspond with allies in England, the Low Countries and elsewhere. Although she was no longer effectively sovereign over her own lands, until her death in 1572 she served as the de facto "Queen of Huguenot France" in their struggle against Catholic France.[69]

Other areas of the Habsburg Empire were just as concerning as the threat from France. Both Luther and Calvin had their spiritual followers in Italy, for example, with fears of Protestantism stimulating a resurgence of Inquisitorial activity in the 1550s and 1560s, and campaigns against reformist theology taking shape into the seventeenth century. Although Italian Protestantism never grow to the scale of French Calvinism or Lutheranism in the Holy Roman Empire, the persistence of its clandestine books, pamphlets, and active exile movements, especially in Calvinist Geneva, kept Italy "an open question" in terms of its final religious resolution for many decades.[70] Although most Protestant cells in the Italian states were in central or northern Italy, with Rome and Venice most notable along these lines, Spain's territories in the south were certainly within reach of this potential religious message.

Accelerating the existential threat posed by the rise of Protestantism was the fear that these new religious movements would unite with the Ottoman Empire, posing a double threat to Catholicism throughout Europe and the Mediterranean. In addition to central Europe, where in Hungary Ottoman and Habsburg leaders vied for influence, Sicily was also a major concern, given the island's vulnerability to Ottoman naval forces and corsairs from North Africa. The arrival of a few English Protestants in Sicily during the 1560s and 1570s gave fuel to this worry, even though most of them arrived following shipwrecks of their commercial vessels, or were captured after naval battles, rather than auguring organized landings of Protestants carried on Muslim warships to assault Catholic Sicily. The Spanish Inquisition's tribunal in Sicily was prepared to dispense with these heretics, with unfavorable results for these unlucky British mariners.[71]

Indeed, Martin Luther spoke favorably of a coalition with the sultan, seeing even the threat of an Islamic incursion as enough to keep Europe's Catholic monarchs set back on their heels. Some Ottoman leaders were intrigued by the idea of promoting dissent within Christendom, and there were examples of court officials and governors aiding Protestant rebels along Habsburg borderlands. Other than a few minor incidents, there was never a strategic decision in Istanbul to provide direct support to Lutheran or Calvinist rebels. The more significant impact that the Ottoman Empire had was in pressuring the Habsburgs to find an accommodation with the Lutheran princes within the Holy Roman Empire, given the needs of first Charles V then Ferdinand I as Holy Roman Emperors to maintain their titles and authority in central Europe.[72]

Spain continued to face threats from the Ottoman Empire and its allies to the south and east, with corsair attacks on Spanish shipping to Italy and the Mediterranean a constant concern. There were even raids as far west as Gibraltar and Granada, involving hit and run attacks, and even kidnapping of Christians for use as galley slaves, from the 1540s to the 1580s. Some of these attacks involved former Muslim subjects of Spain, expelled for refusing to convert to Catholicism, and now returning to punish the lands where they were no longer welcome. For Charles V and Philip II, the war against Islam never ended, despite the victory of the *Reconquista*; there were pauses, shifts in the front lines, with the understanding that the next cataclysmic battle would come at any time.[73]

A full-scale revolt by *Moriscos* against Spanish rule erupted in 1568 in Andalucía and Granada, with approximately 30,000 Muslim and former Muslim subjects (denouncing their forced conversions) revolting against the religious constraints and persecutions they faced. They did not fight alone; in their struggle they were aided by an armed force of 4,000 Turks and Berbers from the Ottoman Empire and Islamic states of North Africa that had infiltrated Spanish shores to support their coreligionists. Although Philip was able to crush the rebellion by 1570, it was a powerful illustration that the war with Islam was not just something far away, but always a threat, with Spain continually on the defensive in the Mediterranean against the Ottoman Empire and its allies.[74]

Charles V, despite his resources, geographic advantages, and military strength, was simply unable to wage war successfully and simultaneously against the French, the Ottomans, and the Protestant princes within the Holy Roman Empire and surrounding states. In 1555, he reluctantly agreed to the Peace of Augsburg, which granted to each state within the empire the right for its prince to choose the state's religion. Many of the Lutheran princes were just as ardently against the Ottomans as Charles, so this agreement, as heartbreaking as it was to the emperor and to all Catholic Christendom, was a necessary step in the direction of religious toleration within Europe. Although the agreement was denounced by Pope Paul III, absent a victory over France or the collapse of Ottoman power, there were few other options for Charles, short of continued warfare at a time when his resources, armies, and finances were at breaking point.[75]

The Treaty of Augsburg between the emperor and the Lutheran Schmalkaldic League was not a declaration of religious tolerance; princes and kings were free to persecute religionists of other sects within their realms. Even so, it was an attempt to end constant warfare between Catholics and Lutherans at a moment when many realized an absolute victory over their theological opponents was no longer possible, at least not within the Holy Roman Empire. The peace did not extend beyond imperial boundaries, so war continued throughout Europe between Catholics and Protestants, as well as between coreligionists.[76] Although Charles V viewed the treaty as a personal failure, since his goal remained the reincorporation of all Christians under the aegis of the Roman Catholic Church, the agreement was consistent with his aim for a peaceful reconciliation and end to religious warfare within Europe. The treaty also foreshadowed the more permanent settlement of the Treaty of Westphalia in 1648, which would put in place sovereign rights, religious autonomy for each state, and mutual diplomatic recognition across confessional boundaries.[77]

With cooperation between the English and Empire, and uncertainties in relation to Italy and the Papal States, in 1525–1526, King Francis began to consider a diplomatic move that would seem unthinkable: an alliance of Catholic France with the Muslim Ottoman Empire. Although this would be a betrayal of Christendom, it was arguably an idea that could revive French power at a critical time. The Ottomans, after all, were threats to both Spain in the Mediterranean and the Holy Roman Empire in south-eastern Europe. The potential for their forces to launch attacks in either direction, in coordination with the French, reduced the likelihood of a full assault on the Valois. Although Francis could argue that he initiated the alliance with the Ottomans to protect Christians in the East, it was clear that the main goal of this arrangement was to threaten Charles V. The Ottomans agreed, happy to see Catholic Europe divided, as this would enable a greater focus on campaigning in south-eastern Europe against Hungary and the lands of Charles V. In his own words, Francis noted his goal "to undermine the emperor's power, to force heavy expenses on him and to reassure all other governments against so powerful an enemy."[78] Gone were the 1540s, when for a brief period it seemed as if Francis and Charles might unite Catholic Europe, with the enthusiastic support of Pope Paul III, against the dual threats of Protestantism and Islam.[79]

Indeed, the French alliance emboldened the Ottomans to launch a major ground campaign against Hungary, seizing most of the country, and nearly taking Vienna in 1529. Although intending to hit the emperor, the French had instead mortally wounded Catholic Hungary.[80] The French and Ottoman Empire formalized a broad-based alliance in 1536, including a commercial treaty, coordination of military operations against the Habsburgs and, most astonishingly, plans to station Ottoman naval forces in Marseilles, the largest French port in the Mediterranean. Islam had arrived in Western Europe again, less than a century after its expulsion in the *Reconquista*, but this time at the express invitation of a Catholic sovereign.[81] Although French and Ottoman forces rarely engaged in joint operations – the 1543 attack on and looting of Nice, allied to the Holy Roman Empire, being an exception – their alliance served as a counterweight to Charles V and his dream of uniting Christendom under his leadership.[82]

While Francis accommodated to Islam, at least concerning Ottoman naval forces and diplomats in France, he was not so gracious with Protestants on French territory. In 1540, he declared those embracing this new faith as guilty of "high treason against God and mankind," authorizing the persecution of Calvinists, Waldensians, Lutherans, and other new branches of Christianity. At least under his rule, there would be no tolerance for the Protestant Reformation; loyalty to the monarchy would only be accepted by those who continued to be similarly loyal to the Catholic Church. His efforts did not succeed in defeating Calvinism in France, however; for the rest of the century there would be too many Huguenots for Catholics to defeat, but not enough to achieve the conversion of France to the ranks of Protestant states.[83]

As many historians have noted, one of the goals of Columbus, and his royal sponsors, was to form an alliance with powerful states in Asia in order to fight against the Ottoman Empire. Indeed, the drive west across the Atlantic was launched because of the inability to go east through the Mediterranean.[84] A brief period of Habsburg–Ottoman peace in the late 1540s, ratified in the 1547 Treaty of Adrianople, did not negate the long-term rivalry. Even though the Holy Roman Empire and the Ottomans periodically renewed this truce, fighting continued between Christians and Muslims throughout south-eastern Europe and the Mediterranean for decades. These maritime conflicts were encouraged by both the French, who sided with the

Ottomans, and Protestant princes, who hoped to see Catholics and Muslims weakened in the struggle.[85]

With Philip II's attentions focused on England, France, the Low Countries, and the global threat of the Protestant Reformation, the long-held Habsburg family mission to wage war against Islam had been delayed. With the French in alliance with the Ottomans, the risk of venturing east across the Mediterranean to reclaim formerly Christian lands or even the Holy Land was even more daunting. Indeed, the results of Spanish inattention to the Ottoman Empire and its Muslim allies throughout the Mediterranean were clear by the 1560s: what had been a string of fortresses and Christian-held cities in North Africa was reduced to Oran and a few small littoral outposts. Indeed, the Ottoman Empire seemed poised to attack not only these territories, but the strategically vital and Christian-held islands of Cyprus and Malta, the latter a Habsburg ally.[86]

After a decisive Catholic naval defeat in 1560 at the battle of Djerba, near Tunis, Philip turned his redoubled efforts to the Mediterranean in an effort to forestall additional Ottoman triumphs or opportunities for their Muslim North African allies in Algiers, Tunis, and Tripoli. The most immediate threat came to the island of Malta, the target of an Ottoman assault in 1565. Spanish forces buttressed the Knights of St. John on the island, a heavily fortified Christian enclave in the central Mediterranean. The knights, with Spanish support, conducted a successful defense of the island against a determined Turkish assault.[87]

After the Venetians lost their island territory of Cyprus in 1571, Spain led a naval counterattack two months later, to pre-empt additional victories by the combined Ottoman navy and army. Philip II's half-brother Don Juan of Austria rallied Christian forces, including Venice, the Papal States, and the Knights of St. John, in a coalition known as the Holy League, which was blessed and endorsed by Pope Pius V. This naval force inflicted a crushing blow against the Ottomans at the sea battle of Lepanto off the coast of Greece, fought in October 1571. This apocalyptic sea battle saw more than 200 war galleys on each side, a battle of cannons, boarding parties, and tens of thousands of Catholic and Muslim sailors and soldiers. Allied with the Knights of Malta, the Papal States, the Venetian Republic, and other Catholic allies, the Spanish defeated the Ottoman navy and their North African allies.[88]

Although the Ottomans would rebuild their navy in subsequent years, and divisions on the Catholic side prevented follow-through to reclaim Cyprus or other territories lost to Islam, the battle did prevent additional territorial losses by Christian states. As had been the case with Emperor Charles V, the victories of King Philip II against Islam concerned his erstwhile allies; even Pope Pius V, who had encouraged a European-wide crusade against Islam, balked at suggestions for a long-term campaign after Lepanto. As with previous Popes, he wanted Christianity to reclaim territory from Islam, including the lost cities of Constantinople and Jerusalem, but was leery of encouraging too great victories by the Habsburgs. A crusade led by papal forces to liberate Jerusalem was an outcome that might be welcomed by all Christendom. A Spaniard able to claim the throne of the Holy Land might be less desirable; one can imagine Paris and London being less than enthusiastic at this potential millenarian turn of events.[89]

Philip was also concerned, as had been his father, about risking his fleet in additional major campaigns; one defeat could fracture the fragile alliances between Catholic powers, as well as reverse years of build-up. This in turn could force Spain into a massive diversion of resources to naval reinforcements, when funds and personnel were always desperately short for campaigns in the Low Countries, Italy, and against France. Although Habsburg ships were generally of better quality than those of the Ottomans, the Turks tended not only to have more naval vessels, but greater potential to recover and rebuild after losses, as happened after Lepanto. This hesitation in pursuing the Ottomans was somewhat ironic, given the ships and treasure Philip would devote in the next decade to the Armada, but then again that climactic battle against England would only take place after he also became king of Portugal, adding Portuguese ships, sailors, and treasure to his naval potential, "an immediate and stupendous expansion of Spanish power."[90]

The result of this decade of conflict was an impasse in the Mediterranean. The Venetians made peace with the Ottomans, rather than suffer ongoing commercial losses and the cost of war. For his part, Philip II by 1580 had by necessity turned his attentions to the ongoing Dutch Calvinist rebellion in the Low Countries. In that year, he had also gained the crown of Portugal, adding the Portuguese empire to his possessions – but also responsibilities for the defense of these far-flung realms.[91] Even more critically, he focused his enmity on the threat of a Protestant power – England – which he equated with heresy and defiance of the Catholic Church.

Notes

1 Tracy, *Emperor Charles V, Impresario of War*, 306.
2 John McGrath, *The French in Early Florida: In the Eye of the Hurricane* (Gainesville: University Press of Florida, 2000), 9.
3 Lynch, *Spain 1516-1598*, 297.
4 Lynn, *Between Court and Confessional*, 97.
5 Kagan and Dyer, eds., *Inquisitorial Inquiries*, 15, 55.
6 Lynch, *Spain 1516-1598*, 298–300.
7 Kagan and Dyer, eds., *Inquisitorial Inquiries*, 36–63.
8 Lynch, *Spain 1516-1598*, 297–298.
9 Jean Ribaut, *The Whole & True Discouerye of Terra Florida* (1563) A Facsim. Reproduction with introd. by David L. Dowd (Gainesville: University of Florida Press, 1964), 6–9.
10 Gonzalo Solís de Merás, *Pedro Menéndez de Avilés and the Conquest of Florida: A New Manuscript* [La Conquista de la Florida por el Adelantado Pedro Meléndez de Valdés]. Translated and edited by David Arbesú (Gainesville: University Press of Florida, 2017), 36, 211.

11 Lynch, *Spain 1516-1598*, 297–298, 414.
12 Paul E. Hoffman, *The Spanish Crown and the Defense of the Caribbean, 1535-1585* (Baton Rouge: Louisiana State University Press, 1980), 15.
13 Hoffman, *The Spanish Crown and the Defense of the Caribbean*, 218.
14 René Laudonnière, *Three Voyages*. Edited and translated by Charles Bennett (Gainesville: University Presses of Florida, 1975), xv–xvi.
15 Solís de Merás, *La Conquista de la Florida*, 38, 212.
16 McGrath, *The French in Early Florida*, 63–65, 169.
17 Mikhail, *God's Shadow*, 388–389.
18 McGrath, *The French in Early Florida*, 75–79. Maltby, *The Black Legend in England*, 68.
19 MacCulloch, *The Reformation*, 516.
20 Charles E. Bennett, *Laudonnière and Fort Caroline: History and Documents* (Tuscaloosa: University of Alabama Press, 2001), 5–6, 13.
21 McGrath, *The French in Early Florida*, 94–95. Bennett, *Laudonnière and Fort Caroline*, 34.
22 Bennett, *Laudonnière and Fort Caroline*, 21.
23 McGrath, *The French in Early Florida*, 106–109.
24 Solís de Merás, *La Conquista de la Florida*, 46, 120.
25 Solís de Merás, *La Conquista de la Florida*, 49, 223.
26 Bennett, *Laudonnière and Fort Caroline*, 37–38.
27 McGrath, *The French in Early Florida*, 146–154.
28 Ribaut, *The Whole & True Discouerye of Terra Florida*, 26–30.
29 Father Francisco López de Mendoza, "Memoire of the Happy Result and Prosperous Voyage of the Fleet Commanded by the Adelantado Pedro Menéndez de Avilés," 1565, in Bennett, *Laudonnière and Fort Caroline*, 163.
30 McGrath, *The French in Early Florida*, 152–155.
31 Bennett, *Laudonnière and Fort Caroline*, 43.
32 McGrath, *The French in Early Florida*, 159–160.
33 Ribaut, *The Whole & True Discouerye of Terra Florida*, 33.
34 Letter, Pedro Menéndez de Avilés, to Philip II, 15 October 1565; "The Capture of Fort Caroline," in Bennett, *Laudonnière and Fort Caroline*, 133, 139.
35 Bartolomé Barrientos, *Pedro Menéndez de Avilés: Founder of Florida*. Translated and edited by Anthony Kerrigan (Gainesville: University of Florida Press, 1965), 69.
36 Roelker, *Queen of Navarre*, 235–236.
37 McGrath, *The French in Early Florida*, 166–167. Olaizola, *Historia del Protestantismo en el País Vasco*, 163.
38 McDermott, *England and the Spanish Armada*, 54, 89–90.
39 Olaizola, *Historia del Protestantismo en el País Vasco*, 239–245.
40 Jeanne D'Albret, Queen of Navarre, *Letters from the Queen of Navarre with an Ample Declaration*. Edited By Kathleen Llewellyn, Emily E. Thompson, and Colette H. Winn (Toronto: Iter Academic Press, 2016), 3.
41 MacCulloch, *The Reformation*, 260.
42 Broomhall, *Women and Religion in Sixteenth Century France*, 119–121.
43 Juan María de Olaizola, *Historia del Protestantismo en el País Vasco; el Reino de Navarra en la encrucijada de su historia* (Pamplona, Spain: Pamiela, 1993), 100–105.
44 Olaizola, *Historia del Protestantismo en el País Vasco*, 106.
45 Kirsi Stjerna, *Women and the Reformation* (Oxford: Blackwell Publishing 2009), 151–157.
46 Stjerna, *Women and the Reformation*, 158–159.
47 MacCulloch, *The Reformation*, 292.
48 Olaizola, *Historia del Protestantismo en el País Vasco*, 126. McCullouch, *The Reformation*, 292–293.

49 Stjerna, *Women and the Reformation*, 161–162.
50 Stjerna, *Women and the Reformation*, 168.
51 Nancy Lyman Roelker, *Queen of Navarre: Jeanne d'Albret, 1528-1572* (Cambridge: Harvard University Press, 1968), 5.
52 D'Albret, *Letters from the Queen of Navarre*, 8. Roelker, *Queen of Navarre*, 114–119. Olaizola, *Historia del Protestantismo en el País Vasco*, 124.
53 Roelker, *Queen of Navarre*, 123–124. Olaizola, *Historia del Protestantismo en el País Vasco*, 121–122.
54 D'Albret, *Letters from the Queen of Navarre*, 8; Letter "To the King," Jeanne to King Charles IX, 16 September 1568, 41; "Ample Declaration," 1568, 63; Stjerna, *Women and the Reformation*, 168.
55 Roelker, *Queen of Navarre*, 174–185.
56 Roelker, *Queen of Navarre*, 153–154, 188.
57 Roelker, *Queen of Navarre*, 188–207.
58 Roelker, *Queen of Navarre*, 213–214.
59 Roelker, *Queen of Navarre*, 216.
60 Roelker, *Queen of Navarre*, 218.
61 Olaizola, *Historia del Protestantismo en el País Vasco*, 132.
62 Roelker, *Queen of Navarre*, 221–222. Olaizola, *Historia del Protestantismo en el País Vasco*, 119, 131–132.
63 Olaizola, *Historia del Protestantismo en el País Vasco*, 130, 134–137, 143.
64 Roelker, *Queen of Navarre*, 222–223, 229–230.
65 Monter, *Frontiers of Heresy*, 84–85.
66 Monter, *Frontiers of Heresy*, 89–92.
67 Roelker, *Queen of Navarre*, 291–292.
68 Mullett, *The Catholic Reformation*, 112–113.
69 D'Albret, *Letters from the Queen of Navarre*, 12–13. Broomhall, *Women and Religion in Sixteenth Century France*, 126; Stjerna, *Women and the Reformation*, 170–173. Roelker, *Queen of Navarre*, 300–308, 311–314. Olaizola, *Historia del Protestantismo en el País Vasco*, 140–160.
70 Simone Maghenzani, "The Protestant Reformation in Counter-Reformation Italy, 1550-1660: An Overview of New Evidence," *Church History*, September 2014, Vol. 83, No.3, 588.
71 Lynn, *Between Court and Confessional*, 149–150, 153.
72 Gábor Ágoston, "The Last Muslim Conquest: The Ottoman Empire and Its Wars in Europe," Zoom, Department of History and the Committee for Early Modern Studies, Penn State University, 8 October 2021.
73 Lynch, *Spain 1516-1598*, 304–310.
74 Lynch, *Spain 1516-1598*, 314–322.
75 Norwich, *Four Princes*, 189.
76 Boehmer, Wiffen, and Wiffen, *Bibliotheca Wiffeniana*, Vol. II, 62.
77 Fernández Álvarez, *España del Emperador Carlos V*, Vol. XX, 871.
78 Norwich, *Four Princes*, 88–89.
79 Fernández Álvarez, *España del Emperador Carlos V*, Vol, XX, 677–678.
80 Norwich, *Four Princes*, 93, 106–108.
81 Norwich, *Four Princes*, 146–147, 151.
82 Norwich, *Four Princes*, 176–178.
83 Norwich, *Four Princes*, 165–166.
84 Mikhail, *God's Shadow*, 386–387, 396.
85 Ágoston, *The Last Muslim Conquest*, 210–211.
86 Rady, *The Habsburgs*, 100–101.
87 Lynch, *Spain 1516-1598*, 325–328.

88 Ágoston, *The Last Muslim Conquest*, 242–243. Lynch, *Spain 1516-1598*, 329–341. Mullett, *The Catholic Reformation*, 117.

89 Lynch, *Spain 1516-1598*, 375–376.

90 Philip Williams, "La guerra en el Mediterráneo durante el siglo vxi," in Álex Claramunt Soto, ed., *Lepanto: La mar roja de sangre* (Madrid: Desperta Ferro, 2021), 2–4. McDermott, *England and the Spanish Armada*, 118.

91 Norwich, *Four Princes*, 236–237, 239–248; Rady, *The Habsburgs*, 100–105.

7 The War in Flanders

The costliest front in Spain's war against the Protestant Reformation, in terms of treasure, casualties, and prestige, was fought in the Habsburg Netherlands. This conflict, known as the Dutch War for Independence, or as the Eighty Years' War, set the Catholic forces of Philip II's worldwide empire against Dutch Calvinist rebels. The Dutch Revolt fought mostly in what are now the modern states of the Netherlands and Belgium, pitted Spanish-led armies of volunteers, conscripts, and mercenaries against a Dutch population resisting taxation, Catholicism, and rule from distant Madrid. Aided sporadically by Elizabethan England, the Dutch persisted in their insurgency, aided by their strength at sea, their home front advantage, and the growing Calvinist consensus among the population. Fought on land, at sea, and in pulpits and the court of public opinion, it may not have been a total war, but involved heavy and ongoing commitment from both sides, with neither Spanish Catholics nor Dutch Calvinists strong enough to win, nor weak enough to be defeated.

Indeed, it was this conflict that shaped not only the religious contours of the late sixteenth century and defined the limits of Habsburg power but led to the permanent division of the region into a Protestant north, which became the modern Netherlands, and a Catholic south, today's Belgium. The identities of both nations were shaped immeasurably by this conflict, with the hard-won independence of the Netherlands becoming a key narrative in its national history, while the future independent Belgium remained in Spanish hands, then passed to the Austrian Habsburgs, then finally to France, before gaining its freedom from Paris in 1830. Even the long war for Dutch independence had an impact on Spain and Madrid's empire. Given Spain's inability either to achieve a final victory over its Calvinist rebels or to extricate itself without threatening its other possessions, one historian's description of this conflict as "a trap from which there was no escape" seems entirely justified.[1] This long war would become an object lesson on how not to extricate oneself from a perpetual imperial entanglement, over which the main goal was not a victory of the insurgency, but to avoid the humiliation of losing.

The most influential work on the Dutch Revolt is Geoffrey Parker's, *The Army of Flanders and the Spanish Road*. His focus is primarily on the military logistics in support of Spain's Army of Flanders, the organized force that for

DOI: 10.4324/9781003197676-8

80 years attempted to crush the rebellion by Dutch Calvinists against the Spanish Empire. He recounts the long slog that was this conflict, with "long sieges" by Spanish infantry against fortified Dutch towns and cities the most common form of campaigning. Almost every year, when Spanish forces emerged from their winter barracks, it was a contest to see which would run out first: Spanish gold and silver to pay their units, or the capacity of Dutch citizens to outlast their besiegers.[2] There was not continuous warfare for the 80 years of the conflict; at times, Spain seemed on the verge of total victory or, less frequently, total defeat. Even so, sporadic ceasefires were more a reflection of temporary exhaustion, rather than a true *modus vivendi* between Catholicism and Protestantism. There was always the expectation of renewed fighting during the reign of Philip II.

While Spain maintained a permanent corps of 10,000–15,000 soldiers garrisoned in the Low Countries all year round, during heavy campaign years and seasons this force could multiply by five to seven times, to as many as 85,000 men under arms, depending on the resources available to the Habsburg monarchy at the time. Spanish infantry, among the best soldiers in Europe, would be supplemented by recruits from other Habsburg lands, local units raised from loyal Catholic areas of the Low Countries, and mercenaries from throughout Europe, attracted by the promise of generous wages. Local troops tended to be the least reliable, given their proclivity to desert and make their way home; conversely, the more distant the soldier, the more loyal they would be to the sovereign who was responsible for their current location.[3]

Although Spain had succeeded in repressing initial Protestant surges in the 1530s and 1540s, by the 1550s Reformed congregations were once again gaining in strength and defiance. In addition to the rise in support for Calvinism in the Low Countries, Spain's campaigns against this theological insurgency became logistically more challenged. Emperor Charles V was reasonably adept at keeping a balance between local imperatives and imperial needs until the 1550s, allowing some measure of autonomy in the Netherlands, in return for generalized locality and tax revenues. His connection was not merely through governance; he had been born in Flanders, spoke Flemish as his preferred language, and personally knew many of the most prestigious noble and merchant families of the Netherlands.

The initial abdication, and then passing, of Charles V changed the dynamics of Habsburg rule over the Low Countries. Philip II knew little of the region, despite having spent time there under his father's tutelage. Unlike Charles, Philip was a Spaniard, not Flemish. Additionally, the strategic situation, and Habsburg communication and logistics lines, deteriorated at the same time as rule passed from father to son. Philip was not interested in compromising with his Dutch subjects nor in accommodating to their traditions of liberty, limited government, and the role of the Estates General in reserving authority to wage war and raise taxes.[4] In April 1565, the Count of Egmont met Philip in Madrid, offering peace in exchange for religious tolerance and greater local autonomy on matters of faith and finances. By June, Philip provided his answer: no. In response, many key nobles withdrew from the Council of State, the local executive body, and either joined the Calvinist opposition or retreated from active participation in politics.[5]

In 1566, the Prince of Orange, William the Silent, a Catholic and a favorite of Philip's father, sent another proposal to the king, offering 40 tons of gold if the monarch would tolerate freedom of conscience in the Netherlands. William and other nobles, although many were themselves Catholic, opposed the increasing dominance of Spaniards in the Low Countries, as well as the actions of Spanish priests in religious tribunals there. Philip refused to consider such an accommodation. William and even more notables withdrew from the Council of State and ended their collaboration with Margaret of Parma, regent of the Netherlands, Philip's half-sister. She had advocated a more moderate policy but was overruled by her brother. In spring 1567, anti-Catholic riots spread across the Low Countries and, although Margaret was able to use a combination of diplomacy and force to tamp these down, Philip was alarmed by this Calvinist resistance and rejected Margaret's proposals for promotion of Catholic education and a light touch against heresy.[6] The king disregarded Margaret's pleading not to send a large army, ignoring her accurate assessment: "the tumults were allayed, the rioters punished, the heretics silenced, the church reinstated in its wonted authority, garrisons put in suspected places, and the whole country settled in a state of perfect order and tranquility."[7] Meanwhile, the king prepared to send more forces to the Netherlands and to reinforce religious persecution of Protestants in the provinces. An insurgency against Habsburg rule, which would become the Eighty Years' War, would soon reignite in response to the arrival of the Duke of Alba.[8]

Although Brussels was Spain's capital in the Low Countries, in many ways Antwerp was the hub. A sprawling city, during the mid-sixteenth century, it controlled major elements of global trade between Europe and the wider world, serving as the "commercial metropolis of the West."[9] With a burgeoning population, which had grown from 55,000 in 1526 to 104,081 in 1568, Antwerp hosted more than one thousand foreign merchants, who controlled global trade in sugar and other commodities from the Americas. This diversity of population, which also included Spanish soldiers and officials, supported an extensive network of printers, bookshops, and readers, with more than half the books printed in the Low Countries produced there. Surprising for a city of its size, it had no university and no bishop. City fathers had prevailed upon Philip II in the early 1560s not to create a new bishopric, as they feared this would extend Inquisitorial work into the Low Countries. Instead, city magistrates tried all cases, whether civil or religious. Among Antwerp's population was a wide range of religious practices, to the horror of one Spanish cleric, who noted: "Lutherans, Zwinglians, Anabaptists, Calvinists, Adamists, libertines, atheists and innumerable other pestilences."[10]

One key challenge for Philip II was bringing reinforcements, whether raised in Spain, Italy, or central Europe. In the 1530s and 1540s, and until the coronation of Queen Elizabeth in 1558, the English Channel had either been friendly waters, or at least neutral to Spanish troop ships and their accompanying combatant vessels. Under the new Protestant queen, however, the numerous English privateers and other maritime adventurers, often in league with the Dutch rebels at sea, closed off this direct route to Antwerp and other Spanish-controlled ports in the Low Countries. While the English navy remained neutral, it did little to make the way safe for Spain. Adding to Philip's maritime difficulties after 1568 was a Huguenot fleet based in La Rochelle, a Protestant port city on the direct Spanish sea lane to the Netherlands. Spain thus faced English, Dutch, and French enemies en route to the Low Countries. Even when Spain was prepared to fight Dutch warships on the way to Habsburg-controlled ports in the Netherlands, the dearth of safe harbors along the way, whether in England or France, meant that bad weather, necessary repairs, or shortages of provisions were far more costly than should have been the case.[11]

In lieu of a maritime option, Spain increasingly sent its forces circuitously via land, on what became known as the Spanish Road.[12] The name for this path imitated the famous Crusader trajectory during the Middle Ages, which posited that Spanish knights, after completing the *Reconquista*, would march across the North African littoral to Jerusalem, paralleling the hoped-for campaigns of the rest of Christian Europe through Constantinople and the Levant. Unlike the medieval Spanish Road, which existed only in the distant dreams of Crusaders, the sermons of priests and Popes, and the pledges of knights, the sixteenth-century Spanish Road saw frequent use to great practical and strategic value. Every year or two, depending on the military situation in the Netherlands and available forces in the midst of other conflicts, Spain would send an army along the Spanish Road – usually 5,000–10,000 Spanish infantry, backed by another 1,000–2,000 cavalry, and usually at least as many camp followers, family members, and non-combatants (clerks, chaplains, quartermasters, blacksmiths, etc.).[13]

The war in the Netherlands was a campaign for Catholicism, as much as for anything else. In these interests, Habsburg forces deploying along the Spanish Road and into the Low Countries saw improvements in the chaplaincy. Rather than secular priests, the army after 1587 was accompanied by a corps of Jesuits, initially 30 of them – "men of courage and integrity" – replacing the less reliable army priests. Scandalously, these previous clerics had taken advantage of wounded soldiers to get themselves written into wills. A war with a religious purpose needed priests devoted to their men, rather than ones taking advantage of their roles as confessors for personal enrichment.[14]

The route to the Netherlands from Italy primarily passed through Spanish-controlled or allied territories, such as Genoa, Savoy, and Lorraine, but at key places navigated through or around enemies of Madrid. Geneva, as the Calvinist center of Europe, was a heavily fortified site along the way. With Spain uninterested in an assault on this city, with forces desperately needed in northern Europe, and the Calvinists unwilling to challenge the most powerful Catholic force in the world, the passages of Spain's army through Genevan terrain were tense, but mostly uneventful. One can easily imagine the scene as Spanish soldiers, perhaps clutching their crucifixes and praying to the Virgin Mary, passed within sight of Swiss lookouts, ready to summon their fellow Calvinist pikemen, crossbowmen, and harquebusiers to the walls against approaching waves of Spanish infantry and cannon fire. While Philip II would have offered celebratory Masses "to see the citadel of Calvinism destroyed ... he was not prepared to delay the dispatch of his elite troops to the Netherlands for the sake of Geneva."[15]

The king was always in a hurry to send the next cohort of reinforcement to the Netherlands, as his forces always seemed on the verge of victory or defeat, with both scenarios calling for more troops. External factors played a key role, as England under Queen Elizabeth provided refuge and resources to the Dutch rebels. Tax increases by Philip II, desperate to raise revenue from his richest provinces for his wars against France and other enemies, also fueled rebellion in the Netherlands, as did the king's plans to increase the number of bishoprics and Inquisitorial tribunals. Resentment in Holland, especially about the provinces' perceived disproportionate tax burden for distant conflicts, grew in parallel to religious discontent. This arose despite the significant external revenues, especially from Castile, raised and devoted to the wars in and around the Netherlands. Philip was effectively drawing a subsidy from a relatively poor Habsburg domain (Castile) to fight a war in the richest one (the Netherlands) against taxpayers in the latter.[16]

To the south and west of the Netherlands waited France, ever prepared to wade into conflicts against Spain, disrupting the plans of Charles V and Philip II for victory. A look at the map should show why this was the case; the Spanish Road passed between or through of French territories and allies. Indeed, on multiple occasions there was some uncertainty about whether Habsburg forces were headed for the Netherlands or to renew the ever-simmering conflict with France. The passage in 1567 of one of the largest Spanish armies ever to make the journey on foot, the Duke of Alba's force of 10,000 well-trained soldiers, provoked concern all along the Spanish Road, with alerts, mobilizations, and plots by Huguenots and others to stop their advance. While nothing came of these discussions and countermeasures, it showed the potential for Spain's adversaries to challenge its overland communications, hindering reinforcements and resupply to the Netherlands.[17]

Finally, Dutch fears that Philip II intended to introduce the Spanish Inquisition to the Low Countries accelerated fears of a wider campaign against Protestants; stories of trials against Spanish Protestants, and the *autos da fe* that followed, came to the region from both Catholic and Calvinist sources, increasing tensions in both directions.[18] The Netherlands was by the 1550s, however, already another front in the global struggle between the Catholic Church and the Protestant Reformation. Although the Spanish Inquisition as an institution did not formally come to the Low Countries, pre-existing ecclesiastical bodies were already fully engaged in combating heresy, buttressing support for the Catholic Church, and implementing Tridentine reforms.

Even so, local rebellions against taxes happened with some frequency in the Low Countries, along with grumbling from broad swathes of the population, as first Charles, then Philip, prevailed upon provincial bodies to impose new taxes and higher rates to fuel the desperate Habsburg need for funds for its many wars against the French Valois, in Italy, and in the Mediterranean. Even though in some cases these wars were fought in or near the Netherlands, there were sentiments that the conflicts were in the interests of the Habsburgs, rather than the local populations, who preferred to sell herring and cloth to the French, rather than to face them in battle in Flanders fields or the waters of the North Sea.[19] Tax rebellions in the sixteenth century were hardly unique to the Dutch; even Castile experienced a fiscal revolt in 1520–1521 against increasing demands of the crown.[20] Similarly, bankers in Antwerp and elsewhere in the provinces became increasingly reluctant to extend credit, initially to Charles V, and later to Philip II. They saw not only the precariousness of Habsburg finances, dependent as they were on shipments of silver from the Americas, but also the unpopularity of the causes for which their loans were being allocated.[21]

Luther had gained initial support in the Low Countries as early as 1519, even though this interest was supplanted, initially by Anabaptism, and then by Calvinism.[22] Calvinist doctrine reinforced the long-standing traditions in the provinces for local autonomy, self-government in cities and towns, and dislike of the centralizing efforts by Charles V and his regents. In this, the new theology coincided well with the outlines of Reform on individual salvation, Bible reading and worship in the vernacular, and resistance to distant princes, whether on the Chair of St. Peter or the thrones of the empire or kingdom of Spain. As elsewhere, the French did everything within their means to encourage local rebellions against Habsburg rule, as did the English, although less consistently. In this context, the efforts by the emperor and later Philip II to seek an English alliance were not only as a counterpoint to France, but also to consolidate their own authority in the Low Countries.[23] As Charles had noted, to preserve Habsburg interests, England and the Low Countries "should be bound together, so that they can provide mutual aid against their enemies," by which he meant principally France.[24]

As early as the 1520s, Antwerp was a center for Protestant printing. By 1522, 12 titles by Luther in Latin and ten in Dutch had been printed there. The Church was well aware of this, with the first burning of Protestant books happening on 13 July 1521, when 400 volumes by Luther were consigned to the flames. Even so, penalties imposed by city magistrates for those convicted of printing Protestant books were initially light, most often the imposition of religious penance or temporary exile. During the three decades after Luther's first appearance, there was only one execution in Antwerp for this cause, that of the printer Jacob van Liesvelt, convicted for a third time in 1545 of printing heretical works. This execution, however, caused a chill among printers, and led to shifts in some production during the 1550s to England and Protestant areas of Germany.[25]

The Catholic Church in the Low Countries had been slow to respond to the religious challenge of this period. Even before Luther, anticlericalism and indifference to the Church were on the increase, with bequests to the Catholic Church, participation in religious fraternities, and veneration of saints in decline for decades before 1517. Antwerp was in the bishopric of Cambrai, more than two hundred kilometers away, which reduced the Church's ability to influence events even more. The slowness of the Church to respond to its own decline, as well as its failure to launch internal reforms, reinforce Catholic teaching, and revive preaching as antidotes to Protestantism, enabled ideas of Luther and Calvin to find ready ears in Antwerp. The first Lutherans executed in the Low Countries were Henrik Voes and Jan van Essen, two Augustinian monks in Brussels, burned at the stake on 1 July 1523. Soon, however, it was the ideas of John Calvin that became most popular in the region. By the 1550s, with the influence of Calvin and contact with French Huguenots, Calvinism had begun to spread rapidly. The first execution of a Dutch Calvinist leader came on 16 October 1551, with the killing in Antwerp of Jan van Ostende.[26]

To combat Reformation ideas throughout the Low Countries, on 29 April 1550, Charles published "The Perpetual Edict," soon renamed by Protestants "the bloody edict," which imposed verifiable religious orthodoxy in Habsburg lands, including requiring foreigners to provide letters from their home priests, and empowering the Inquisition and diocesan tribunals to investigate heresy. Because of its importance to global trade, and concerns by the emperor that the decree could discourage foreign residents, Antwerp was exempt, instead covered by its own decree on 25 September 1550. City magistrates there retained control over rooting out heresy. Between 1550 and 1566, 306 accused Protestants were tried. Of these, 131 were executed and 90 exiled. The remaining 85 received lighter sentence, were acquitted, pardoned, or avoided trial.[27]

Despite the rising affiliation of the Dutch with Calvinism, there remained strong pockets of Catholic devotion throughout the Low Countries. Amsterdam's elected city government remained dominated by Catholic officeholders until 1578; the southern half of the Spanish Netherlands was especially loyal to the Church, with ethnic Walloons in what is today's Belgium embracing the Counter-Reformation. Although they were less effective in fighting against neighboring Dutch Calvinists in the northern regions of the Netherlands, Walloons proved reliable fighters elsewhere on the front lines of the Spanish Empire. Sending Walloons to Italy and Italians to the Low Countries, and Spaniards everywhere but Spain, was the most effective policy for Philip II. Foreign fighters were almost always the most loyal, least likely to rebel, and even more unlikely to feel sympathy for local populations.[28]

On multiple occasions, Philip II had opportunities to compromise with his subjects in the Low Countries. Indeed, many leading Dutch citizens were willing to maintain their loyalty to their Spanish king, provided he extended toleration to their religious faith. To Philip, however, even more than had been the case with his father, "heretics and rebels" were one and the same, indivisible in his thinking. After all, if the Dutch were loyal to him, why could they not also be to his faith, the one true Church? To accommodate to Calvinists or Lutherans would be to admit that there were multiple ways to worship God and follow his Son, beyond the authority of the Chair of St. Peter and the apostolic succession since the time of Jesus. Although as king, Philip would accept temporary accommodations and truces with his enemies, it was another thing entirely to do so in his own realms. Allowing Protestant sects to coexist under a Catholic monarch would to Philip II call into question the legitimacy of his dynasty and its special mission as the right arm of Catholicism, and redefine as wasted efforts the decades of struggle by Philip and his father against the Reformation. Later monarchs might follow this path, but Philip would rather bankrupt his kingdoms and expend every last soldier and sailor than accept the followers of John Calvin and Martin Luther as equivalent to those of the Roman Catholic Church.[29]

Given the wealth of the 17 provinces of the Low Countries, Philip II could not abandon them without surrendering tremendous resources, which he needed for use throughout his empire. Antwerp in the mid-to-late sixteenth century was "the greatest commercial centre in Europe," a global hub within Europe, extending to the Americas, Asia, and Africa through Dutch, Spanish, and Portuguese fleets.[30] The industries of the region, including textiles, metallurgy, shipbuilding, printing, and agriculture, supplied Habsburg soldiers, as well as civilian populations throughout the empire. Especially amid costly counterinsurgency warfare in the Low Countries, Philip II desperately needed any revenues he could generate to fund his army in Flanders. In his long-term vision, once he had successfully quelled this uprising, he hoped to devote these same resources elsewhere; Spain did not lack for enemies and wars in Europe and beyond.

Even beyond the economic value of the Low Countries was the prestige of their possession. Inheriting these domains from his father, Philip II could not countenance the thought of surrendering them, no matter the cost, especially for reasons of their theological dissent. The success of Calvinism in gaining converts among the Dutch actually reduced the chance that Philip would allow the provinces to slip from his grasp either through military defeat or for reasons of dynastic necessity. One can imagine the king trading the provinces for wealthier ones – perhaps for gains in Italy or at the expense of France, or as dowry for a highly beneficial marriage – but hardly as a result of desires by his subjects for religious and political freedom. Even his marriage to England's Queen Mary, which saw their potential heir inheriting the Low Countries, England, and Spain, would have kept these territories united in union with England.[31]

By 1562, the Low Countries were seeing widespread public disturbances against both Habsburg tax and religious policies. This resistance included non-compliance with taxes, reduced willingness to serve in official capacities, and a more open embrace of Reformist theology, including the conversion of formerly Catholic parishes into centers for Lutheran, Anabaptist, and increasingly Calvinist Protestant religious services. Books by Protestant authors were widely available and read, in flagrant violation of decrees by the king. Loyal Catholic bishops were at times unable to take up residence in their diocese because of hostility from the Calvinist population; the same bishops could not launch investigations against heresy, much less conduct religious trials of the accused.

In 1566, Margaret of Parma, Regent of the Netherlands and Philip's half-sister, allowed a brief period of toleration, while awaiting the king's decision on a petition from the Dutch nobility asking for toleration. Philip's response, sending an army under the Duke of Alba and asking for the resignation of Margaret, accelerated hostility to Spanish Habsburg rule. He revoked her decree on toleration, noting emphatically that abiding any heresy was "a great offense to the honor of God and to the authority of His church."[32] While Philip bristled at the accommodations Margaret had made to local sensitivities, she had built positive relationships with some key nobles, ecclesiastical, and intellectual figures in the Netherlands. Philip's reaction ensured that this good will would not be transferable to the Duke of Alba, the tenacious and uncompromising military commander and new governor general of the Low Countries. Margaret resigned and left the Netherlands for Italy.[33]

Alba's introduction of special religious and military courts, most infamously the "Council of Troubles," to impose harsh justice, his occupation of the region with the largest forces assembled to date in the Netherlands, and his alignment with Philip II's refusal to consider any religious accommodations to heresy, transformed Spanish relations with the Dutch population.[34] Many in the population would look back with nostalgia on 1566–1567 as the "wonder year," a brief period of religious coexistence in the Low Countries, before Philip's reversal and military initiatives. Initially, the force of the king's actions and personality gained momentum and authority, but as his financial resources began to show limitations, the rebellion gained steam, with Alba as a symbol of hatred and loathing, and reducing what lingering dynastic loyalties Philip II still enjoyed. The campaign of Alba and the imposition of religious tribunals and new bishoprics, including in Antwerp, caused a dramatic shift into Holland not only of the center of Protestant activity, but of Antwerp's previous role as a global trading hub, printing, and banking center. Catholicism would win in Antwerp, but at the expense of the city's leading role as a cosmopolitan center. With Anglo-Spanish trade at historic lows, unrelenting campaigns against Protestantism, and the emergence of alternative centers for finance and trade, including London, the city entered an enduring decline as a global hub.[35]

The Duke of Alba and his army arrived in August 1567, and for the next six years attempted to use military force, special tribunals, arrests, and repression to stamp out heresy. He united a divided population against Philip II, with even some Catholics joining the resistance, led by Prince William of Orange, a former Habsburg ally. The execution of the Count of Egmont and other nobles enraged the population and encouraged even many hardline advisers to Philip II to urge compromise, rather than continue the bloody campaign. Spain was winning the battles but losing the country. Philip finally removed Alba in December 1573, with victory no closer than in 1567. It was not because the king disagreed with the duke's methods, but instead because Spain had no funds – even Alba had faced mutinies from unpaid soldiers. By fall 1575, Philip was out of money not only to provision his military in Flanders, but across his entire empire, declaring bankruptcy in September of that year, while still refusing to negotiate with the rebels.[36]

The dispatch of Alba "was probably a serious mistake" as he "accomplished by cruelty what others would have done" through diplomacy, incentives, and more moderate use of military means. Although his depredations have been at times exaggerated, with direct deaths closer to one thousand than the tens of thousands alleged by Protestant sources, he alienated even moderates in the Netherlands. While his forces quelled the rebellion, it was a peace of exhaustion and defeat of Dutch Calvinists, not a return of their loyalty. Only the constant presence of an army of occupation would henceforth keep the provinces quiet.[37]

Beginning in 1568 and lasting until the final settlement of the Thirty Years' War in the 1648 Treaty of Westphalia, Spain fought against an iterative Calvinist insurgency in the Low Countries. Although Spain's global assets were tremendous, fueled by precious metals from the Americas, spices from Portuguese colonies, and trade with Africa and Asia, the war against Dutch Calvinists proved exhausting. Continual cycles of Spanish tactical victories, followed by Habsburg resource challenges, and Calvinist counterattacks, proved a predictable, and understandably frustrating, story in the Low Countries. By the late 1570s, previous Spanish victories had been erased, with Protestant ascendancy in the north. The conversion to Calvinism and other Protestant sects in the 1560s by many members of the nobility, including high-ranking lords such as William of Orange, helped accelerate the rebellion in the Netherlands against Philip II and his conception of an indivisible Catholic monarchy over an empire free of dissent and heresy.[38] William, who had warned both Philip and Margaret of the results of the king's intransigence, noted in spring 1566: "by imitating the French Catholics in their severity, we, like them, involve our country in the dreadful miseries of civil war."[39]

The arrival of Alba in 1567 also encouraged England under Elizabeth to provide more direct and forceful aid to Dutch Protestants. Spain, rather than France, was poised to become the most powerful continental power, should its efforts to reverse the Protestant Reformation in the Low Countries succeed. English financial aid, naval cooperation with the Sea Beggars, providing asylum to Dutch Calvinists and Spanish Protestants, and ongoing efforts to interdict Spanish maritime communications, were outgrowths of the arrival of Alba with his force of direct occupation in the Netherlands.

Dutch resistance, however, proved challenging and, after initial successes, Spanish financial resources, and commitments elsewhere, forced reversals in their direct control over the region. Although in 1572, Elizabeth expelled the Sea Beggars, the Dutch rebel fleet, this did not appease Philip, who continued to lose ground against the insurgency.[40]

Indeed, for several years, 1577–1584, Spanish forces were essentially driven from most of the Netherlands. While much of the south remained majority Catholic, and cities such as Amsterdam went over to the Reformation later than smaller communities in the north, Calvinism held sway everywhere during this period. Effective Calvinist political and military leadership, Spanish engagements elsewhere, ongoing resentment against Spanish rule even apart from religious issues, and the challenge of fighting a war so far away from Philip II's base in Iberia, all led to this period of Protestant ascendancy in the region. While in Flanders and other parts of the southern Netherlands, the population remained majority Catholic, even there the Calvinist minority was at times able to expel local Catholic leaders, drawing on resources and personnel from the north, where the rising popularity of Calvinism seemed inexorable after the 1560s.[41]

Despite the battlefield losses, and the tremendous resources required to regain lost territory, Philip II refused to come to terms with the Dutch rebels that included any concessions on the religious question, even with the promise that he could retain sovereignty, revenues, and access to the resources of the provinces. The price for an end to the insurgency, and the Calvinist insurgents recognizing him as king, was religious tolerance. For Philip, this was an impossible request; he refused to be "the ruler over heretics," instead expending countless more lives and treasure to retain the provinces for Catholicism. The king insisted that a return to Catholicism was a precondition for a peace settlement, a non-starter in discussions with the ardent local Calvinists that his armies faced throughout the Netherlands.[42]

While the direct enemy in this case, intractable Dutch Protestants on land and at sea, lost many battles to the formidable military forces available to Philip II, the greater challenges for Spain were the distances involved and the persistence of other rivals, including the Ottoman Empire, the Valois dynasty in France, and Queen Elizabeth's England. For the Spanish king, the enduring struggle was not only to recruit, deploy, pay, and maintain large ground forces, but to determine where to send these forces against multiple threats. The Netherlands was the longest and most consistent war of Habsburg Spain, but hardly the only place where it faced threats. As one historian noted, "as a world leader Philip of Spain had much else on his mind."[43] Even more significantly, hardline Catholic military and religious leaders, and their counterparts among Dutch Calvinist nobles and clergy, consistently sabotaged attempts at compromise, even when supported, albeit reluctantly, by key leaders.[44]

Spain and the Ottoman Empire both changed their approaches to religious liberty in the seventeenth century, moving from insisting on religious unity to accepting diversity. Spain in the sixteenth century was irreconcilable against tolerating Protestantism within its empire. Indeed, promising negotiations toward peace in the Netherlands foundered repeatedly – 1567, 1575, 1577, and 1589 – over Spain's refusal to respect the religious liberties of the Dutch, who had embraced Calvinism. By the early 1600s, in 1609 and 1621, Spain ended its insistence that the Dutch return to Catholicism as a condition of a peace treaty. By this later date, however, Spain was fully embroiled in the Thirty Years' War (1618–1648), by the end of which it was forced by the provisions of the Treaty of Westphalia to surrender all temporal and spiritual authority over the Low Countries. The Dutch victory, driven by external events, finally ended the Eighty Years' War.

Toleration, in this case emerging only when there were no other options, was not implemented in Habsburg lands, because the territories that had most desired it succeeded in breaking away. In 1648, Spain not only had to accept that Calvinism would hold sway in the Dutch Republic; it had to surrender these lands in the treaties that ended the Thirty Years' War.[45] The Habsburgs remained throughout their military and political entanglement in the Low Countries "unable to win yet determined not to lose," until external forces, and the settlement of the Thirty Years' War, ended their rule over the region.[46] It had taken the Dutch 80 years to expel the Spanish Habsburgs from the Netherlands, a fight prolonged and exacerbated by the bitter religious warfare so central to Habsburg identity and campaigns in Europe and beyond.

The end of this war, the longest in the history of Spain's crusade against Protestantism, signaled at the same time the end of this struggle. While Spain would not embrace tolerance for another two centuries, no longer would it fight wars primarily because of the religion of the adversary. While the war against Dutch Calvinism had been a religious war, it had also been one fought over dynastic ambitions, to keep the Dutch down, the French and English out, and Spain's prestige high. In the end, it accomplished these goals until the end, and even thereafter. The Netherlands would not become a dependent of any other major power; the fight for Dutch independence succeeded not only against Spain, but as a deterrent to the ambitions of other European states, perhaps tempted by the wealth of the Low Countries.

Although the Treaty of Westphalia came during the reign of Philip IV, the grandson of Philip II was fulfilling the Habsburg mandate to continue fighting in the Netherlands. This defeat is most correctly understood as the final collapse of Philip II's grand strategy and global imperatives: to fight the Protestant Reformation on all Habsburg lands, to the bitter end. While King Philip II did not succeed in defeating the followers of Calvin and Luther, neither was he overwhelmed by them. Philip II's vision of Spanish monarchy, inextricable from Europe's religious civil war, essentially ended in 1648. The remaining years of Philip IV (to 1665) and especially those of his son and successor, Charles II (1665–1700) were ones of strategic decline.

Notes

1 Lynch, *Spain 1516-1598*, 386.
2 Parker, *The Army of Flanders and the Spanish Road*, 10–11.
3 Parker, *The Army of Flanders and the Spanish Road*, 25–29.
4 Robert Watson, *The History of the Reign of Philip the Second, King of Spain* (London: Thomas Tegg, 1839), 50.
5 Patterson, *With the Heart of a King*, 202. Watson, *The History of the Reign of Philip the Second*, 56–58.
6 Patterson, *With the Heart of a King*, 208–209. Watson, *The History of the Reign of Philip the Second*, 114–115, 122–124.
7 Watson, *The History of the Reign of Philip the Second*, 131–132.
8 Boehmer, Wiffen, and Wiffen, *Bibliotheca Wiffeniana*, Vol. III, 18–21. Watson, *The History of the Reign of Philip the Second*, 125.
9 Guido Marneff, *Antwerp in the Age of Reformation, 1550-1577*. Translated by J.C. Grayson (Baltimore: Johns Hopkins University Press, 1996), xi.
10 Marneff, *Antwerp in the Age of Reformation*, xi, 4–5, 20–21.
11 Parker, *The Army of Flanders and the Spanish Road*, 77–79.
12 Parker, *The Army of Flanders and the Spanish Road*, 56–57.
13 Parker, *The Army of Flanders and the Spanish Road*, 87.
14 Parker, *The Army of Flanders and the Spanish Road*, 171–172.
15 Parker, *The Army of Flanders and the Spanish Road*, 61–64.
16 Tracy, *The Low Countries in the Sixteenth Century*, XIV, 134–135. Parker, *The Army of Flanders and the Spanish Road*, 145–147.
17 Parker, *The Army of Flanders and the Spanish Road*, 64–67.
18 Lynn, *Between Court and Confessional*, 33.
19 Tracy, *The Low Countries in the Sixteenth Century*, XII, 259–266.
20 Homza, *Religious Authority in the Spanish Renaissance*, xviii.
21 Tracy, *The Low Countries in the Sixteenth Century*, XI, 72–73, 81–82, 84–87, 91–93, 95–96.
22 Lynch, *Spain 1516-1598*, 393–394.
23 Lynch, *Spain 1516-1598*, 133–135.
24 Lynch, *Spain 1516-1598*, 252.
25 Marneff, *Antwerp in the Age of Reformation*, 39–40, 42.
26 Marneff, *Antwerp in the Age of Reformation*, 48, 52–55, 58, 61, 63, 80–81.
27 Marneff, *Antwerp in the Age of Reformation*, 82–84.
28 Mullett, *The Catholic Reformation*, 169. Parker, *The Army of Flanders and the Spanish Road*, 30–31.
29 Lynch, *Spain 1516-1598*, 378.
30 Lynch, *Spain 1516-1598*, 387–388.
31 Lynch, *Spain 1516-1598*, 389–390.
32 Marneff, *Antwerp in the Age of Reformation*, 111–112.
33 Watson, *The History of the Reign of Philip the Second*, 134.
34 Watson, *The History of the Reign of Philip the Second*, 135.
35 MacCulloch, *The Reformation*, 300–301. Marneff, *Antwerp in the Age of Reformation*, 88, 105, 111–113, 120–121, 125–126, 141. McDermott, *England and the Spanish Armada*, 91.
36 Patterson, *With the Heart of a King*, 210–213. Watson, *The History of the Reign of Philip the Second*, 52.
37 Maltby, *The Black Legend in England*, 47–49.
38 Tracy, *The Low Countries in the Sixteenth Century*, IX, 53–55.
39 Watson, *The History of the Reign of Philip the Second*, 119.
40 McDermott, *England and the Spanish Armada*, 54, 73–77, 87.

41 Tracy, *The Low Countries in the Sixteenth Century*, VIII, 548–549; X, 293–294.
42 Parker, *The Army of Flanders and the Spanish Road*, 132.
43 MacCulloch, *The Reformation*, 358.
44 MacCulloch, *The Reformation*, 356–357.
45 Parker, *The Army of Flanders and the Spanish Road*, 112–113.
46 Lynch, *Spain 1516-1598*, 402.

Conclusion

Philip II – The Triumphant Failure

The war for Europe between Spanish Catholicism and the Protestant Reformation ended without a total victory for either side. Spain was not overcome by the Protestant Reformation in the sixteenth century, nor did it lose any of its key territories to the insurgent faiths of Calvinism or Lutheranism during the following century after 1517. However, at multiple points its strategic position, domestic politics, and status as a global power were threatened by these theological challenges. By the 1550s Protestant movements had become inextricably linked to multiple enemies of Catholic Spain, from England to the Low Countries to German princes within the Holy Roman Empire. The ultimate endurance of Spain as a Catholic state does not diminish the potential that Protestantism had during this era, nor the possibility that it could have plunged Spain into the religious and political tumult seen elsewhere. The uncertain, brutal, and unpleasant crises of theology and governance experienced by France, England, and the Holy Roman Empire, where civil war, religious conflict, and atrocities on all sides plagued these years, did not come to Spain.

While there were significant differences between these realms, the primary institutional difference between the Catholic Church in these nations and that of Philip II's kingdom was the existence in Spain of the Holy Office of the Spanish Inquisition. The persistence and effectiveness of this body, one could argue, spared Spain from the widespread religious violence that pervaded and scarred Europe throughout the sixteenth century. The relatively modest numbers of deaths ordered by the Spanish Inquisition for heresies, including Protestantism, compared quite favorably in absolute numbers and percentages of casualties to those lost to religious wars and persecutions on all sides in France, England, the Holy Roman Empire, the Low Countries and elsewhere during the century. In these states and regions, it was in many ways the weakness of the respective monarchies, unable to consolidate the population under a single religion, that led to conflict. Philip II was, after all, in addition to being king of Spain, Lord of the Netherlands, but in the Low Countries he lacked the tool of the Spanish Inquisition or the defined boundary of the Pyrenees to help screen out Reformation ideas. His efforts to introduce similarly effective tribunals there, as well as in England when he was husband to Queen Mary, failed to generate popular support or widespread

DOI: 10.4324/9781003197676-9

effectiveness. Indeed, even the fear of the Spanish Inquisition was a major element in resistance to Spanish influence in England and the Netherlands.

At the time of his death in 1598, King Philip II left this world in both victory and defeat, triumphant on many battlefields and the king of an empire more powerful, feared, and glorious in secular and religious achievements than the one he inherited. Spanish ships laden with silver traversed the Atlantic, bringing untold treasures into the king's reach and subsidizing his vast armies, fleets, and building projects. Spanish soldiers stood sentinel across Europe and the Americas, from Italy to the Netherlands, from Florida to Peru. After many failed attempts, and the mysterious death of one crown prince, Philip II would hand over his realms to his son and heir, the future Philip III. At the same time, Philip II had faced unparalleled defeats on many fronts, and died with many disappointments. One wonders what the last thoughts of this king were on 13 September 1598, dying in his beloved El Escorial palace, holding a crucifix that had belonged to his father and mother, and listening to his chapel choir sing hymns.[1]

Unable to create the universal Catholic empire of his dreams and those of his father, nor to achieve a final triumph over any of his enemies – French Catholics, Ottoman Turks, English Tudors, German Lutherans, or Dutch Calvinists – he had spent vast fortunes, lost countless armies and navies, and bankrupted his empire four times. Even so, neither had his foes defeated him permanently. After the defeat of his Spanish Armada, he rebuilt his navy. After each mutiny or defeat in the Low Countries, he rallied a new army for dispatch to his rebellious provinces, extracted needed revenues from the long-suffering population of Castile, promissory notes based on future shipments of silver from the Americas, or loans from increasingly skeptical bankers. Spain endured, remained undivided, and no major lands or territories slipped from Philip's grasp during his lifetime. While one might argue he had lost England, during his time as husband to Queen Mary, he had never been king of England; the loss of that kingdom to Queen Elizabeth and to the Church of England's brand of Protestantism was not something for which Philip could be truly blamed.

The Spanish Catholic Church remained notably robust, especially in comparison to its counterparts in western Europe. Over the course of the sixteenth century, Protestantism had reclaimed over Catholicism in much of Europe, from England to the Netherlands to Scandinavia to the northern states of the Holy Roman Empire. Although eventually Catholicism triumphed in Italy and France, even in these strongly Catholic countries the ideas of Luther and Calvin gained wide support for a time. The Spanish Church, however, remained resolutely loyal to Roman Catholicism, with strong parishes, effective religious orders, and the overarching institution of the Spanish Inquisition providing a strong bulwark against heresy, as bishops promoted and reinforced spiritual education at the local level after the conclusion of the Council of Trent in 1563. Indeed, by 1600 there were more active Catholic bishoprics in Spain alone than in all of these other European regions combined.[2]

At the height of the insurgent Protestant Reformation, in the middle of the 1500s, there were no kingdoms, territories, or principalities without the potential for the replacing of orthodox Catholicism with one or more of these new Christian faiths. Spain's retention of Catholicism, through the collaboration of the Habsburg monarchy and the Spanish Inquisition, was no certain thing. While one can make the argument that Protestantism was barely a threat to Catholicism in Spain, events across Europe show that previously ardently Catholic states such as France and England could find themselves in civil war or alternating between religious faiths at the discretion of mercurial monarchs. The life of Don Carlos, son of Philip II and heir to the throne of Castile and other Habsburg domains, show the potential for this kind of tumult even in Spain.

When Philip came to the throne of Spain in 1555, in a sense the war against Protestantism was already over, at least for those who advocated for the absolute extirpation of the ideas of Calvin and Luther from Europe. It was simply not possible for all Protestants to be killed, driven into exile, or forcibly reconverted back to Roman Catholicism. The Peace of Augsburg, signed by Charles V and German Lutheran princes, enshrined the principle that the ruler chose the religion of the state. [3] With that concession, Christendom was destined to remain divided, absent an apocalyptic war of extermination, beyond even the deaths wrought by the Thirty Years' War of the seventeenth century, when 20–25% of Europe's population died from combat, disease, and starvation.[4] Not even Philip, merciless toward Protestants in his own realms, and Muslims without, would likely have wished for a conflict deadlier than this.

In many ways, the reign of Philip II was a triumph; he greatly expanded the domains left to him by his father, adding Portugal and the Portuguese Empire. With his fourth wife, Anna, he produced a legitimate and reasonably able heir, the future Philip III. Other than England, which was never properly his, he did not lose any important lands to rebellion or foreign occupation. His battle standards had achieved dramatic victories over the Ottomans, the French, the Dutch, and even the English, and although some of these triumphs were ephemeral, none of the counterattacks threatened the survival of his regime. Nowhere in his lands was he forced to tolerate any of the Protestant faiths, whether Calvinist, Lutheran, or Anglican, as legitimate Christian denominations alongside Catholicism. In his territories, he left behind a legacy of Spanish Habsburg art, architecture, and government that would prevail culturally for another century, until the death of Charles II, great-grandson of Philip II. Dear to Philip II's heart and indispensable to his realm, the Spanish Inquisition had revived significantly as an institution during his lifetime.

The Catholic Church was, ironically in some ways, immeasurably stronger for having faced the challenge of the Protestant Reformation. The penetrating theological questions posed by Luther and Calvin, the proliferation of written works from the Bible to sermons to hymns in the vernacular, and the public criticism of the corruption and incompetence of the Catholic Church, led to a strengthening of Catholic educational efforts, theological consistency, and self-policing of concubinage, nepotism, indulgences, and other practices at odds with newly reinforced orthodox Catholicism. An observer of the time might have referred to a verse from Proverbs, translated into English in the widely used Geneva Bible: "Yron sharpeneth yron, so doeth man sharpen the face of his friend." If we take Protestants and Catholics as pieces of iron, even if the title of "friend" might not apply during the sixteenth century, the sentiment seems accurate.[5] Absent the hard questions posed by Martin Luther and John Calvin, especially the pointing out of hypocrisy and corruption within the Church, the Reformist impulses of the Council of Trent would likely not have emerged within sixteenth-century Catholicism.

For Philip II, despite his many triumphs, there was always another enemy. While he won enough victories to preserve his realms, these were not substantial enough to forestall future conflicts. After Lepanto, the Ottomans built new fleets. Malta remained Christian, but Cyprus fell to the Turks. Most importantly, however, no matter the defeats and disappointments he faced, there was always Spain. The realm he left behind, despite the bankruptcies and battlefield losses, was more coherent as a nation and a kingdom than when he first put on its crown.

Philip II was not alone in attempting to combat the Protestant threat, even if he was singularly effective. Certainly, the kings of France and the Holy Roman Emperors tried to extirpate Lutheranism and Calvinism from their realms. The close collaboration of Church and state was the ideal during this period, regardless of country or theological affiliation, with Spain seen as a model for close collaboration between both. As Geoffrey Parker has noted, "(r)eligious faith provided perhaps the most effective means of securing and keeping allegiance in early modern Europe, even in the teeth of military repression and atrocities."[6] Even in England, Queen Elizabeth seems to have imitated some of the persecutory policies of her half-sister Mary and brother-in-law Philip, with tribunals and heresy trials supported by the authority of the state. These were conducted, of course, in the interests of the Church of England and Queen Elizabeth as its Defender of the Faith, rather than in the interests of realigning with Rome. "One faith and one king" was not a uniquely Hispanic aim, even if in the sixteenth century Spain remained uniquely successful in achieving this unity.[7]

Nor, as one historian has noted, did the persecutions of the Spanish Inquisition have an overall negative impact on Spain's economy; the wealthiest period of Spain coincided with the high point of Inquisitorial activity. While there were certainly individual losses of highly skilled professionals and negative impacts on specific industries, neither the expulsion of the Jews in the fifteenth century nor the global campaign against Protestantism in the sixteenth century caused Spain's economic challenges of the seventeenth century. While one could argue that Spain's wars against English and Dutch Protestantism were a major factor in the kingdom's multiple bankruptcies, these financial declarations were the result of excessive spending, not economic decline.[8]

By every measure, the Spanish Inquisition succeeded in its primary task, with few negative repercussions for itself or the monarchy during the sixteenth century. It was, in the assessment of one historian, at least within the boundaries of Habsburg Spain, "respected everywhere, enforcing strict obedience to orthodox Catholic doctrine without employing excessive physical cruelty" throughout the nation, even in areas of Spain distant from the royal court or protective of local laws and privileges.[9] Focused on the Protestant threat at mid-century, the Spanish Inquisition's reputation and popularity among the Catholic population remained strong, even as the targets of its investigations and trials moved from *conversos* to Lutherans to Moriscos to moral crimes under Church law, especially bigamy, witchcraft, and homosexuality.[10] For many Habsburg subjects, the Spanish Inquisition was not a fearsome institution of torture and punishment, hiding around every corner watching for the slightest failing. Instead, the Holy Office was "a police court of morals and suppressers of the unusual," protecting against "gypsies, witches, Judaizers, crypto-Muslims, Lutherans, and increasingly, bigamists, homosexuals, and (immoral) priests," all of which were dangers to the health, morals, and piety of the Catholic nation.[11] To contradict the famous line of the Monty Python comedy troupe, in Spain, everyone expected the Spanish Inquisition.[12]

A Latin-language history of the Spanish Inquisition, first published in Madrid in 1598, claimed that the greatest achievement of the Holy Office in its first century was the successful suppression of the Lutherans in Spain. Luis de Páramo, who authored this work, served the Holy Office as an Inquisitor in Palermo. In his evaluation of this campaign as the height of the Inquisition's success. the author included the trials of Protestants in Valladolid and Seville, as well as the process against Archbishop Bartolomé Carranza, former primate of Spain.[13] On the timeline of the Spanish Inquisition, the primary effort against Protestantism was relatively brief, but for Páramo, it defined the institution more than any other initiative taken by this network of tribunals and religious officials.

This assertion, quite remarkable given the Spanish Inquisition's initial mandate to extirpate false converts from Judaism, reveals a sixteenth-century understanding that it is time to reconsider: the Reformation's threat to Spanish Catholicism was an existential one. As such, supporting the enhanced activity of the Spanish Inquisition during the period of the Reformation was a rational and appropriate response not only by the Catholic Church, but by the Habsburg monarchy that was its unremitting advocate. The Habsburg wars against Calvinist rebels in the Low Countries, Lutheran principalities in the German Empire, and sea-borne efforts against Protestant pirates, were obvious battle lines. Absent the concerted, consistent, and thorough efforts of the Spanish Inquisition, as well as its allies on the state and society, Spain could have gone the way of France or the Holy Roman Empire – divided by decades of religious civil war – or even England, with an independent national church, eventually hardening into a branch of Protestantism. King Phillip II of Spain and his father, Holy Roman Emperor Charles V, were in this sense right, given the context of the time, to refuse an accommodation with Protestant Reformers, or to allow religious tolerance within their lands. To do so would have destroyed the legitimacy of their respective reigns, at a time when religious and dynastic loyalties were the primary justification for kingdoms and empires.

Other Catholic writers in the 1580s and 1590s made similar arguments, asserting not only the threat that the Protestant Reformation had posed, but that the Spanish Inquisition had been indispensable to the elimination of this threat within Spain, and in serving as an example to other tribunals in regions that remained faithful to the Catholic Church. In 1581, Tomás Cerdán de Tallada noted that without the Inquisition, Spain might well have suffered the religious conflicts of Northern Europe.[14] Marco Antonio de Camós y Requeséns commented in 1592 that Protestants represented "a danger to the stability of kingdoms" with destruction of both states and true religion following in their wake.[15] The Jesuit priest Pedro de Ribadeneira used biological and mythological terms to describe the Protestant threat to Catholic Spain:

> heresy is the breath of Satan, and a fire from hell, and a corrupt and pestilential air, and a cancer that grows and spreads without remedy, and a disease so dangerous and acute that it penetrates the innermost parts and corrupts and infects souls, and not only kills with its touch, like the viper, or with its look, like the basilisk, or with its breath, like the dragon, but in all these ways and many others destroys, ends, and consumes everything.[16]

These writers took seriously the campaign against Luther and Calvin and argued that the measures taken by Philip II and the Spanish Inquisition were necessary as the minimum for the preservation of Spain as a Catholic state.

To the sixteenth-century mind, certainly before Protestant Reformers suggested the idea that politics could be separate from religious faith, loyalty to the state was considered identical with adherence to the confession of the kingdom. Islam in the Ottoman Empire, Eastern Orthodoxy in the Russian Empire, and Catholicism in much of western Europe, especially in Spain, were linked completely with the state. Heresy – belief in unapproved theologies– was therefore equivalent to treason. Even today, the penalty for treason in many nations is death; this was a universal punishment in the early modern period for the same crime. For those suspected of treason to the state, there might be a brief trial, or just summary execution by agents of the king, but the insecurity of kings, and the frequency with which they were overthrown by relatives, even their own sons, meant that it was better to kill a few – or even many – innocents rather than risk missing the one regicide or conspirator who saw the crown as more fitting for another head. In this context, the methods of the Inquisition – questioning those accused as to their knowledge of the faith – could they recite Catholic prayers? What did they believe about original sin? When had they last been to confession? Had they read forbidden books or heard forbidden ideas? – were relatively moderate for the times.

The most frequent punishments meted out – attending extra masses, paying penances of time, rituals, or donations to the Church, public confessions of their sins, exile – were far preferable to execution, often through terribly frightful, painful, and extended methods – in the name of the king.

To Spain's kings and Inquisitor Generals, the domestic threats posed by followers of Luther and Calvin were just as real and dangerous as the military challenges faced by Spanish soldiers and sailors in France, the Low Countries, the English Channel, and elsewhere. The success of the Holy Office in Spain, which did not suffer the religious tumult of France, England, or the German states, illustrates that this pivot to address the threat of the Protestant Reformation was timely and effective. Indeed, in their employment of the Spanish Inquisition, their continued prosecution of external wars, and the survival of their dynasty, the historical evidence does appear to show that Charles V, Holy Roman Emperor, and his son, Philip II, that Most Catholic King, assessed their situation accurately. Especially until the consolidating and reforming achievements of the Council of Trent, which defined Catholicism not only on its own terms, but in contrast to Protestantism, the ambiguity of this new religious interpretation added to the danger it posed to devout Catholic monarchs. In a sense, the Reform impulse could seem more terrifying during the initial decades when the lines between Catholicism and Protestantism were unclear, since absent clear lines of doctrine, even faithful believers could be unwittingly influenced by the ideas of Luther and Calvin.[17]

Philip II not only feared the Reformation as a theological threat to a unified Christendom, but he also feared encirclement by an alliance of Protestant powers. This strategic concern, as much military as religious, was borne out by efforts by his enemies to make common cause. For example, Queen Jeanne of Navarre did write to Queen Elizabeth of England in 1568, justifying the taking of arms against Catholic kings, and asking for her continued favor in this endeavor.[18] For her part, Elizabeth provided military aid, diplomatic support, and refuge to Calvinist rebels against Spain, French Huguenots, and even Spanish Protestants. While a formal alliance between Europe's Protestant powers did not emerge, the threat of one, or at least the danger of coordinated attacks on Habsburg domains, loomed large in the fears of Philip II. Had Europe's Protestants succeeded in coordinating their campaigns against the Habsburgs and their allies, perhaps following Luther's encouragement toward a coalition with the Ottoman Empire, the leading Catholic power would have been hard-pressed to fend off these simultaneous and encircling threats in Europe, the Mediterranean, and on the world's oceans. These two monarchs illustrate another key challenge to the king: the identification of women with the Protestant Reformation, including as leaders of enemy states, as defendants brought before the Spanish Inquisition, and material supporters of warfare against the Habsburg monarchy. With the rise of literacy among the middle and upper classes, women also became writers of Protestant or Protestant-sympathizing letters, theology, and other works. In these efforts, women, as well as men, operated in defiance of campaigns by the Spanish Inquisition and the broader Catholic Church to repress the flowering of Reformist opposition throughout the empires of Charles V and Philip II in Europe and the world beyond.

While Spain did see limited efforts to bring Reformist ideas to its population, there was none of the tumult that so wracked every other major European state in central and western Europe. The Habsburg lands were not entirely free from insurrection and civil unrest– the simultaneous uprisings in 1640 of Portugal and Aragon during the Thirty Years' War being only the best example – none of which were launched under the inspiration of Luther or Calvin. Some credit must be given to the successors to both Philip II and Elizabeth I; neither Philip III of Spain nor James I of England (formerly of Scotland) wished to continue the continual warfare of their predecessors. Even for Spain, with its vast empire and wealth from the Americas, at times simultaneous warfare against England, France, and the Dutch was too much to continue bearing.[19]

Spanish Catholicism emerged from the existential struggle against Protestantism in Spain, throughout Habsburg lands, and across the globe as a stronger, more coherent, and more theologically orthodox institution. Gone were "the wild prophecies, millenarian expectations, and spiritual wonders of unofficial religion," replaced by a revitalized Church hierarchy, an increasingly literate and trained secular and regular clergy, and an embrace of sacramental and mystical Catholicism, with clear guidelines on religiously acceptable and unacceptable behaviors.[20] The theological clarity and reforms from the Council of Trent were implemented with serious intent in Spain, although of course unevenly given resource and personnel disparities. Rural communities often had fewer parish priests per capita, a dearth of available clerics for pastoral assignment compounded by the location of many monasteries and convents near urban areas.

Even so, the Spanish Church of 1600, 1620, and 1640 was one of a better educated clergy, more knowledgeable and literate parishioners, more pastoral bishops, and a more consistent and competent ecclesiastical structure. While there would not be a concerted effort to introduce Protestant Christianity again into Spain until the nineteenth century, after the dissolution of the Spanish Inquisition, the Spanish people and their clergy were institutionally and theologically more resolute against these ideas because of the sixteenth-century struggle against Calvinism and Lutheranism. The greater threat to Spanish Catholicism, from the nineteenth century onward, would not be a rival Christian belief or theology, but the advent of non-belief, in agnostic or atheist forms.

Taken in the context of the lifespan of the Spanish Inquisition, the campaign against Protestantism in the peninsula was of relatively small scope; by one historian's estimate 8% of the approximately 49,000 trials by the Holy Office between 1540 and 1700 were of Protestants. Most of these were clustered in the 1550s and 1560s, but cases continued in small numbers thereafter. Even assuming death sentences were imposed on 10% of convicted Protestants, more than twice the 3.5% rate for all crimes (such as blasphemy, Judaism, and witchcraft), there were likely fewer than 400 publicly executed through being "released to the secular authorities."[21] While perhaps there continued to be underground Spanish Protestants on the peninsula, hidden away from the authorities and continuing to meet in small groups, if so their existence was precarious and has not yet been validated by significant primary sources from the period. Small numbers of Spaniards continued to live in exile, chiefly in England and Geneva, but of decreasing demographic and theological significance. [22]

In many ways, the work of the Inquisition was subsumed by these successful pastoral efforts to educate and integrate the Spanish people into Catholicism. With the waning of Protestantism and other heresies from Spain, by the early seventeenth century the Holy Office was essentially where it had been a hundred years earlier, before the Protestant irruption began in Germany. In the seventeenth century, it would not be a rival theology that threatened Catholic unity in Spain and beyond, but instead the rising secularism of the Enlightenment, a movement that even more than the Reformation threatened the unity of monarchy and Church in western and southern Europe.

While prosecutions by the Spanish Inquisition of Protestants declined dramatically after the 1570s, they did occur. Foreigners continued to make up a disproportionately large percentage of those accused of this heresy, with the specific nationalities depending as much on Spain's contemporary foreign policies as on the beliefs of those in question. When Spain was at peace with England, few English sailors and merchants found themselves before Inquisitorial tribunals. When Spain and France were at peace, printers and other skilled artisans faced fewer ecclesiastical travails south of the Pyrenees. The dramatic decline in numbers and prominence of Spanish Protestants, however, through the work of the Spanish Inquisition, voluntary emigration, and the gradual ebbing of the religious ferment of the sixteenth century, ended at least the internal dynamic of Spanish Catholicism's global war on the Protestant Reformation.

At the same time, the mandate of the Holy Office widened throughout the sixteenth century and into the seventeenth and eighteenth centuries, adding moral and other offenses against the Christian family, such as adultery, bigamy, homosexuality, and incest, as spiritual sins against the moral order, as well as being crimes against society. Especially during times of alliance with England and other Protestant states, prosecutions for that specific kind of heresy dwindled to nothing. Even cases against *conversos* occurred occasionally during the following centuries until the Spanish Inquisition's final abolition in 1834, but in practice there were almost no Protestants, converted Jews or Muslims in Spain to pursue. Former obsessions of the Inquisition, such as *Alhumbrados* and Erasmians, similarly no longer existed in Spain. Only general moral offenses remained widespread enough to warrant investigation and prosecution, but clearly these could be handled by Spanish civil or other ecclesiastical courts.[23]

An exception to this broadening of mission was dealing with witchcraft in Spain. Unlike elsewhere in Europe and the Americas, witchcraft and assorted accusations never became a significant area of interest for the Catholic Church in Spain, or specifically for the Inquisition. While the Spanish Inquisition did investigate thousands of cases, the penalties for these crimes tended to be light, with few executions. Some authors have argued this came from a generalized skepticism about witchcraft in Spain, the disappearance of pagan ideas hundreds of years earlier in Spain compared to elsewhere in Europe, the lack of fiscal incentives for the Inquisitorial pursuit of sorcery (given the typical poverty of those accused), or the possibility that those who elsewhere would have been charged as witches were subsumed into other categories.[24] Indeed, the Spanish Inquisition seems to have been employed against the ideas of the French Revolution more frequently and seriously than against admitted practitioners of witchcraft in Spain, or those merely accused of these demonic entanglements.[25]

The Protestant Reformation not only challenged Catholicism in Spain but emboldened the enemies of Charles V and Philip II. Absent the alliance between these Habsburg monarchs and the Spanish Inquisition, the existential threat of this alternative version of Christianity could have overcome the Catholic Church in the Iberian Peninsula. Without Spain as the strong right arm of the Church, "the champion of Catholicism," it is not difficult to wonder what might have followed thereafter in Europe.[26] Absent the ardent advocacy for the Catholic Church, and the vast resources of the Habsburg monarchy, the theological insurgencies of Luther, Calvin, and other Reformers could have triumphed, rather than just on the northern and western extremes of Europe, across the continent to the frontiers of Eastern Orthodoxy in Russia and Sunni Islam in the Ottoman Empire.

By the middle of the seventeenth century, the fires of religious warfare had ebbed in Europe. The Treaty of Westphalia, which in 1648 ended the Thirty Years' War, recognized the legitimacy of the several branches of Christendom and the autonomy of each nation to choose, leaving to monarchs the authority to decide for their subjects which would be allowed. Spain, no longer the world's most powerful nation, but still a major power, recognized that England would remain Protestant, acquiesced to the independence of the Dutch Republic, and ceased to see its sole mission in the world as unrelenting wars against Calvinists, Lutherans, and Anglicans. Indeed, despite multiple wars fought against England in particular, a slow realignment between England and Spain began, reviving at the same time the traditional rivalry with France, just across the English Channel.

Commercial interests, complementary economies, and shared antipathy toward Paris prevailed again, once religion was no longer the primary term defining the existence of the two monarchies. Despite brief Anglo-Spanish conflicts in 1625 and 1655, by 1661, it was a general sentiment in London that "indeed, we do naturally all love the Spanish and hate the French."[27] This echoed comments made by King James I to Juan Fernandez de Velasco, Constable of Castile, at the celebration of the peace treaty with England in 1604. He praised Spain's many good characteristics, as well as the hope that the young Princess Isabella, then two years old, would find "the means of preserving the kingdoms of Spain and England in friendship and union, unlike that other hostile Elizabeth who had caused so much mischief."[28] For an English king to make such a declaration, even given that he was the son of Mary, Queen of Scots, was a note showing how much had changed in a short period of time. James would even seek a Spanish princess, and older sister of Isabella, as a bride for Charles, Prince of Wales, even though that particular plan failed.

Spain survived the Protestant Reformation, but of equal importance is that the Reformation survived Spain. In this sense, both Spanish Catholicism and the movement associated with the Reformations of Luther, Calvin, and Henry VIII were simultaneously triumphs and failures. Having survived the threats from their most determined enemies, at the same time they failed to destroy that which they viewed as the most nefarious force in the world. Catholicism and Protestantism alike (in its several forms) aspired to unite all Christians, indeed all of humanity, under their particular vision of the path to salvation. By the end of the sixteenth century, it was clear that many roads would remain, even if in the minds of their theological rivals their opponents' path was one leading to perdition. While future European world conflicts would not be fought primarily over religious differences, the results of the war for Europe between Spanish Catholicism and the Protestant Reformation would leave a legacy in terms of confessional boundaries and national identities that would remain significant for centuries.

Notes

1 Patterson, *With the Heart of a King*, 315.
2 MacCulloch, *The Reformation*, 388.
3 Rady, *The Habsburgs*, 119.
4 Rady, *The Habsburgs*, 141.
5 Proverbs 27:17. Geneva Bible, 1587. https://biblehub.com/parallel/proverbs/27-17. htm.
6 Parker, *Success is Never Final*, 4.
7 Pérez, *The Spanish Inquisition*, 196–199.
8 Pérez, *The Spanish Inquisition*, 177–179.
9 Monter, *The Frontiers of Heresy*, 321.
10 Monter, *The Frontiers of Heresy*, 321–323.
11 Edwards, *The Spanish Inquisition*, 97.
12 "The Spanish Inquisition (Monty Python)," accessed 20 March 2022, https://en.wikipedia.org/wiki/The_Spanish_Inquisition_(Monty_Python).
13 Luis de Páramo, *De Origine et Progressu Sanctae Inquisitionis (On the Origin and Progress of the Holy Inquisition)* (Madrid: 1598). Páramo was an Inquisitor in Palermo, Sicily.
14 Tomás Cerdán de Tallada, in "Verdadero govierno desta monarchía, tomando por su propio subiecto la conservación de la paz," in Ronald W. Truman, *Spanish Treatises on Government, Society and Religion in the Time of Philip II* (London: Brill, 1999), 194.
15 Marco Antonio de Camós y Requeséns, in "Microcosmia y govierno universal del hombre christiano, para todos los estados y qualquiera de ellos," (Barcelona, 1592), in Truman, *Spanish Treatises on Government, Society and Religion in the Time of Philip II*, 239.

16 Truman, *Spanish Treatises on Government, Society and Religion in the Time of Philip II*, 287.

17 Mullett, *The Catholic Reformation*, 32–33.

18 D'Albret, *Letters from the Queen of Navarre*, letter, "To the Queen of England," 16 October 1568, 49.

19 Óscar Alfredo Ruiz Fernández, *England and Spain in the Early Modern Era: Royal Love, Trade, Diplomacy, and Naval Relations, 1604-1625* (London: Bloomsbury Academic, 2020), 6, 11, 19.

20 MacCulloch, *The Reformation*, 410, 668–669.

21 Pérez, *The Spanish Inquisition*, 173–174.

22 Luttikhuizen, *Underground Protestantism in Sixteenth Century Spain*, 228, 261–262.

23 Pérez, *The Spanish Inquisition*, 93–94, 100. Lynn, *Between Court and Confessional*.

24 Homza, *Religious Authority in the Spanish Renaissance*, 180–181. Pérez, *The Spanish Inquisition*, 79–83.

25 Pérez, *The Spanish Inquisition*, 94–98.

26 Pérez, *The Spanish Inquisition*, 205.

27 McDermott, *England and the Spanish Armada*, 317, 327.

28 William Brenchley Brye, ed. and trans., *England as Seen by Foreigners in the Days of Elizabeth & James the First*. Originally published in 1865 (New York: Benjamin Blom, 1967), 121.

Bibliography

Primary Sources

Archivo Histórico Nacional (AHN). Madrid, Spain: Inquisición, 1531–1583.

Barrientos, Bartolomé. *Pedro Menéndez de Avilés: Founder of Florida*. Translated and edited by Anthony Kerrigan. Gainesville: University of Florida Press, 1965.

Bénéton, Philippe, ed. *The Kingdom Suffereth Violence: The Machiavelli/Erasmus/ More Correspondence and Other Unpublished Documents*. Translated by Paul J. Archambault. South Bend, Indiana: St. Augustine's Press, 2012.

Bennett, Charles E., ed. *Laudonnière and Fort Caroline: History and Documents*. Tuscaloosa: University of Alabama Press, 2001.

Boehmer, Eduard, Benjamin Barron Wiffen, and Benjamin B. Wiffen. *Bibliotheca Wiffeniana. Spanish Reformers of Two Centuries from 1520; Their Lives and Writings, According to the Late Benjamin B. Wiffen's Plan and with the Use of His Materials*, vols. 1–3. New York: B. Franklin, 1971.

D'Albret, Jeanne. Queen of Navarre, *Letters from the Queen of Navarre with an 'Ample Declaration.'* Edited by Kathleen Llewellyn, Emily E. Thompson, and Colette H. Winn. Toronto: Iter Academic Press, 2016.

Fitzsimon, Henry S.J. *A Catholike Confvtation of M. John Riders Claymé of Antiqvities, and a Calming Comfort against His Caveat*. Rouen, France: 1608.

Harrison, G.B., ed. *The Letters of Queen Elizabeth I*. Westport, Connecticut: Greenwood Press, 1981.

Hume, Martin A.S. ed., *Calendar of Letters and State Papers Relating to English Affairs*, Archives of Simancas, Vol. II. Elizabeth, 1568–1579. London: Her Majesty's Stationery Office, 1894.

Kellison, Matthew, Doctour of Divinitie. *A Treatise of the Hierarchie and Divers Orders of the Church Against the Anarchie of Calvin*. Doway, France: Gerard Pinchon, 1629.

Laudonnière, René. *Three Voyages*. Edited and translated by Charles Bennett. Gainesville: University Presses of Florida, 1975.

Monjo Bellido, Emilio, ed. *Obras de los Reformadores Españoles del Siglo XVI*, Vols. I–IX. Seville: Editorial MAD, 2006–2011.

Olivar-Bertrand, R. *La revolución erasmista y los españoles*. Quito, Ecuador: Casa de la Cultura Ecuatoriana, 1976.

Persons, Robert. *The Jesuit's Memorial for the Intended Reformation of England under their Firft Popish Prince*. With Intro by Edward Gee, London: Rose and Crown, 1690. Originally written in 1596 in Seville.

Procesos de protestantes españoles en el siglo XVI. Madrid: Revista de Archivos, Bibliotecas, y Museos, 1910, Microfilm. Biblioteca Nacional, Madrid: Archivo de Simancas.

Ribaut, Jean. *The Whole & True Discouerye of Terra Florida.* (1563) A facsimile reproduction with introduction by David L. Dowd. Gainesville: University of Florida Press, 1964.

Schäfer, Ernst Hermann Johann. *Protestantismo Español e Inquisición en el Siglo XVI*, Vol. 2. Translated and edited by Francisco Ruiz de Pablos. Seville: MAD, 2014.

Solís de Merás, Gonzalo. *Pedro Menéndez de Avilés and the Conquest of Florida: A New Manuscript [La Conquista de la Florida por el Adelantado Pedro Meléndez de Valdés]*. Translated and Edited by David Arbesú. Gainesville: University Press of Florida, 2017.

Usoz y Rio, Luis, Benjamín B. Wiffen and Eduardo Boehmer, ed. *Reformistas antiguos españoles.* Barcelona: Librería de Diego Gomez Flores, 1848–1863, 20 volumes.

Whelan Richardson, Regina, ed. *The Salamanca Letters: A Catalogue of Correspondence (1619–1871) from the Archives of the Irish Colleges in Spain in the Library of St. Patrick's College, Maynooth, Ireland.* Maynooth, Ireland: St. Patrick's College, 1995.

Secondary Sources

Ágoston, Gábor. *The Last Muslim Conquest: The Ottoman Empire and its Wars in Europe.* Princeton: Princeton University Press, 2021.

de Alberti, Leonora and Annie Beatrice Wallis Chapman. *Los mercaderes ingleses y la Inquisición Española en las Islas Canarias.* Translated from the English by José Delgado Luis. Original edition. London: Royal Historical Society, 1912. Tenerife, Canarias: Publidisa, 2010.

Alonso Burgos, Jesús. *El luteranismo en Castilla durante el siglo XVI: autos de fe de Valladolid de 21 de mayo y de 8 de octubre de 1559.* San Lorenzo de El Escorial: Editorial Swan, 1983.

Alvarez-Villa, Daphne and Jenny Guardado. "The Long-Run Influence of Institutions Governing Trade: Evidence from Smuggling Ports in Colonial Mexico." *Journal of Development Economics* 144 (2020): 102453.

Angeles, F. Delor. "Bibliographical Data on the Philippine Inquisition." *Silliman Journal* 23 (Third Quarter 1976): 239–260.

Bainton, Roland. *Women of the Reformation: From Spain to Scandinavia.* Minneapolis, Minnesota: Augsburg, 1977.

Balasch Blanch, Enric and Yolanda Ruiz Arranz. *Atlas Ilustrado: La Inquisición en España.* Madrid: Susaeta, 2014.

Bataillon, Marcel. *Erasmo y España: Estudios sobre la historia espiritual del siglo xvi.* Mexico City: Fondo de Cultura Económica, 1965.

Bayne, C.G. *Anglo-Roman Relations, 1558–1565.* Oxford: The Clarendon Press, 1913.

Borreguero Beltrán, Cristina and Asunción Retortillo Atienza. *La memoria de un hombre.* El Burgalés Francisco de Enzinas en el V centenario de la reforma protestante. Burgos, Spain: Universidad de Burgos, 2019.

Brady, Thomas A., Heiko A. Oberman, and James D. Tracy. *Handbook of European History, 1400–1600.* Leiden, Netherlands: Brill, 1994.

Brenchley Brye, William, ed. and trans. *England as Seen By Foreigners in the Days of Elizabeth & James the First.* New York: Benjamin Blom, 1967. Originally published in 1865.

Broomhall, Susan. *Women and Religion in Sixteenth Century France*. New York: Palgrave Macmillan, 2006.

Bruquetas, Fernando and Manuel Lobo. *Don Carlos: Príncipe de las Españas*. Madrid: Cátedra, 2016.

Buringh, Eltjo and Jan Luiten Van Zanden. "Charting the 'Rise of the West': Manuscripts and Printed Books in Europe, a Long-Term Perspective from the Sixth through Eighteenth Centuries." *The Journal of Economic History* 69, no. 2 (June 2009): 409–445. Cambridge University Press.

De Castro, Adolfo. *The Spanish Protestants and their Persecution by Philip*. Translated by Thomas Parker. London: Charles Gilpin, 1851. (Published contemporaneously with Spanish edition, through cooperation with the author). *Historia de los protestantes españoles y de su persecución por Felipe II*. Cadiz: Revista Médica, 1851.

Chambers, Liam and Thomas O'Connor, eds. *College Communities Abroad: Education, Migration and Catholicism in early modern Europe*. Manchester: Manchester University Press, 2018.

Chuchiak, John F. IV, ed. and trans. *The Inquisition in New Spain, 1536–1820: A Documentary History*. Baltimore: Johns Hopkins University Press, 2012.

Claramunt Soto, Álex, ed. *Lepanto: La mar roja de sangre*. Madrid: Desperta Ferro, 2021.

Crews, Daniel. *Twilight of the Renaissance: The Life of Juan de Valdés*. Toronto: University of Toronto Press, 2008.

Croft, Pauline. "Englishmen and the Spanish Inquisition 1558–1625." *The English Historical Review* 87, no. 343 (April 1972): 249–263.

Cruz, Anne J. and Mary Elizabeth Perry, eds. *Culture and Control in Counter-Reformation Spain*. Minneapolis: University of Minnesota Press, 1992.

Del Valle, D.G. *Anales de la Inquisición*. Madrid: Gregorio Hernando, 1848.

Domínguez Nafría, Juan Carlos, ed. *100 impresos españoles sobre la Inquisición: Instrucciones, edictos, cedulas, relaciones de autos de fe y otros*. Madrid: Bibliotheca Sefarad, 2018.

Downey, Kirstin. *Isabella: Warrior Queen*. New York: Doubleday, 2014.

Elvy, Peter. "A Tale of Two Sitters: Juan and Alfonso de Valdés." *Bulletin for Spanish and Portuguese Historical Studies* 40, no. 1 (2015): 105–106.

Edwards, John. *The Inquisitors: The Story of the Grand Inquisitors of the Spanish Inquisition*. Stroud, Gloucestershire, UK: Tempus, 2007.

Edwards, John. *The Spanish Inquisition*. Stroud, Gloucestershire, UK: Tempus, 1999.

Edwards, John. "The Spanish Inquisition Refashioned: the Experience of Mary I's England and the Valladolid Tribunal, 1559." *Hispanic Research Journal* 13, no. 1 (2012): 41–54. DOI: 10.1179/174582011X13183287338095.

Escobar Golderos, Mario. *La historia de una obsesión: Felipe II y su época*. Madrid: Consejo Evangélico de Madrid, 2001.

Fernández Álvarez, Manuel. *España del Emperador Carlos V (1500–1558, 1517–1556)*, Vol. XX, introduction by Ramón Menéndez Pidal. Madrid: Espasa Calpe, 1999.

Fernández Campos, Gabino. *Reforma y contrarreforma en Andalucía*. Seville: Editorial MAD, 2006.

Fowler, Jessica J. "Process and punishment: alleged alumbrados before the Mexican Holy Office, 1593–1603." *Colonial Latin American Review* 29, no. 3 (2020): 357–375.

García Hernán, David, ed. *La historia sin complejos: La nueva visión del Imperio Español (estudios en honor de John H. Elliott)*. Madrid: Actas, 2010.

Gerhard, Peter. *Pirates on the West Coast of New Spain, 1575–1742*. Glendale, California: Arthur H. Clark, 1960.

Giles, Mary E., ed. *Women in the Inquisition: Spain and the New World*. Baltimore: Johns Hopkins University Press, 1999.

Gilly, Carlos. "Juan de Valdés, traductor y adaptador de escritos de Lutero en su Diálogo de Doctrina christiana," *Miscelánea de Estudios Hispánicos, Homenajée de los hispanistas de Suiza, a Ramon Sugranyes de Franch*. Carrer Ausiàs Marc, Catalonia: Publicacions de L'Abadia de Montserrat, 1982.

González Ancín, Miguel and Otis Towns. *Miguel Servet en España (1506–1527)*, expanded edition. Tudela, Spain: Imprenta Castilla, 2017.

Gorrochategui Santos, Luis. *The English Armada: The Greatest Naval Disaster in English History*. London: Bloomsbury Academic, 2018.

Green, Vivian. *A New History of Christianity*. New York: Continuum, 1996.

Greenleaf, Richard. *The Mexican Inquisition of the Sixteenth Century*. Albuquerque: University of New Mexico Press, 1969.

Greenleaf, Richard E. *Zumárraga and the Mexican Inquisition, 1536–1543*. Washington, DC: Academy of American Franciscan History, 1961.

Griffin, Clive. *Journeymen-Printers, Heresy, and the Inquisition in Sixteenth Century Spain*. Oxford: Oxford University Press, 2005.

Hammer, Paul E.J. *Elizabeth's Wars: War, Government and Society in Tudor England, 1544–1604*. London: Palgrave Macmillan, 2003.

Hoffman, Paul E. *The Spanish Crown and the Defense of the Caribbean, 1535–1585*. Baton Rouge: Louisiana State University Press, 1980.

Homza, Lu Ann. *Religious Authority in the Spanish Renaissance*. Baltimore: Johns Hopkins University Press, 2000.

de Ibáñez, Yolanda Mariel. *El Tribunal de la Inquisición en México (siglo xvi)*. Mexico City: Universidad Nacional Autónoma de México, 1979.

Irwin, Joyce. *Womanhood in Radical Protestantism, 1525–1675*. New York: Edwin Mellen Press, 1979.

Kagan, Richard and Abigail Dyer, eds. *Inquisitorial Inquiries: Brief Lives of Secret Jews and Other Heretics*. Baltimore: Johns Hopkins University Press, 2011.

Kinder, A. Gordon. "Two Previously Unknown Letters of Juan Pérez de Pineda, Protestant of Seville in the Sixteenth Century." *Bibliothèque d'Humanisme et Renaissance* 49, no. 1 (1987): 111–120. http://www.jstor.org/stable/20677441

Lea, Henry Charles. *A History of the Inquisition of Spain and the Inquisition in the Spanish Dependencies*. Introduction by Lu Ann Homza. New York: I.B. Tauris, 2011. Originally published in 1906–1908.

de León de la Vega, Manuel. *Los protestantes y la spiritualidad evangelica en la Espana del siglo XIV*, vols. 1 and 2. Oviedo, Spain: Self-published, 2012.

Lindberg, Carter. *The European Reformations*, 2nd edition. Chichester, UK: Wiley-Blackwell, 2010.

Lipscomb, Suzannah. *The King is Dead: The Last Will and Testament of Henry VIII*. New York: Pegasus Books, 2016.

Llorente, Jose A. *La Inquisicion y los espanoles*. Originally published 1812. Madrid: Castellote, 1973.

Longhurst, John. *Erasmus and the Spanish Inquisition: The Case of Juan de Valdés*. Albuquerque: University of New Mexico Press, 1950.

Longhurst, John E. "Julián Hernández: Protestant Martyr." *Bibliothèque d'Humanisme et Renaissance* 22, no. 1 (1960): 90–118.

Longhurst, John E. *Luther's Ghost in Spain (1517–1546)*. Lawrence, Kansas: Coronado Press, 1969.

Lopes Don, Patricia. *Bonfires of Culture: Franciscans, Indigenous Leaders, and the Inquisition in Early Mexico, 1524–1540*. Norman: University of Oklahoma Press, 2010.

López Muñoz, Tomás. *La Reforma en la Sevilla del XVI*, Vol. I and II. Seville: Editorial MAD, 2011.

Lowery, Woodbury. *The Spanish Settlements within the Present Limits of the United States*. New York: Russell & Russell, 1959.

Luttikhuizen, Frances. *La Reforma en España, Italia, y Portugal, Siglos XVI y XVIII: Bibliografía Actualizada*. Seville: Editorial MAD, 2007.

Luttikhuizen, Frances. *Underground Protestantism in Sixteenth Century Spain*. Bristol, Connecticut: Vandenhoeck & Ruprecht, 2017.

Lynch, John. *Spain 1516–1598: From Nation State to World Empire*. Oxford: Blackwell, 1991.

Lynn, Kimberly. *Between Court and Confessional: The Politics of Spanish Inquisitors*. Cambridge: Cambridge University Press, 2013.

Maltby, William S. *The Black Legend in England: The Development of Anti-Spanish Sentiment, 1558–1660*. Durham, North Carolina: Duke University Press, 1971.

Marshall, Peter. *Religious Identities in Henry VIII's England*. Aldershot, UK: Ashgate, 2006.

Marshall, Peter and Alec Ryrie, eds. *The Beginnings of English Protestantism*. Cambridge: Cambridge University Press, 2002.

Martínez, Emilio. *Recuerdos de Antaño: los mártires españoles de la Reforma del Siglo XVI y la Inquisición*. Valladolid: Consejo Evangélico de Castilla y León, 2009.

Massing, Michael. *Fatal Discord: Erasmus, Luther, and the Fight for the Western Mind*. New York: HarperCollins, 2018.

Mattingly, Garrett. *Catherine of Aragon*. New York: Quality, 1990. Originally published in 1941.

MacCulloch, Diarmaid. *The Reformation: A History*. New York: Viking 2003.

McDermott, James. *England and the Spanish Armada: The Necessary Quarrel*. New Haven: Yale University Press, 2005.

McDonald, Grantley. "'Burned to Dust': Censorship and Repression of Theological Literature in the Habsburg Netherlands during the 1520s." in *Church, Censorship and Reform in the Early Modern Netherlands*, edited by Violet Soen, Dries Vanysacker and Wim François, 27–52. Turnhout, Belgium: Brepols, 2017.

McGrath, John. *The French in Early Florida: In the Eye of the Hurricane*. Gainesville: University Press of Florida, 2000.

Mikhail, Alan. *God's Shadow: Sultan Selim, His Ottoman Empire, and the Making of the Modern World*. New York: W.W. Norton, 2020.

Monter, E. William. *Frontiers of Heresy: The Spanish Inquisition from the Basque Lands to Sicily*. Cambridge: Cambridge University Press, 1990.

Mullett, Michael A. *The Catholic Reformation*. London and New York: Routledge, 1999.

Netanyahu, Benzion. *The Origins of the Inquisition in Fifteenth Century Spain*. New York: Random House, 1995.

Newcombe, D.G. *Henry VIII and the English Reformation*. London: Routledge, 1995.

Nieto, José C. *Juan de Valdés y los orígenes de la Reforma en España e Italia*. Mexico City: Fondo de Cultura Económica, 1979.

Henry Servier. *Protestantism in Spain, Its Progress and Its Extinction by the Inquisition, with an Account of the Principal Martyrs*. Translated from the French. Dublin: J. Porteous, 1835.

Norwich, John Julius. *Four Princes: Henry VIII, Francis I, Charles V, Suleiman the Magnificent and the Obsessions that Forged Modern Europe*. New York: Atlantic Monthly Press, 2016.

de Olaizola, Juan María. *Historia del Protestantismo en el Pais Vasco; el Reino de Navarra en la encrucijada de su historia*. Pamplona, Spain: Pamiela, 1993.

Parker, Geoffrey. *The Army of Flanders and the Spanish Road, 1567–1659. The Logistics of Spanish Victory and Defeat in the Low Countries' Wars*. Cambridge: Cambridge University Press, 1972.

Parker, Geoffrey. *Success Is Never Final: Empire, War, and Faith in Early Modern Europe*. New York, NY: Basic Books, 2002.

Pastore, Stefanie. *Una herejía española: conversos, alumbrados e Inquisición (1449–1559)*. Madrid: Marcial Pons, 2010.

Patterson, Benton Rain. *With the Heart of a King: Elizabeth I of England, Philip II of Spain, and the Fight for a Nation's Soul and Crown*. New York: St. Martin's Press, 2007.

Peebles, Kelly Digby. "Renée de France's and Clément Marot's Voyages: Political Exile to Spiritual Liberation." *Women in French Studies* 2018 (2018): 33–60.

Pérez, Joseph. *The Spanish Inquisition: A History*. Translated by Janet Lloyd. New Haven, Connecticut: Yale University Press, 2005.

Pettegree, Andrew. *Brand Luther*. New York: Penguin: 2016.

Próspero Gachard, Luis. *Don Carlos y Felipe II*. Barcelona: Editorial Lorenzana, 1963.

Rady, Martyn. *The Habsburgs: To Rule The World*. New York: Basic Books, 2020.

Rodríguez-Salgado, M.J. *The Changing Face of Empire: Charles V, Philip II and Habsburg Authority, 1551–1559*. Cambridge: Cambridge University Press, 1988.

Ruiz Fernández, Óscar Alfredo. *England and Spain in the Early Modern Era: Royal Love, Trade, Diplomacy, and Naval Relations, 1604–1625*. London: Bloomsbury Academic, 2020.

Ruiz de Pablos, Francisco. "Carlos V y su persecución del Protestantismo." *Cuadernos de Historia Moderna* 43, no. 2 (2018): 505–518.

Saint-Saëns, Alain, ed. *Young Charles V (1500–1531)*. New Orleans: University Press of the South, 2000.

Sanchez, Mark G. *Anti-Spanish Sentiment in English Literary and Political Writing 1553–1603*. Leeds, UK: University of Leeds, Ph.D. dissertation, 2004.

Sarasa Sanchez, Esteban. "La Casa Real de Aragon y Castilla: Los Trastámara (1410–1516)." in *Reyes de Aragón: Soberanos de un Pais con futuro. Ramiro I-Juan Carlos I (1035–2011)*, edited by Guillermo Redondo Veintemillas and Carmen Morte Garcia, 164–81. Zaragoza, Spain: Gobierno de Aragón, 2011.

Schäfer, Ernst Hermann Johann. *Protestantismo Español e Inquisición en el Siglo XVI*, Vol. 1. Translated and edited by Francisco Ruiz de Pablos. Seville: MAD, 2014a.

Schäfer, Ernst Hermann Johann. *Protestantismo Español e Inquisición en el Siglo XVI*, Vol. 3B. "Documentos para la historia de la comunidad protestante de Valladolid." Translated and edited by Francisco Ruiz de Pablos. Seville: MAD, 2014b.

Schmidt, H.D. "The Idea and Slogan of 'Perfidious Albion." *Journal of the History of Ideas* 14, no. 4 (October 1953): 604–616.

Skidmore, Chris. *Death and the Virgin Queen*. New York: St. Martin's Press, 2010.

Soen, Violet, Dries Vanysacker and Wim François Church, eds. *Censorship and Reform in the Early Modern Netherlands*. Turnhout, Belgium: Brepols, 2017.

Spach, Robert C. "Juan Gil and Sixteenth-Century Spanish Protestantism." *The Sixteenth Century Journal* 26, no. 4 (1995): 857–879. DOI: 10.2307/2543791.

Stjerna, Kirsi. *Women and the Reformation*. Oxford: Blackwell Publishing, 2009.

Tellechea Idígoras, José Ignacio. *Fray Bartolomé Carranza de Miranda (Investigaciones históricas)*. Pamplona, Navarre: Gobierno de Navarra, 2002.

Thomas, Hugh. *The Golden Age: The Spanish Empire of Charles V*. London: Penguin Books, 2010.

Toribio Medina, José. *El Tribunal del Santo Oficio del la Inquisición en las Islas Filipinas*. Santiago, Chile: Imprenta Elzeviriana, 1899.

de la Torre, José Ignacio. *Breve Historia de la Inquisición*. Madrid: Nowtilus, 2014.

Tracy, James D. *The Low Countries in the Sixteenth Century: Erasmus, Religion and Politics, Trade and Finance*. Aldershot, Hampshire, UK: Ashgate Publishing, 2005.

Tracy, James D. *Emperor Charles V, Impresario of War: Campaign Strategy, International Finance, and Domestic Politics*. Cambridge: Cambridge University Press, 2002.

Tracy, James D. *Europe's Reformations, 1450–1650*. Lanham, Maryland: Rowman and Littlefield, 1999.

Vargas-Hidalgo, Rafael, ed. *Guerra y diplomacia en el Mediterráneo: Correspondencia inédita de Felipe II con Andrea Doria y Juan Andrea Doria*. Madrid: Ediciones Polifemo, 2002.

Villalon, Andrew. "The 1562 Head Injury of Don Carlos: A Conflict of Medicine and Religion in Sixteenth-Century Spain." *Mediterranean Studies* 22, no. 2 (2014): 95–134.

Warnicke, Retha. *The Rise and Fall of Anne Boleyn*. Cambridge: Cambridge University Press, 1989.

Warren, Adam. *Medicine and Politics in Colonial Peru: Population Growth and the Bourbon Reforms*. Pittsburgh: University of Pittsburg Press, 2010.

Waterforth, Rev. W.S.J. *England and Rome: Or, The History of the Religious Connection between England and the Holy See, from the year 179, to the Commencement of the Anglican Reformation in 1534*. London: Burns & Lambert, 1854.

Watson, Robert. *The History of the Reign of Philip the Second, King of Spain*. London: Thomas Tegg, 1839.

Wernham, R.B. *After the Armada: Elizabethan England and the Struggle for Western Europe, 1588–1595*. Oxford: Oxford University Press, 1984.

Wilkinson, Alexander S. *Iberian Books: Books Published in Spanish or Portuguese or on the Iberian Peninsula before 1601*. Leiden, Netherlands: Brill, 2010.

Wilson, Derek. *Sir Francis Walsingham: A Courtier in an Age of Terror*. New York: Carroll & Graf Publishers, 2007.

Woodworth, Allegra. "Purveyance for the Royal Household in the Reign of Queen Elizabeth." *Transactions of the American Philosophical Society* 35, no. 1 (1945): 1–89.

Index